Beyond Borders

IASIL Essays on Modern Irish Writing

Edited by

Neil Sammells

Beyond Borders: IASIL Essays on Modern Irish Writing

Edited by

Neil Sammells

Sulis Press

First published in 2004
by Sulis Press, Newton Park
Bath BA2 9BN

Printed by Antony Rowe Ltd, Chippenham, Wilts

Cover design by Herrstein Design

ISBN
0 9545648 2 0   hardback
0 9545648 1 2   paperback

British Library Cataloguing in Publication Data
A catalogue record of this book is available from the British Library

Contents

Preface

These essays on modern Irish writing have been developed from papers delivered at the annual conference of the International Association for the Study of Irish Literatures, held at Bath Spa University College in 2000. They are not intended as a 'best of' that event, nor even as exemplifying the entire range and spread of the papers and panels which made up the conference, which featured discussions of Irish writing from the early modern period to the present day. Instead, the aim has been to bring together essays which cohere and reflect upon each other. This has involved a concentration on prose, poetry and plays from the 'modern' period; that is to say, from the 1880s and the beginnings of the Irish literary renaissance to the present.

What the selection does demonstrate, with its spread of contributors from Europe and North America, is the particular strength of IASIL: the way in which the association brings together comparative international perspectives on Irish writing (the annual conferences regularly feature contributions from flourishing Irish Studies networks in South America, Japan and Australasia as well). The title of this collection, 'Beyond Borders', is, first, an attempt to capture that bringing together of voices from different national cultures and scholarly contexts. Second, each of the essays discusses, more or less explicitly, borders both literal and metaphorical in Irish writing. Sometimes this involves showing how Irish writers look beyond national borders for influences and analogues; other contributors focus on aspects of the powerful politics of place in Irish culture. Sometimes the borders are less tangible, but no less substantive: the dividing lines that separate genres, languages, gender, race. Again and again the contributors emphasise the transgressive potential of much modern and contemporary Irish writing as it crosses and recrosses those borders, attempting to challenge convention and authority, to dissolve fixities, certainties and controls: corrosive and transformative of partition in its manifold forms.

I wish to thank IASIL for the opportunity to convene its annual conference at Bath, and the contributors to this collection for their patience and the constructive ways they have responded to my queries and comments as the chapters evolved from the original conference presentations. I am grateful to Jan Relf and Caroline Netherton for their work on the manuscript, and, in particular, to Elaine Cordy for the doggedness with which she laboured at producing the final copy.

Neil Sammells

The Victorian Celt Stereotyped, Historicised and Imagined

SIMON TREZISE

THE CELT STEREOTYPED

What did the term 'Celt' mean during the period from the middle to the late nineteenth-century? Ernest Renan, writing from a Breton perspective, defined the term logically: the Celts were those people who spoke the Celtic languages in Ireland, Scotland, Wales, Brittany and Cornwall.[1] Other commentators had more questionable ways of defining the Celt, although these questionable ways tended to be presented in the authoritative voice of 'science'. Victorian scientific commentators classified human beings in terms of physical characteristics but were not content to remain in this sphere: they linked the superficial appearance of people with subjective judgements about the qualities that the physical appearance was assumed to signify. An Anglo-Saxon Sherlock Holmes went to work using 'science' to de-code the meaning of the appearance of the Celtic or Irish 'Moriarty' figure. Meet, for instance, the 'dolichocephalous' or long-headed Celts. These are:

> quick in temper and very emotional, seldom speaking without being influenced by one feeling or another;

more quick than accurate in observation; clear thinkers,
but wanting in deliberation; they have a fertile and vivid
imagination; love the absolute in thought and principle;
dislike expediency and doubt; sympathetic with the
weak, patriotic, chivalrous. Disposed to a sentimental
melancholy, yet hopeful and sanguine. Often witty and
eloquent...[2]

This Celt has some attractive qualities but he is also on the
slippery slope that descends towards the monstrous, simian
Paddy in the *Punch* cartoons of the period.[3] How would a
Victorian in 1885 read between the lines of this passage? Some
Victorians, not caring about the history of oppression which
could have resulted in a Celtic tendency to sadness, might have
read 'sentimental melancholy' to mean 'sad for no good
reason'. For some readers, 'sympathetic with the weak' meant
'dangerously inclined to join foolish causes such as that of
Irish nationalism or the Home Rule movement'. For others,
'quick in temper' meant 'violent'; 'fertile imagination' meant
'liar'; to 'dislike expediency and doubt' meant being 'unable to
make sensible compromises'. This long-headed Celt needs
help: someone has to make his observations of the world
accurate; his wit and eloquence must be tempered by
moderation and 'common sense'; his imagination must be
compensated for with 'deliberation'. But a modern reader with
the benefit of an historical knowledge of anti-Irish prejudice,
might speculate about the human beings hidden and distorted
in this stereotype: should the Celtic 'love of the absolute' be
read to mean 'willing to hold ideals and not only hold ideals,
but act on them'; should the Celt who dislikes 'expediency' be
read as 'a person of convictions and honour'? The modern
reader needs to penetrate this voice of science in order to hear
the human voice of the Celt that is apparently so 'influenced'
by 'feeling'.

The Victorian voice of science presents other types of Celt
in relation to the long-headed variety. Consider, for example,

the 'brachycephalous' or short-headed Celt, detected by the 'Holmes and Watson' team in northern and eastern parts of the Scottish Highlands: 'These people have strong attachments and feelings, but more forethought and self-control; are gloomy, fervent, humorous' (246). Like their misguided long-headed cousins, these Celts are humorous, but are prone to melancholy; they have 'attachments' to places and possibly political causes; they are even 'fervent', a state of being which may make one susceptible to bad influences. However, although they have strong feelings, they have even more 'forethought and self-control': in this important respect, these are useful Celts not very different from 'us', (Holmes and Watson), those whose tremendous reasoning powers and attention to detail can explain the world and track down the villain.

Now let Holmes introduce the 'Irish' or 'Sancho Panza' variety of Celt. This type is (of course) instantly identifiable due to its large head, dark complexion, 'short stature' and 'coarse features'. It derives from primitive Cro-Magnon man, is 'said to be pretty common in the Hebrides' and can also be detected in the Highlands, Spain and the West of Ireland. This type of Celt seems to have few saving graces: 'Though the head is large, the intelligence is low, and there is a great deal of cunning and suspicion' observes Dr John Beddoe (1826-1911), a leading anthropologist of the period (10, 246). The choice of Sancho Panza as one of the terms to classify this Celt is intriguing. Cervante's Sancho is a sympathetic figure and is more in touch with reality than the chivalric but deluded Don whom he serves. The voice of science, however, is probably thinking of Sancho as a poor illiterate, only good enough to ride an ass, and foolish enough to dream that one day he too will be a governor. In fact, Sancho's dream is Caliban's dream: 'this isle is mine, by Sycorax my mother'. In *Punch*, however, it is made clear that while the Irish, Fenian Caliban may want to govern his country (the innocent Miranda-Hibernia), it really belongs under the control of the British Prime Minister who has a magic staff of power (Gladstone-Prospero).[4] Here, the voice of science and the voice of Mr Punch speak in unison. Sancho Panza-Caliban is closely linked to the 'prognathous' Celt, the one whose large mouth and projecting jaw 'proves' with 'scientific' logic that he is a near descendant of the ape. He is to be found in influential writings by Thomas Carlyle and Charles Kingsley and in numerous visual caricatures of the Irish Celt in *Punch* and elsewhere. Such is the power of the caricaturist to attach a character to his victims, that the simian quality was then projected onto the actual human faces of Irish people at home or abroad. One observer, who preferred Welsh Celts to Irish Celts, commented that 'the Irishman's frightful prognathous jaw, as seen in Munster and Connemara, is unknown in Wales, as is also the coarse lip which, in a lesser degree, is likewise distinctive of the Milesian race ...'. The Irishman is blamed for introducing or preserving 'a mouth scarcely improved since the much remoter date when we were apes'.[5] The voice of science was sometimes ambivalent about the significance of the prognathous face. Dr John Beddoe, for example, found it to be typical of Welsh bards and therefore associated it with eloquence. On the other hand, his statistics could be used to support the idea of the prognathous and ape-like Irishman: in 1885 Beddoe calculated that only 6% of the English but 20% of the Irish were prognathous (10).

Beddoe also helped to support the idea of a common genetic ancestry for all of the Celtic nations. He developed an influential 'Index of Nigrescence' which was used to distinguish racial types by measuring the quantity of melanin in the skin, the iris of the eye and hair follicles. According to this system of measurement, the further West you travelled in England, Ireland and Scotland, the more dark people you found. The highest point on the index was found in parts of Wales and Western Ireland. The Cornish are described as 'the darkest people in England proper' (258). Science and racial prejudice combine here. It was not only that the educated tourist travelling west might care to observe these dark 'other' beings, but the dark West, especially in the aftermath of the Irish Famine, was imagined as coming east. Beddoe refers in passing to 'the undoubted fact that the Gaelic and Iberian races of the west, mostly dark haired, are tending to swamp the blond Teutons of England by reflux migration. At the same time...the relative increase of the darker types through the more rapid multiplication of the artizan class, who are in England generally darker than the upper classes, should be kept in view' (270). Beddoe does not acknowledge or explain the source of his statistics about artisans: perhaps the only basis for this assertion is the amount of dirt involved in some skilled and manual labour. What this evidence suggests is that the Celt was endowed with racial characteristics that were considered to be markers of inferiority.

Sophie Bryant claimed to be able to identify a Celt without relying on external characteristics: 'In a Saxon assembly we easily recognise the presence of a stray Celt, apart from accent or physique, and even after a long course of naturalisation in England'.[6] Celtic people who have lost or disguised their accent cannot hide from this gaze. It is not necessary to rely on the externals of Celt and Saxon in order to identify them. The Holmes-like penetrating gaze reaches a deeper reality where a permanent, undisguisable essence of the Irish Celt is revealed. But this essence is located at an unstable point where the conscious mind is linked to the unpredictable emergence of the unconscious. According to Bryant's proto-Freudian reading, the Irish exhibit in their behaviour a

> *high degree of liability in the subconscious to pass into the conscious...*

> From this all the observed manifestations follow; it explains them. The psychological quality is no doubt correlated with a physiological quality, i.e., a high tension in the nervous structures, making them liable to explode on very slight stimulus. Thus it may be that our quick-witted Irishman is what he is because

he differs from the Teuton in the very quality of his
nerve structure. (538)

Bryant loves her Irish people but she is still defining them
mainly within the terms of the prevailing stereotype: they are
emotional and irrational, liable to uncontrolled behaviour. On
the other hand, the imagination which is a vice in many
descriptions of the Celt, here becomes a virtue. Her Irish are
not only 'quick-witted' but have the ability to make the world
of the imagination and of feelings available to the conscious
mind. This is related to but different from the kind of Celt
imagined by Matthew Arnold: a dreamy person with access to
a world of dreams, a person who is hopeless in the realm of
politics but an asset in the world of culture. Bryant's Celts, on
the contrary, retain an ability to link the world of imagination
to the world of practical politics. Her Celts excel in the art of
government, empire, diplomacy and collective action:

> The ability of a Celtic group to adopt a common
> standpoint notwithstanding great diversity has been
> abundantly tested...an Irish crowd mobilises with
> strange swiftness, and Irish politicians, even when
> sworn enemies, can co-operate with a rapidity
> embarrassing to governments. (541)

Bryant found many common characteristics between the
various Celtic nations within Britain but the majority of
observers ranked and differentiated them. Ireland is
improvident and 'wild'; Scotland provident and 'stern'.
Beddoe does not take long to put all the Celts in their place:
'the Welsh rise most in commerce, the Scotch coming after
them, and the Irish nowhere. The people of Welsh descent and
name hold their own fairly in science; the Scotch do more, the
Irish less'(142). Some are concerned to talk up the contrast
between the Irish and the Welsh. Beddoe argues that the Welsh
and the Irish have 'a common element, in both physical and

moral nature' but 'Prudence, frugality, caution, and secretiveness distinguish the Welshman...from the Irishman'(261-2). Francis Power Cobbe found a 'vast' difference between the Welsh and the Irish. Her preference for the Welsh can be summed up in one phrase: 'Instead of a Home Rule meeting, there is an eisteddfod'.[7]

THE CELT HISTORICISED

There is a perceptible hierarchy amongst the kinds of Celt surveyed here. Bryant's Celts and the short-headed Highlanders are mostly on a level with the Holmes and Watson types observing them. All other Celts are beneath their surveyors, and the Celt consistently at the very bottom of the hierarchy is the Irish Celt. The reasons for this have been explored by others but can be repeated, developed and clarified here. Linda Colley has shown that the so-called United Kingdom came into being during the eighteenth century less because of an internal motivation for union, than because of two external factors that could overcome regional and cultural differences within Britain: war and religion.[8] The nation was forged (in both senses of the word) by means of proving, in various bloody ways, that the true Briton was not a Jacobite or a Frenchman. The Britons could not easily define what they were, but they could easily define what they were not. The fact that they seemed to win most of their wars assisted them in proving their identity and superiority. As for the differences in accent and tradition among Welsh, Scots and English, that might be overcome by the universal bonding cement of English Protestantism. A Scot or a Welsh or Cornish person could be joined as one through the medium of the Protestantism preached in the churches and through the Protestant values preserved in popular chap-books, *The Pilgrim's Progress*, Foxe's *Book of Martyrs*, and interpretations of history glorifying Queen Elizabeth's victory over a Catholic Spanish empire. The fact that the Welsh and Scots were vigorous in their complaints about Catholic Irish immigration suggests the power of religion to cover ethnic and cultural links. However, during the Victorian period, war—one of those factors identified by Colley as a fortifier of nationhood—was considerably diminished in significance. The Crimean conflict, the Boer War and many conflicts of empire need to be taken into account, but during Victoria's reign there were no national wars involving Britain on the Napoleonic scale. Between the Crimean and the Boer Wars, the main means of reassuring the nation that it truly was a nation was religion. This inevitably meant that the Celtic nations, with their past and present links to Catholicism, as well as countries with strong Catholic traditions such as France and Spain, were under suspicion. Their cultural tradition posed worrying questions for the powerful Protestant fiction—that figment of the collective imagination which was what mainly stood between the nation and a realisation of its own fictional nature.

This enables us to contextualise Cobbe's reason for accepting the Welsh and loathing the Irish: 'Ireland is ultra-Catholic, Wales ultra-Protestant'.[9] Charles Kingsley's popular novel *Westward Ho!* (1855), which glorifies Protestant Elizabethans and vilifies Catholic Spaniards and Irish persons, also helps us to understand the tensions of the age. As George Eliot pointed out, Kingsley spends much of his time 'riding down' Jesuits.[10] Kingsley, however, could not sustain his attack on the Catholics and Irish: the novel was completed during the Crimean war and Kingsley was disturbed to discover that many of the troops dying at the front as a result of cold, cholera and incompetence, were Catholic Irish. During the novel he glosses over Walter Raleigh's part in the atrocities in Ireland in the sixteenth century but has to admit to the virtues of the Irish when he refers to the Crimean war. Unlike the 'successful' wars fought when the nation was being forged, this war—the first war to be made public by way of the new phenomenon of war-reporting—provided worrying evidence of incompetence and corruption within the nation. This is one symptom of the wider problem: when war fails to restore and maintain identity, other means must be found.

The other factor taking us beyond Colley's analysis of the pre-Victorian period is the impact of Darwinism. From 1859 onwards, believers in a Protestant Genesis had to cope with the march of science and the age of Victorian exploration. The prognathous human face was associated with the appearance in zoos of apes and Orang Utans, now seen by the public for the first time. The theory of evolution proposed by Darwin and Wallace (*The Origin of Species*, 1859) was angrily rejected by many, partly on the grounds that it was insulting to the dignity of a human species that preferred to think it had been made by God rather than having evolved from an ape. An effective way of distancing oneself from animal ancestry was to put the Celt between you and the past: if the human did derive from the ape, it was the primitive or dark skinned races that were closest to the point of origin. Perceptions of Darwinism combined with the 'science' of Beddoe to bolster assumptions about the contrast between superior, fair Saxons and inferior, dark Celts.

This returns us to the question of the kind of reader produced by the many texts about and images of the Celt. The principal reason for the Victorian interest in the Celt is the need to produce the 'Saxon'. It was essential to the welfare and continuity of the nation's self-image to create and re-create the true 'Briton' who 'never, never' shall be a slave; and, as we have seen, this is a time when war could not fulfil this role, and a unifying national religion was seriously under question from science. Matthew Arnold was brought up by his father Thomas Arnold, Headmaster of Rugby, to think of the 'Celt as separated by an impassable gulf from the Teuton'.[11] Despite this gulf, the Celt is present, not absent. He is needed in the background in order to foreground what it means to be Saxon. As Bryant explains: 'We know the Teuton by his divergence from the Celt, and the Celt by his divergence from the Teuton'

(533). In 1848, that year of revolutions in Europe, the 'nation' announced:

> Thank God we are Saxons! Flanked by the savage Celt on the one side and the flighty Gaul on the other...we feel deeply grateful from our inmost hearts that we belong to a race, which if it cannot boast the flowing fancy of one of its neighbours, nor the brilliant *esprit* of the other, has ample compensation in [a] social, slow, reflective, phlegmatic temperament.[12]

Within the language of simple stereotypes, the Saxon was everything the Celt was not. The Celt was dark; the Saxon was fair. The Celt was imaginative but impractical; the Saxon was a hard-headed man of action. The Celt was untrustworthy and work-shy; the Saxon was a sturdy worker. The Celt was anarchical and violent; the Saxon was orderly and law-abiding. The Celt was an animal; the Saxon was a man. Stereotypes of race and gender coalesce here. The Celt was inclined to be hysterical like a woman; the Saxon kept his eyes on reality as a man should. The Celt had attractive and charming qualities but these were out-weighed by his fundamental weaknesses. The Celt would get into trouble without strong paternal guidance. It was for the Saxon to lead and the Celt to follow. History demonstrated that the Celt lost battles and that the Saxon won them. The tension between dark Celt and fair Saxon is evident in Tennyson's popular Arthurian epic, *The Idylls of the King*. Tennyson gives King Arthur dark Celtic ancestors, but he also gives Arthur a supernatural birth and makes him fair. A figure with Celtic origins who represents Celtic resistance to the Saxons has to be partially Saxonised in order to be a satisfactory hero for the Victorian English. (Tennyson's Arthur is in fact closely modelled on the Teutonic Prince Albert.)

The Celts were not always entirely dehumanised, although they were routinely patronised. Beddoe quotes Cobbe speaking of the Irish and the Welsh: "' the love of justice and truth, the backbone of every Englishman's nature, is replaced by the imperfect substitute of personal loyalty or general kindliness'" (261). More usually, the Irish Celt is given the worst treatment of all the Celts, not merely patronised but dehumanised. Arnold, despite his Cornish links, wanted a Celt who belonged in the past as a political force and in the present only as a cultural one:

> I know my brother Saxons, I know their strength, and I know that the Celtic genius will make nothing of trying to set up barriers against them in the world of fact and brute force, of trying to hold its own against them as a political and social counter-power, as the soul of hostile nationality. To me there is something mournful...in hearing a Welshman or an Irishman make pretensions—natural pretensions, I admit, but how hopelessly vain!—to such a rival self-establishment.... It is not in the outward and visible world of material life that the Celtic genius of Wales and Ireland can at this day hope to count for much; it is in the inward world of thought and science. What is *has* been, what is *has* done, let it ask us to attend to that, as a matter of science and history; not to what it will be or will do, as a matter of modern politics'.[13]

Wales (despite the Rebecca riots), Scotland (despite the Jacobite past) and Cornwall (despite rumours about wrecking) could play the role of an exotic, rural 'other' which offered a holiday from Saxon, urban reality. This Celtic territory was glamorous but not part of the real business of life. Ireland, however, was a place where cultural difference was combined with the reality of political and violent action. Ireland was a stubborn and threatening 'other', both over the water and at home within the mainland cities. This sense of an irreducible 'Irishness' is sustained from the middle to the late-nineteenth century within England. In 1848, just after the Irish Famine and the fears of immigration it produced in England, Carlyle conceded that the Irish had been the victims of English injustice but then constructed an Irish stereotype that justified even more injustice. This Irishman has 'wild Milesian features, looking false ingenuity, restlessness, unreason, misery and mockery'; he is 'uncivilised' and lives in world of 'squalor and unreason', 'falsity and drunken violence'. A danger within his own sphere, he is also a threat to society: he is 'the ready-made nucleus of degradation and disorder'. He is characterised as sub-human, prone to 'laughing savagery' and 'squalid apehood'.[14] In 1885 Beddoe spoke in more moderate terms but still in a way that gives the Irish a special status. Beddoe did not think that Irish immigration had changed the racial mix of the English: 'the great Irish immigration of late years is not at present ethnologically, very important; for the Irish are amongst us, but not of us, and generally intermarry among themselves'(139). 'Amongst us but not of us': this a phrase that can stand as a sign for the prevalent English attitude to the Irish in this period.

THE CELT IMAGINED

How did the scientific observer of the Celt collect the evidence so necessary to his scientific pose? This is Beddoe's improbable account of the way he worked when in Ireland:

> I measured a considerable number (thirty or more) of living heads, and observed the eyes and hair of hundreds of subjects. The heads were almost all got by stratagem. Whenever a group of eligible peasants had collected around our party, two of us would get up a dispute as to which had the larger head, and I was called in to settle the doubt with my callipers and tape. The interest of Paddy was quickly excited; before I had finished several of the bystanders would be wagering on

the respective sizes of their own heads, and begging me
to settle their differences by measurement.[15]

Beddoe provides hints that the individuals he is content to
lump together as 'Paddy' did not all react to him in exactly the
same way. He reveals that 'such people, if approached directly,
always broke away at once, suspecting some concealed
mischief devised by "Government"'. Regarding the most
inferior type, the Sancho-Panza Celt, he comments: 'it is
curious, psychologically, that the most exquisite examples of it
never would submit to measurement' (10). Given the history of
John Bull and his 'Other Island', the modern reader finds it
'curious' that anyone willingly submitted to such
investigations and wonders how many fell for transparently
obvious ruses designed to elicit information.

This leads to the question of whom we should trust to take
us beyond the Victorian stereotypes. The famous Irish literary
Renaissance was inspired by men and women, from Douglas
Hyde to Yeats and Lady Gregory, who claimed to work very
differently from the men of science. They set out to revive and
restore the dignity and culture of a nation, not by measuring
the people but by listening to them. They recorded the many
tales that they heard in Gaelic and Hiberno-English, and
indirectly gave us some knowledge of the tale-tellers, the
individual human beings who had been subsumed by
stereotypes and statistics. Synge was keenly aware that the
caricatures of *Punch* had made 'the Irish character a sealed
book to Englishmen'.[16] He set out to open this book, not by
idealising the Irish peasant but by listening to him:

When a benevolent visitor comes to his cottage seeking
a sort of holy family, the man of the house, his wife and
all their infants, too courteous to disappoint him, play
their parts with delight. When the amiable visitor,
however, is once more in the boreen, a storm of good-
tempered irony breaks out behind him, that would

surprise him could he hear it. This irony I have met with
many times…and I have always been overjoyed to hear
it. It shows that in spite of relief works, Commissions
and patronising philanthropy—that sickly thing—the
Irish peasant, is neither abject nor servile (224).

This is a vivid contrast to Beddoe's account of his methods.
Synge does not stereotype his subjects. He knows that human
beings are capable of acting parts; he knows that they wear
masks but he is watching when they remove them.

The intention here is not to use a folklorist's perspective to
explore the tales that Yeats, Synge and Lady Gregory collected
or invented. Neither is it to dismiss their work as the creation
of a stereotyped peasant which was of more use to the Anglo-
Irish Protestant ascendancy than to the Irish tale tellers,
although this question does need to be considered. Rather, it is
to contrast the reader produced by the texts that the revival
created with the reader produced by the Victorian men of
science and the *Punch* cartoonists. The focus is on one
example of the work of the Irish Renaissance, some of the
lesser known prose writings of J.M. Synge: *In Wicklow, West
Kerry and Connemara*. This text is chosen because it
represents a particular type of work produced at the close of
the Victorian period by writers with Irish allegiances. It is a
type of work firmly attached to a sense of place, a text that
sends you to topography and from topography back to the text.
This is one of the ways for a suppressed nation to find itself:
the land and its people become a source of identity that escapes
stereotyping.

Jack B. Yeats observed that Synge 'was by nature well
equipped for the roads' and that he seemed more interested in
meeting and listening to people than reading books (402-3).
J.M. Synge's prose records of his travels in Ireland between
1898 and 1905 bring us close to the territory of Ireland as
experienced by a walker and by a listener to the voice of the

people. Here is Synge not only observing but also participating in the cliff-scapes of West Kerry:

> I turned up a sharp, green hill, and came out suddenly on the broken edge of a cliff. The effect was wonderful. The Atlantic was right underneath; then I could see the sharp rocks of several uninhabited islands, a mile or two off, the Tearaught further away, and, on my left, the whole northern edge of this island curving round towards the west, with a steep heathery face, a thousand feet high. The whole sight of wild islands and sea was as clear and cold and brilliant as what one sees in a dream, and alive with the singularly severe glory that is in the character of this place. (86)

Synge finds that the actual, live interaction between participative observer and place can be better than the idealisation of a place in memory:

> Often, when one comes back to a place that one's memory and imagination have been busy with, there is a feeling of smallness and disappointment...This morning, however, when I went up the gap between Croagh Martin and then back to Slea Head, and saw Innishtooskert and Inishvickillaun and the Great Blasket Island itself, they seemed ten times more grey and wild and magnificent than anything I had kept in my memory. The cold sea and surf, and the feeling of winter in the clouds, and the blackness of the rocks, and the red fern everywhere, were a continual surprise and excitement .(280)

Synge is sensitive to people as well as place. He can tell the difference between true and false local knowledge. He was critical of the urban 'carmen' who drove well-intentioned but

ignorant Government inspectors through rural districts and
were their chief guide as to the views of the people. According
to Synge, these 'carmen' found out how to tell the inspectors
what they wanted to hear: town prejudice about rural ways was
then dressed as local wisdom (321). Synge attempted to
position himself *with* rather than *above* the country people that
he met during his travels. Rather than passing through a place,
he tried to see the world from that place's point of view. For
example he undermined talk of the 'sloth and ignorance' of
country people by re-defining why a person might be 'slow' to
adopt new ways:

> The people have traditional views and instincts about
> agriculture and live-stock, and they have a perfectly
> natural slowness to adopt the advice of an official
> expert who knows nothing of the peculiar conditions of
> their native place. (340)

Synge records places respectfully, through the voices of those
who live and work in them. He enables us to overhear the
repartee at the Wicklow country fair: 'a man said to a seller:
"You're asking too much for them lambs."   The seller
answered : "If I didn't ask it how would I ever get it?"...'(225).
He enables us to hear the tramp describing the solitude and
independence of his life: 'When he was too old to wander in
the world, he learned all the paths of Wicklow, and till the end
of his life he could go the thirty miles from Dublin to the
Seven Churches without, as he said, "putting out his foot on a
white road, or seeing any Christian but the hares and
moon"'(203). From Synge's written record, we can hear this
young woman's voice:

> The women in this place have little time to be
> spinning, but the women back on the mountains do
> be mixing colours through their wool till you'd
> never ask to take your eyes from it. They do be

throwing in a bit of stone colour, and a bit of red
madder, and a bit of crimson, and a bit of stone
colour again, and, believe me, it is nice stuffs they
do make that you'd never ask to take your eyes
from. (320)

Synge shows that even a little use of the Irish language can
change the perceptions of an observer. This is his encounter
with a beggar-woman who can speak the poetry of the people:

We gave her a few halfpence, and as she was moving
away with an ordinary 'God save you!' I said a blessing
to her in Irish to show her I knew her own language if
she chose to use it. Immediately she turned back
towards me and began her thanks again, this time with
extraordinary profusion. 'That the blessing of God may
be on you,' she said, 'on road and on ridgeway, on sea
and on land, on flood and on mountain, in all the
kingdoms of the world'—and so on, till I was too far off
to hear what she was saying. (287)

Thanks to Synge we can visualise remote Dinish Island and the
'quality' who visit it through the eyes of a local ferryman:

And isn't it a queer thing to be sitting here now thinking
on those times, and I after being near twenty years back
on this bit of a rock that a dog wouldn't look at, where
the pigs die and the spuds die, and even the judges and
quality do come out and do lower our rents when they
see the wild Atlantic driving in across the cursed stones.
(304)

Synge's 'Celts' are not stereotypes. They are not
sentimentalised or vilified. They are individuals who share a
common language and culture but who live in particular places
and know particular forms of labour. Synge does not survey

them, he shows them surveying their world; he does not speak
at them or *about* them, he lets them speak for themselves.
When they speak they judge both their own behaviour and
those who would judge them. Synge's texts produce a reader
who crosses the border from the dehumanised images of *Punch*
to the human, from the haughty tone to the compassionate,
from the abstract to the particular, from no particular place to,
exactly, Dinish Island. They position a reader alongside the
workers in the landscape, not above them. They enable the
reader to imagine distinctive voices and individual lives.

The word 'imagined' in the sub-title of this final section,
draws on the long and complex literary tradition from
Shakespeare's famous lines about the lunatic, the lover and the
poet, to Coleridge's *Biographia Literaria* and 'Frost at
Midnight'. The word 'imagined' here particularly relates to
that theory of imagination and art outlined by Shelley and
George Eliot. Eliot explains it as follows:

> The greatest benefit we owe to the artist, whether
> painter, poet, or novelist, is the extension of our
> sympathies. Appeals founded on generalisations and
> statistics require a sympathy ready-made…but a picture
> of human life such as a great artist can give, surprises
> even the trivial and selfish into that attention to what is
> apart from themselves….Art is the nearest thing to life;
> it is a mode of amplifying experience and extending our
> contact with our fellow-men beyond the bounds of our
> personal lot. (110)

The reader of all the texts discussed here can escape from
pernicious caricature, vague generalisation and manipulable
statistics to Synge's world of firm particulars and human
sympathies. The Celt stereotyped poses disturbing questions.
The Celt historicised enables us to contextualise and
understand some of these questions. The Celt imagined is the
figure who offers an opportunity to answer these questions.

NOTES

1. Ernest Renan, *The Poetry of the Celtic Races and Other Studies*, trans. W.G. Hutchison, London 1896, 1-2.

2. John Beddoe, *The Races of Britain: A Contribution to the Anthropology of Western Europe*, London 1885, 245-6. Further references are to this edition and are given in the text in parentheses.

3. L. Perry Curtis Jr., *Apes and Angels: The Irishman in Victorian Caricature*, revised edition, Washington and London 1997.

4. *Ibid.*, 168.

5. Francis Power Cobbe, 'The Celt of Wales and the Celt of Ireland', *The Cornhill Magazine*, 36 (1877), 666.

6. Sophie Bryant, 'The Celtic Mind', *The Contemporary Review*, 72 (1897), 533. Further references to this article are given in the text in parentheses.

7. Power Cobbe, *op.cit.*, 664.

8. Linda Colley, *Britons: Forging the Nation 1707-1837*, London 1992, 11-43.

9. Power Cobbe, *op.cit.*, 633.

10. A.S. Byatt and N. Warren, eds, *George Eliot: Selected Essays, Poems and Other Writings*, Harmondsworth 1990, 312.

11. Matthew Arnold, 'On the Study of Celtic Literature' in R.H. Super, ed., *Matthew Arnold: Lectures and Essays in Criticism*, Ann Arbor 1973, 298.

12. Quoted in Raphael Samuel, *Island Stories: Unravelling Britain*, London 1998, 60.

13. Arnold, *op.cit.*, 1866, 298.

14. Thomas Carlyle, 'Chartism' in *Thomas Carlyle: Selected Writings*, edited by Alan Shelston, Harmondsworth 1988, 171-2.

15. John Beddoe, *Memories of Eighty Years*, London 1910, 180-181.

16. J.M. Synge, *Collected Works: Prose*, edited by Alan Price, London 1966, 2, 397. Further references are to this edition and are given in the text in parentheses.

Yeats and Pearse in Dialogue

ROBERT TRACY

It was a Poet's Rebellion with too much literature.

Roscommon Herald, 27th May 1916

On the 24th April 1916, Easter Monday, Padraic Pearse strode out from beneath the iconic portal of Dublin's General Post Office at 12:45 p.m. Standing on a chair between two pillars, he read aloud a printed document which he had carefully composed, proclaiming the establishment of the Irish Republic.[1] Pearse, the newly designated President of the Republic's Provisional Government, and Commander-in-Chief of the army of the Republic, wore the grey-green military uniform and a bush hat of the Irish Volunteers, and a ceremonial sword.

A little past noon, members of the Volunteers and of the Irish Citizens Army, on what had seemed a routine practice march along Dublin's O'Connell Street, had suddenly halted, wheeled, and charged into the Post Office. Driving out

the postal staff and any stray customers, they began to prepare
the building for defence against the inevitable attack by units of
the British Army. As Pearse read his Proclamation, members of
the Volunteer and of the Citizen Army were seizing and fortify-
ing other strategic or symbolic points throughout the city of
Dublin. He hoped that similar events were taking place elsewhere in Ireland. Pearse read his Proclamation from a printed
broadsheet about the size of an average page of newsprint. His
text had been secretly printed a day earlier, on an old balky press
in the basement of Liberty Hall, the headquarters of the Irish
Transport and General Workers' Union and of the Union's military branch, the Citizen Army. Twenty-five hundred copies
were printed, and while Pearse read they were being distributed
around Dublin, some handed to passers-by, some posted on
walls, one, held down by four paving stones, spread out on the
plinth of Nelson's Pillar. The Proclamation that Pearse read is
now a sacred text, the birth certificate of independent Ireland –
though in fact the independence it so decisively declared would
only be won after fierce guerrilla warfare in 1912-21, and later
painstaking negotiations with successive British governments.
Irish independence would be claimed, seized, struggled for, and
eventually achieved, but the Irish Republic did not fully gain
complete independence until 1949.

Pearse's Proclamation is a remarkable statement. It declares
Irish independence to be a fundamental right, guarantees religious and civil liberty, and repudiates any intention of punishing
or subduing those in Ireland who traditionally supported British
rule. In promising that a 'permanent National Government' will
be 'elected by the suffrages of all' Ireland's 'men and women,'
the Proclamation affirms for women a right then denied by
Great Britain and the United States, and indeed by almost every
country in the world.

Since 1916 Pearse's Proclamation has rightly been examined
as a political document, in a sense the fundamental law of the
Republic of Ireland. But it is also a work of imaginative literature, a dramatic monologue written to be performed in a dramatic setting under particularly dramatic circumstances. As a
backdrop, Pearse chose the Post Office's classical portico, an

assertive reminder of British rule, its typanum adorned with the British royal arms in stone. As he read, the elegant building behind him became the military/ political headquarters of the Republic. He faced Nelson's Pillar, a monument to Britain's triumph over the ideas of the French Revolution, ideas which were echoed in the Pearse's text. Before him, and away on either side, stretched the broad dimensions of O'Connell Street – still officially Sackville Street, but already O'Connell Street to Irish nationalists. High above his head, the portico supported a statue of Hibernia, flanked by the statues of Mercury and Fidelity.

Pearse spoke for Ireland - Hibernia - and as he read, he too was flanked by two representative figures.[2] One was Thomas Clarke, a member of the Irish Republican Brotherhood since 1878, veteran of sixteen years' solitary confinement in English prisons, and after 1907 the reviver and reorganizer of the IRB in Ireland. Clarke was the keeper of the Fenian flame that Pearse hoped to 'fan' and a visible guarantor of that 'apostolic succession' of Irish rebels that Pearse considered a necessary component of revolutionary orthodoxy.[3]

Pearse's other companion was James Connolly, no less a nationalist, but standing also for new ideas about political equality and civil rights. Their presence beside Pearse emphasised the dual nature of the Rising, nationalist but also democratic, democratic but also nationalist, and reinforced the Proclamation's mixture of almost mystical exhortation and advanced social doctrine.

From where he stood, Pearse could see to his right O'Connell's monument, to his left Parnell's, his predecessors in the struggle to gain for the Irish people the right to rule themselves in Ireland. His green uniform was a modern version of the uniform Robert Emmet had worn to lead the last Dublin rising against British rule, on 23 July 1803. Emmet too had proclaimed Ireland's independence, and hoped 'to establish a free and independent republic in Ireland'.[4] As both exemplar and rebel he was much in Pearse's mind during Easter Week. 'Robert Emmet's memory haunted the mind and personality of Pearse', his pupil and first biographer, Desmond Ryan, recalled.[5] Pearse's Emmet was a hero of romance with whom he could identify: a 'dreamer...student...recluse' who became 'a man of action...a leader of men'.[6] No failure, as the world judges these things, was ever more complete, more pathetic than Emmet's, Pearse declared in 1914; but 'he has left us a prouder memory' than the memory of any Irish victory: 'It is the memory of a sacrifice Christ-like in its perfection'.[7] In the middle of Easter Monday afternoon, remembering that Emmet's insurrection lasted only two hours, Pearse checked his watch and exclaimed, 'We've already put Emmet's revolt in the shade'.[8] On Thursday he told Desmond Ryan, 'Emmet's insurrection was nothing compared to this...Dublin's name will be glorious forever'.[9]

Pearse's green uniform also subtly echoed the new green flag- with 'Irish Republic' painted on it in gold letters-that had just been raised above the Post Office, at the South of Prince's Street corner, and the green in the tricolour, the green, white and orange flag of Fenians, now flying above the north or Henry Street corner of the building. His sword invoked those images of antique heroism and chivalry that often filled Pearse's imagination. Emmet too had carried a sword.

Setting and costume, then, reinforced Pearse's text, enhanced its dramatic impact, if only on his immediate companions and the few Dubliners within the sound of his voice. But the text itself is central. In its strategies we can recognise a romantic literary mind striving to achieve a powerful emotional effect. Pearse creates a mystical presence, a personified Ireland, to stand with him and his comrades. 'What stood in the Post office/With Pearse and Connolly?'Yeats was to ask many years later in his play *The Death of Cuchulain* (1939).

Yeats was thinking of the doomed heroic Cuchulain, for whom Pearse had, Yeats said, 'a cult'.[10] But in the Proclamation Pearse implicitly evokes the more emotive presence of Mother Ireland, at once Poor Old Woman, maiden in distress, and the Warrior Queen, a dispossessed woman, usually young, representing Ireland: Cathleen Ni Houlihan, Erin, Dark Rosaleen.[11] He artfully identifies this figure, a traditional subject of Irish loyalties, with a more abstract and political concept, the 'Irish Republic'. But even the Republic is less a theory of government than another mystical object of loyalty and devotion. Ireland,

Mother Ireland, and the Irish Republic become a single concept, evoking a combination of traditional loyalties, as did the traditional green flag and the equally traditional tricolour breaking out above Pearse's head as he stood on a chair and read his Proclamation.

How strongly his evocation of Cathleen entered the popular mind is shown by the icons available in Ireland by the summer of 1916, as Pearse and his companions began to assume the status of national heroes. Cathleen, often in chains, has represented Ireland as maiden in distress, England's helpless victim in the nineteenth century political iconography.[12] After the Rising, a popular print showed an idealised Volunteer in the sleep of death; beside him, with laurelled head bowed, Cathleen weeps over a fallen tricolour, while an angel consoles her by pointing heavenwards. In another print a militant Cathleen unfurls the tricolour in a ray of sunlight above a trench where Volunteers fire rifles or reel back wounded; the print is captioned 'The Birth of the Irish Republic'.[13]

In composing the Proclamation, Pearse drew on his own earlier political writings, especially those exploring Ireland's republican or separatist tradition, and on the doctrine of the already existing but invisible Irish republic as held by the nineteenth century Irish Republican Brotherhood or Fenians. The IRB/Fenians insisted that the Irish Republic did not need to be declared or inaugurated because it had been in existence, though unrecognised, for an unspecified period of time, perhaps since Emmet's rebellion. Its existence was real, though hidden; its concealment in no way affected its legitimacy and it was entitled to the loyalty of all Irish men and women. As founded by James Stephens on St. Patrick's Day, 1858, the IRB imposed an oath which began, 'I (name) do solemnly swear allegiance to the Irish Republic, *now virtually established* [italics mine]; that I will take up in arms at a moment's notice to defend its integrity and independence'.[14] Pearse and the other leaders of 1916 had taken that oath. The Republic 'now virtually established' was in fact a fiction, a literary creation existing only in the imagination, and in the printed texts which gave it a purely textual reality. But it was a powerful fiction.

But along with his reiteration of Fenian doctrine in the Proclamation, Pearse also entered, perhaps deliberately, into a dialogue with W.B. Yeats, who had unknowingly initiated that dialogue with his play *Cathleen Ni Houlihan* (1902). We know that
Lady Gregory was at least the co-author of the play.[15] But to
Pearse it was Yeats's. In any case, his response to the play's subject and theme: Ireland, personified as Cathleen, suddenly appears, in an ordinary place among ordinary people, demanding
that at least one of them do something extraordinary. She demands that a young man go out to fight for her and perhaps die
for her, promising in return not victory, but only that his sacrifice will be remembered and preserved in patriotic litanies and
ballads. The sudden and unexpected appearance of Padraic
Pearse outside the G.P.O. on Easter Monday, with his Proclamation summoning the people of Dublin to join the rising, implicitly recalls Yeats's Cathleen and her call to an action that h-
as no real promise of success. After the suppression of the Rising, and the execution of its leaders, Yeats would continue the
dialogue with 'Easter 1916', his response to the Rising and
especially to Pearse's Proclamation. He continued to brood
over a possible connection between *Cathleen ni Houlihan* and
the Easter Rising until his death.

In 'The Man and the Echo', written in 1938, Yeats pondered
his own possible responsibility for the 1916 Rising and some of
its consequences: the executions, the later erratic career of Maud
Gonne, the destruction of so many Big Houses in the Irish War
of Independence (1919-21). 'Did that play of mine send
out/Certain men the English shot?[16] Yeats famously asked, a
question Paul Muldoon briskly answered some forty years later
with ' "Certainly not" 'adding, 'If Yeats had saved his pencil-
lead/Would certain men have stayed in bed?'[17] Most historians
would comfort–or annoy Yeats by denying him credit or
blame for these events, and so, as he implies, for the emergence
of an independent Ireland. Nevertheless, Yeats did play his role
in preparing for the rising by initiating the dialogue that Pearse
would take up in the Proclamation of the Irish Republic.

Cathleen ni Houlihan (1902) – as the play in question–had a
strong effect on Pearse, and indeed on many Irish nationalists

who saw its first production, with Maud Gonne playing the title
role and so symbolically embodying the mysterious fugitive
spirit of the Irish nation. 'When I was a child I believed that
there was actually a woman called Erin', Pearse tells us in *The
Spiritual Nation* (13 February 1916), one of a series of pam-
phlets he wrote explaining his political ideas in the months preceding the Rising:

> ....and had Mr. Yeats' "Kathleen Ni Houlihan" [sic] been
> then written and had I seen it, I should have taken it not
> as an allegory, but as a representation of a thing that
> might happen any day in any house. This I no longer be-
> lieve as a physical possibility, nor can I convince mys-
> elf that a friend of mine is right thinking that there is
> a mystical entity which is the soul of Ireland, and which
> expresses itself through the mind of Ireland. But I believe
> that there is really a spiritual tradition which is the soul of
> Ireland, the thing which makes Ireland a living nation
> ...This spiritual thing is distinct from the intellectual
> facts in which chiefly it makes its revelation, and it is
> distinct from them in a way analogous to that in which
> a man's soul is distinct from his mind.[18]

In Pearse's Proclamation, paragraphs three, four, and five are
specifically political and explain the principals that will guide
the new Irish Republic. But the other three paragraphs, and especially the first and last, invoke God, the 'dead generations'
who have preserved Ireland's 'tradition of nationhood', and
claim to speak for Ireland herself, that mystical elusive woman
who in Yeats's play summons Michael Gillane to her service.
Pearse and his fellow signatories of the Proclamation summon
'Irishmen and Irishwomen' to serve the newly proclaimed Irish
Republic. In Pearse's words, Ireland – here personified as 'she'
'summons...through us...her children to her flag' to fight and,
if need be, 'to sacrifice themselves'. If Cathleen/Ireland spoke
through Yeats's words and Maud Gonne's performance to demand voluntary sacrifice, Pearse and his fellow signatories are

the collective medium through which the eternal spirit of Ireland speaks to make the same demand.

In Yeats's play, the Old Woman, who is Cathleen, personifies an Ireland robbed of her land and independence. She is said to appear during troubled times. Yeats too has taken the IRB oath to the invisible Republic[19] and the mysterious but not exactly human Cathleen is a successful metaphor for that persistent but elusive concept. Cathleen appears in a Killala cottage in 1798 to entice young Michael to join General Humbert's French army and go out and die for Ireland. She casts a kind of spell over Michael by singing about one 'yellow- haired Donough' who died for her and listing others who resisted foreign rule:Red Hugh O'Donnell, O'Sullivan Beare, Brian Boru. In the Proclamation, Pearse reminds his readers that 'six times in the past three hundred years...the Irish people have asserted their right to national freedom...in arms'. Yeats's rebels are heroic figures from a remote past. In his pamphlet *Ghosts* (Christmas 1915) Pearse celebrates the six more recent rebellions he refers to in the Proclamation: that of the Catholic Confederation (1641-48); the struggle between James II and William of Orange (1689-91); the Rising of 1798; Robert Emmet's Dublin insurrection; William Smith O'Brien's equally brief attempt at Ballingarry, County Tipperary (29 July 1848); the Fenian Rising (5 March 1867).[20] But both Yeats and Pearse offer their catalogue of rebel leaders as constituting a tradition that justifies armed rebellion. Because we Irish have done this before, we must do it again, as a redemptive act for ourselves and our generation.Yeats's Michael leaves his cottage and his bride-to-be to assist in forging a link in Pearse's chain, the doomed Rising of 1798. His commitment—his willingness to participate in a blood sacrifice—regenerates Cathleen. She is transformed from an old woman to a 'young girl' with 'the walk of a Queen'. As for Michael, she does not promise him victory, but only a 'hard service...pale cheeks'.[21]

Pearse begins the Proclamation with a phrase in Irish: '*Poblacht na hEireann*': 'the Republic of Ireland'. By using Irish, albeit sparingly, he grounds the Proclamation in the vanishing native language, and evokes that language, an object of his af-

fection and loyalty. Pearse taught Irish and established a bilin-
gual school, St.Enda's. He wrote stories, plays, and poems in
Irish, and spoke Irish whenever he could, dreaming of the day
when it would be the national vernacular. 'I have spent the best
fifteen years of my life teaching and working for the idea that
language is an essential part of the nation', he declared in Janu-
ary 1914.[22] A month later, he described the Gaelic League,
which Douglas Hyde had founded in 1893 to restore the Irish
language to daily use, as 'the most revolutionary influence that
has ever come into Ireland. The Irish Revolution really began
when the seven proto-Gaelic Leaguers met in O'Connell
Street'.[23] Pearse wrote songs in Irish, hoping the Volunteers
would sing them as they marched. He began his 'Oration at the
Grave of O'Donovan Rossa'(August 1915) with four paragraphs
in Irish, and praised Rossa as both Fenian and Gael, one of who
dreamed of Ireland as 'not free merely, but Gaelic as well; not
Gaelic merely, but free as well'.[24]

For Pearse the Irish language offered 'Irish Nationalism...renewed communication with its origins'.[25] The language
was a kind of disembodied avatar of Cathleen Ni Houlihan, and
so of Ireland. The language was fugitive, neglected, spoken only
in the poorest of districts, scorned by the Anglo-Irish literary
and educational establishments as a mud cabin argot fit for talking of pigs, potatoes, grotesque superstitions, and rustic inde-
cencies. Now it can at once express and reveal the Republic,
which has also been in hiding, a fugitive like the Poor Old
Woman of Yeats's play.

The Irish Republic becomes a mother summoning 'her children' – an image Yeats would weave into 'Easter, 1916'... our
part/ To murmur name upon name/ As a mother names her
child'.[26] She has long been concealed, carrying out the secret
military training of those who are to fight for her. There is an
ambiguity between mother and warrior queen as Cathleen
merges into Scathach, the fierce warrior woman who directed
Cuchulain's secret military training until he was ready to emerge
as Ulster's champion, master of all warlike arts. Pearse suggests
the same dual identity in a poem of 1916, ' I am Ireland':

I am Ireland;
I am older than the Old Woman of Beare.[27]

Great my glory:
I that bore Cuchulain the valiant.

Great my shame:
My own children that sold their mother.

I am Ireland:
I am lonelier than the Old Woman of Beare.

In 'An Dord Feinne' (the chant of Fianna, or Fenians), originally written in Irish, Ireland, the 'woman that was sorrowful', was 'in chains…thou sold to the Galls'[strangers], but she becomes the warrior queen 'Gráinne Mhaol and a thousand heroes/Proclaiming the scattering of the Galls!':

Gráinne Mhaol is coming from over the sea.
The Fenians of Fál as a guard about her,
Gaels they, and neither French nor Spaniard,
And a rout upon the Galls![28]

The personified Irish Republic of the Proclamation 'now seizes…the right moment' to emerge and 'strike for her freedom'. The Irish Republic speaks 'through us', Pearse and his fellow signatories. It is Ireland as Cathleen Ni Houlihan, Dark Rosaleen, Eriu, Eire, who speaks with Pearse's voice, as Ireland/Cathleen speaks through the voice of the actress playing the Old Woman in Yeats's play. Ireland/ Cathleen is revivified, as she is in the play, when young men are again willing to die for her. Her health and vigour restored by the imminent blood sacrifice, she becomes a warrior queen.

In the play, the Old Woman's summons to 'her children' to fight for her, and Michael's obedience to that summons, depend for their effect on the audience knowing that the young Irishmen who joined General Humbert in 1798 were slaughtered after they had surrendered. She does not promise victory or national

independence, only that those who fight for her will be remembered in songs:

> They shall be remembered for ever.
> They shall be alive for ever,
> The shall be speaking for ever,
> The people shall hear them forever.[29]

In 'The Mother', a poem written shortly before the Rising,[30]
Pearse echoes Yeats, imagining his own mother mourning her
'two strong sons' who die for Ireland, but at the same time celebrating their bravery:

> They and a few,
> In bloody protest for a glorious thing,
> They shall be spoken of among their people,
> The generations shall remember them,
> And call them blessed.[31]

If Pearse's poem borrowed from Yeats, Yeats borrowed
back in 'Easter 1916' where his image of 'murmur[ing] name
upon name / As a mother names her child' recalls lines from
'The Mother':

> But I will speak their names to my own heart
> In the long nights;
> The little names that were familiar once
> Round my dead hearth.

Pearse's Proclamation is a dramatic monologue, in which he
adopts the voice of the hidden Ireland, traditionally personified
as mother and warrior queen, speaking first in the suppressed
and furtive Irish language, and identified with the shadowy Irish
Republic of Emmet's Rebellion and the Fenians. Now that Republic has emerged, a real presence like the Christ of Easter, in
the most conspicuous setting Dublin offered, and in the clear
light of noon. Spirits that appear in daylight are not mere spirits;

Christ's appearance on Easter morning was evidence of physical resurrection.

The Proclamation ends with the names of the seven who signed it 'on behalf of the Provisional Government', and in fact were the Provisional Government. In one sense, the names emphasized the traditions that the Proclamation combines. Thomas Clarke's name, like his presence, connected the Rising with the Fenian/IRB tradition; Connolly's affirmed the presence of the labour movement; Pearse and Plunkett were known as the leaders of the Volunteers. The signatures announce and guarantee the unity of the three groups until then seen as separate – a unity Pearse made visible by reading the Proclamation flanked by Clarke and Connolly. But the seven names also constitute a premature martyrology. By signing, each man offered himself as a participant in the act of blood sacrifice Pearse imagined for them, either in battle or before a firing squad. To sign was to sign one's own death warrant should the Rising fail –and none of the seven seem to be under any illusion that it would succeed. By signing, each of the seven deliberately pre-inscribed himself on the long list of Irish martyrs, courting death in a way that Tone and perhaps Emmet had not. In a sense they included themselves in the sacrificial rhetoric of Pearse's text.

The list of names at the foot of the Proclamation also recalls *Cathleen ni Houlihan,* and Yeats would partially adapt it into 'Easter, 1916'. When Yeats's Cathleen lists some of those who have died for her, then sings of those who are about to do so, she promises in her song that they shall be remembered for ever in the songs and stories of the people. In effect, they pass into poetry, into art, to become the 'terrible beauty' of Easter, 1916, icons in an imagined gallery of successive heroes. In the poem, Yeats fulfils the promise his Cathleen had made in the play, and at the same time partially echoes the list of signatories with which the Proclamation ends:

> I write it out in a verse—
> MacDonagh and MacBride
> And Connolly and Pearse
> Now and in time to be,

> Wherever green is worn,
> Are changed, changed utterly:
> A terrible beauty is born.[32]

In celebrating the Easter Rising as the birth of 'a terrible beauty' Yeats, with some justification, treated Pearse's Proclamation and the Rising itself as primarily aesthetic events, ritual dramas rather than political acts. The Rising was in fact a decisive political act, especially after the executions of its leaders. But Pearse seems to have planned it to enact, and composed the Proclamation to explain, a dramatic ritual of sacrifice. That sacrifice was to take its place in a succession of such acts—the six preceding rebellions against British rule, performed, as both Yeats and Pearse imply, to nourish and sustain the soul or spirit of Ireland. Greek drama was also at once a religious and civic ritual, performed to ensure the continuation of the *polis* and nourish its values.

Yeats's literary movement developed Irish art as a necessary preamble to the achievement of an independent Irish nation: the Irish must learn aesthetic self-contemplation to be truly rather than merely nominally independent. Pearse's Proclamation is written in a similar spirit, to create an image of Irish heroism and sacrifice as a preamble to Ireland's achievement 'of the august destiny to which it is called'. It was indeed a 'terrible beauty' that he presented for his reader, listeners, spectators, and those who would come later to contemplate. Yeats's play begins a dialogue on the nature of Irish heroism and its need—indeed, its right—to be commemorated in poetry; Pearse in the Proclamation speaks as Cathleen Ni Houlihan to summon Irishmen and Irishwomen to heroism; Yeats draws on his own play and on Pearse's dramatic monologue to fulfil, in 'Easter, 1916', Cathleen's promised celebration of their heroic deeds in poetry.

NOTES

1.   See Appendix.
2.   Piraras F. MacLochlainn, *Last Words: Letters and Statements of the Leaders Executed After the Rising at Easter 1916*, Dublin 1971, 37,178.
3.   P.H. Pearse, *Collected Works: Political Writing and Speeches*, Dublin 1922, 205, 226.
4.   Richard R. Maddan, *The United Irishmen, Their Lives and Times*, vol. 3, London 1860, 546-556.
5.   Desmond Ryan, *Remembering Sion*, London 1934, 119.
6.   Pearse, *Political Writing, op. cit.*, 81-2.
7.   *Ibid,* 69.
8.   Max Caulfield, *The Easter Rebellion*, London 1965, 130.
9.   Thomas M. Coffey, *Agony at Easter: The 1916 Irish Uprising*, New York 1969, 189.
10.   W.B. Yeats, *The Letters of W. B. Yeats*, ed. Allan Wade, London 1954, 991.
11.   For Pearse's debt to the *aisling* see Ruth Dudley Edwards, *Patrick Pearse: the Triumph of Failure*, London 1977, 202, and Richard Kearney, *Myth and Motherland*, (Derry 1984)reprinted in *Ireland's Field Day*, Notre Dame, Indiana, 1986, 76-8.
12.   L. Perry Curtis, Jr. *Images of Erin the Age of Parnell*, Dublin 2000.
13.   Redmond Fitzgerald, *Cry Blood Cry Erin*, London 1966, 112, 119; Kearney, *op. cit.*, 75.
14.   John Devoy, *Recollections of an Irish Rebel*(1929), Shannon 1969, 272.
15.   R.F. Foster, *W.B. Yeats: A Life: Vol. I: the Apprentice Mage 1865-1914*, Oxford 1997, 168-9.
16.   W.B. Yeats, *The Poems*, ed. Richard J. Finneran, New York 1983, 345.
17.   Paul Muldoon, *Meeting the British*, Winston-Salem, N.C., 1987, 45-46.
18.   Pearse, *Political Writing op. cit.*, 300-301.
19.   Foster, *op. cit.*, 112-3.
20.   Pearse, *Political Writing op. cit.*, 234-39.
21.   W.B. Yeats, *The Collected Plays of W.B. Yeats*, New York 1953, 57, 54-6.
22.   Pearse, *Political Writing op. cit.*,106.
23.   Dorothy Marcardle, *The Irish Republic*, New York 1965, 61. Pearse's comment is quoted from *The Irish Volunteer*, 7 February 1914.
24.   Pearse, *Political Writing op. cit.*, 135.
25.   *Ibid.*, 72.
26.   Yeats, *The Poems, op. cit.*, 180-82.
27.   P.H. Pearse, *Collected Works: Plays, Stories, Poems*, Dublin 1918, 323.
28.   *Ibid.*, 332.
29.   Yeats, *Collected Plays, op. cit.*, 56.
30.   Edwards, *op. cit.*, 263-4.
31.   Pearse, *Plays, Stories, Poems, op. cit.*, 333.
32.   Yeats, *The Poems, op. cit.*, 182.

Appendix

The Proclamation is as follows:

Poblacht na h-Eireann
the Provisional Government
of the IRISH REPUBLIC
to the People of Ireland

IRISHMEN AND IRISHWOMEN: In the name of God and of
the dead generations from which she receives her old tradition
of nationhood, Ireland, through us, summons her children to her
flag and strikes for her freedom.

Having organised and trained her manhood through her secret revolutionary organisation, the Irish Volunteers, and the
Irish Citizen Army, having patiently perfected her discipline,
having resolutely waited for the right moment to reveal itself,
she now seizes that moment, and, supported by her exiled children in America and by the gallant allies in Europe, but relying
in the first on her own strength, she strikes in full confidence of
victory.

We declare the right of the people of Ireland to the ownership
of Ireland, and to the unfettered control of Irish destinies, to be
sovereign and indefeasible. The long usurpation of that right by
a foreign people and government has not extinguished the right,
nor can it ever be extinguished except by the destruction of the
Irish people. In every generation the Irish people have asserted
their right to national freedom and sovereignty; six times during
the last three hundred years they have asserted it in arms. Standing on that fundamental right and again asserting it in arms in
the face of the world, we hereby proclaim the Irish Republic as a
Sovereign Independent State, and we pledge our lives and the
lives of our comrades -in –arms to the cause of its freedom, of
its welfare, and of its exaltation among the nations.

The Irish Republic is entitled to, and hereby claims, the allegiance of every Irishman and Irishwoman. The Republic guarantees religious and civil liberty, equal rights and equal opportunities to all its citizens, and declares its resolve to pursue the hap-

piness and prosperity of the whole nation and all of its part's, cherishing all the children of the nation equally, and oblivious of the differences carefully fostered by an alien government, which have divided a minority from a majority in the past.

Until our arms have brought the opportune moment for the establishment of a permanent National Government, representative of the whole people of Ireland, and elected by the suffrages of all her men and women, the Provisional Government, hereby constituted, will administer the civil and military affairs of the Republican in trust for the people.

We place the cause of the Irish Republic under the protection of the Most High God, whose blessing we invoke upon our arms, and we pray that no one who serves that cause will dishonour it by cowardice, inhumanity, or rapine. In this supreme hour the Irish Nation must, by its valour and discipline and the readiness of its children to sacrifice themselves for the common good, prove itself worthy of the august destiny to which it is called.

Signed on Behalf of the Provisional Government

THOMAS J. CLARKE

SEAN Mac DIARMADA,   THOMAS Mac DONAGH,
P.H.PEARSE,   EAMONN CEANNT,
JAMES CONNOLLY,   JOSEPH PLUNKETT.

Yeats, Pearse and the Sublime Subaltern

PAUL MURPHY

This essay focuses on a paradoxical phenomenon intrinsic to Irish national ideology and the dynamics of Irish state formation during the early years of the twentieth century, particularly as it is revealed in the dramatic representation of the subaltern figure of the peasant in W.B. Yeats's *Cathleen ní Houlihan* (1902) and Pádraic Pearse's *The Singer* (1917). I use these two plays to illustrate my argument because they represent significant landmarks in what D.P. Moran famously described as the 'Battle of Two Civilizations',[1] between two ultimately incompatible visions of how Ireland was to be constituted both culturally and politically. F.S.L. Lyons has formalised this conflict as being specifically between the proponents of 'Irish Ireland versus Anglo-Irish Ireland',[2] in which the ideology of Irish Ireland and its social praxis as Catholic *bourgeois* nationalism gradually displaced British colonialism and its manifestation in the waning Protestant Anglo-Irish Ascendancy, to achieve hegemony in the establishment of the Free State in 1922. While the 'Two Civilizations' model implies a social polarisation which, *prima facie*, might seem to reduce the complexity of a much broader social spectrum, nevertheless the emphasis on the conflictual nature of Irish cultural politics is useful in understanding the significance of dramatic representation during the period leading up to the foundation of the Free State.

In the 1900s, 'the outcome of the struggle to capture the concept of "the peasant", in order to mobilise it as a sentimental connection between the various contending groups of intellectuals and the people-nation, gave a particular form of definition and concretisation to that people-nation.'[3]   While Anglo-Irish and Irish-Irish polemic 'frequently overlapped on the matter of materialism versus anti-materialism, albeit for conflicting strategic reasons, the conflicting concepts which both held of the pure peasant as the quintessence of the nation acted to crystallize their differences.'[4] This conflict famously came to a head in the protests surrounding the opening performances of   J.M. Synge's *The Playboy of the Western World* in 1907, where Synge's Anglo-Irish vision clashed head on with the orthodoxy of Irish-Irish Catholic Nationalism.[5]

What both these conflicting visions have in common in their evocation of the Peasant is the equivalence of poverty with purity, where the national essence is materialised in the form of subaltern figures whose continued subordination was the necessary condition of the economic consolidation of the Free State. It is this contradiction between social subordination and symbolic valorisation which is of concern here, and this phenomenon of the pure peasant as national essence can paradoxically but effectively be described as the sublime subaltern. In what follows here, the notion of the sublime subaltern will be situated in relation to current debate surrounding the issue of subaltern studies in the Irish context; followed by a brief analysis of Yeats's and Pearse's representation of the Peasant figure as a paradoxical trope whose symbolic valorisation is undercut by the subordinate status of the social group which that trope dramatically re-presents.

The contemporary debate over the symbolic representation of the subaltern in the Irish cultural context, exemplified by the recent work of David Lloyd[6] and Colin Graham,[7] has centred around the application of the Italian Marxist Antonio Gramsci's theories to the field of post-colonial criticism. David Lloyd offers a critique of post-colonial Irish nationalism and state formation by suggesting that, ultimately:

both imperialism and nationalism seek to occlude troublesome and unassimilable manifestations of difference by positing a transcendent realm of essential identity. The limitations of an oppositional nationalism become apparent in post-colonial states where political unification around the concept of national identity obscures continuing exploitations of class and cultural difference, and where the aim of a cultural education that retains its hegemonic forms continues to be the production of subjects fitted to the requirements of global economic imperialism.[8]

Lloyd contends that it:

is indeed precisely the inadequacy of the organizing narrative of state formation to represent such struggles, and the failure of the state itself to respond even to that dimension of feminist and labour demands whose expression takes shape within the forms of legal discourses on rights and citizenship, that has required the opening of further studies in the longer duration of labour and women's history. What such studies may yet clarify is the extent to which the failures of the state lie in the peculiar conjunction of modernity and non-modernity that forms the cultural substrata of the post-1922 Irish states. [9]

Referring to the Subaltern Studies group of historians in India and their seminal application of Gramsci's formulation of subaltern historiography[10] to post-colonial criticism, Lloyd suggests that:

in the wake of a still dominant 'revisionist' history, Irish historiography has yet to produce anything as self-conscious and theoretically reflective as *Subaltern Studies*. Nevertheless, it is clear that the last fifteen years or so has seen the emergence of a large corpus of non-elite histories: histories of agrarian movements, local histories, social histories of the complex intersections of class and colonization in rural Ireland, women's history, in the form both of biographical work and, more recently, of studies of women's movements and social history.[11]

Colin Graham has similarly argued that Subaltern Studies have had 'important effects on thinking concerning the category of the subaltern which need to be understood in order to read the subaltern into an Irish context.'[12] The editor of the first six volumes of *Subaltern Studies,* Ranajit Guha, states that the aim of the collection is to 'promote a systematic and informed discussion of subaltern themes in the field of South Asian studies, and thus help to rectify the elitist bias characteristic of much research and academic work in this particular field.'[13] In *Elementary Aspects of Peasant Insurgency in Colonial India,* Guha explains how the subaltern classes of peasants and small farmers were effectively 'written out' as agents of their own history by the historiographers of the British Raj. The British administration meticulously recorded acts of 'insurgency' by the subalterns which, when read against the grain, can be used to argue for the existence of a 'rebel consciousness' inscribed in the midst of the historical discourse which sought to marginalise and efface the subaltern, 'to acknowledge the peasant as the maker of his own rebellion is to attribute, as we have done in this work, a consciousness to him.'[14]

The notion of retrieving a 'subaltern consciousness' was problematised with the intervention of Gayatri Chakravorty Spivak who argued that to 'investigate, discover, and establish a subaltern or peasant consciousness seems at first to be a positivist project—a project which assumes that, if properly prosecuted, it will lead to a firm ground, to some *thing* that can be disclosed.'[15] As the 'colonized subaltern *subject* is irretrievably heterogeneous',[16] Spivak recommends an alternative to the quasi-archaeological approach employed by the Subaltern Studies group: 'what I find useful is the sustained and developing work on the *mechanics* of the constitution of the Other; we can use it to much greater analytic and interventionist advantage than invocations of the *authenticity* of the Other.'[17]

Colin Graham suggests that in the field of Irish post-colonial criticism Spivak's critique of Subaltern Studies' methodology and her emphasis on the 'mechanics of the ordering of subaltern/dominant relations rather than searching for an authentic site of pure insurgency' is the 'starting point of reading the gendered-subaltern.'[18] Graham contends that disagreements about the status of gender in the Irish cultural context show that 'gender in Ireland, because it is figuratively central to nationalist ideologies and yet subversive of them, will enable a critique of subalternity, nationalism, colonialism and post-colonialism which will unveil the mechanics of their constitution of the gendered Other.'[19]

Graham's advocacy of Spivak's emphasis on the 'mechanics' of the 'constitution' of the subaltern informs the methodological approach of this essay, in the sense that, rather than essentialising the subaltern subject as 'some *thing* that can be disclosed', the aim is to show that the subaltern is *already* essentialised within hegemonic discourse, and to explain *how* the subaltern is essentialised as a fantasy object which is symbolically central but maintains its disruptive power through the contradiction of the social subordination of the subject which that fantasy object represents. If we understand 'fantasy object' in the sense offered by the radical psychoanalytic theories of Jacques Lacan as the '*objet petit à*',[20] then an analysis of the essentialisation of the subaltern as the supporting or anaclitic element within ideology can be enhanced. Lacanian theory can be somewhat complex and, while it defies simplification, Jacqueline Rose offers a concise definition of the major elements of Lacan's triadic paradigm:

Lacan termed the object of language the symbolic, that of the ego and its identifications the imaginary (the stress, therefore, is quite deliberately on symbol and image, the idea of something which 'stands in'). The real was then his term for the moment of impossibility onto which both are grafted, the point of that moment's endless return.[21]

One can perhaps begin to understand the *objet petit à* as the impossible moment of the Real in the oxymoronic sense as a 'materialised absence' or an 'empty' signifier, which functions as the receptacle for semiotic investment in a manner similar to object cathexis[22] in the Freudian sense. As Lacanian theorist Slavoj Žižek explains:

> the Real [is] that which resists symbolization: the traumatic point which is always missed but none the less always returns, although we try—through a set of different strategies—to neutralise it, to integrate it into the symbolic order. In the perspective of the last stage of Lacanian teaching, it is precisely the symptom which is conceived as such a real kernel of enjoyment, which persists as a surplus and returns though all attempts to domesticate it, to gentrify it...to dissolve it by means of explication, of putting-into-words its meaning.[23]

It is by way of these shared senses of *objet petit à* and symptom that we can understand how the subaltern is essentialised as a sublime object which is used as the mainstay of the competing ideologies of both Anglo-Irish and Irish-Irish Ireland. As Žižek suggests, '[t]he function of ideology is not to offer us a point of escape from our reality but to offer us the social reality itself as an escape from some traumatic, real kernel.'[24] This traumatic kernel of the Real which the Symbolic order of ideology attempts to incorporate can be understood as the social antagonisms implicit to class hierarchy which is manifest symptomatically in both drama and ideology in the trope of the Peasant. After 1922, the hegemony of Irish Ireland established itself through the social praxis of Catholic *bourgeois* nationalism, an ideological fantasy space which effectively structured the reality of the Irish people-nation in their practical, quotidian experience. If we interpret Yeats's romantic notion of Ireland as *The Land of Heart's Desire*[25] in the Lacanian sense, then we can conceive of an ideological fantasy space which is constituted around the essentialisation of subaltern groups whose status as symptoms disrupts the structural integrity of the competing ideologies which inhabit that national fantasy space. It is then possible to see the 'transcendent realm of essential identity' in the heart of nationalism as being ironically replete with the 'troublesome and inassimilable manifestations of difference'[26] which it seeks to occlude.

Yeats's *Cathleen ní Houlihan* (1902) represents a subtle shift in strategy consequent to the opprobrium that surrounded his earlier play, *The Countess Cathleen* (1899), as Yeats's Anglo-Irish vision manifests itself in a motif which is subtextually insinuated under the prevailing leitmotif of anti-colonial propaganda. The aristocrat/peasant dyad returns but is cleverly imbued with the spirit of revolutionary nationalism, as The Poor Old Woman named Cathleen ní Houlihan who symbolises Mother Ireland calls upon her faithful sons, typified in the young Michael Gillane, to shed blood in a war of national liberation so that she may be reborn as a 'young girl' with the 'walk of a queen'.[27] The setting for the play in the '[i]nterior of a cottage close to Killala, in 1798'[28] could hardly have been more emotionally charged for a Catholic Nationalist audience, as *Cathleen ní Houlihan* represents Yeats's closest approximation to an ideological suture between the two conflicting visions of Anglo-Irish and Irish-Irish Ireland, by playing on the symbolic ambiguity surrounding the relationship between Cathleen and Michael.   From an Irish Ireland perspective Cathleen ní Houlihan represents one of many personifications of Ireland as republican matriarch, variously described in nationalist folklore and legend as the Shan Van Vocht or Dark Rosaleen.[29] Michael accordingly represents the patriotic Catholic nationalist subject, faithfully performing his duty to retrieve his nation's sovereignty from foreign domination. The benefits of his blood sacrifice will be reaped by future generations when colonial Ireland as Poor 'Old' Woman will be reborn as a 'young'

Catholic nationalist republic. From an Anglo-Irish Ireland viewpoint Cathleen ní Houlihan represents the personification of the Ascendancy as aristocratic matriarch, who calls upon her peasantry/tenantry to unite with her against a common foreign enemy and consolidate their shared territory *à la* Samuel Ferguson's 'green point of neutral ground, where all parties may meet in kindness and part in peace'[30] once political autonomy from England had been achieved. In this perspective the plot echoes the standard scenario in Standish O'Grady's *History of Ireland:The Heroic Period* [31], where the Celtic Warrior swears allegiance and performs deeds of heroic self-sacrifice to the noble Chieftain. What is crucial in this reading is that the body-politic of Old Mother Ireland would be reborn as a 'young girl' specifically with the 'walk of a queen', implying the renewal of a decidedly aristocratic style of leadership. Victory in this mythopoeic history of the 1798 rising would mean that the 1800 Act of Union never took place and the Ascendancy maintained their governance of a newly independent Ireland.

In either reading of the play the central dynamic relies on the compliance of the agent of revolutionary Irish history, personified as the Western Peasant in the form of Michael Gillane. In the Irish Ireland reading, the subordination of the subject's individual desires and aspirations is the *sine qua non* of the achievement of the Catholic Nation State. By answering Cathleen's call Michael is transformed from a 'classed' subject with a specific historical location into a 'national' subject whose symbolic universality transcends historical particularity. Michael epitomises the good citizen whose loyalty to the state is so intrinsic that interpellation within republican nationalist ideology seems a perfectly natural occurrence. In the Anglo-Irish Ireland reading the subordination of the subject's immediate interests involves a temporary amnesia concerning the class inequality and colonial legacy of the Ascendancy/peasantry relationship, which is the necessary condition for maintaining Ascendancy hegemony. This faith in Ascendancy leadership is the categorical imperative in achieving an aristocratic Arcadia, where noble and peasant exist in a harmonious society devoid of middle-class interference or aspiration. Michael's compliance embodies the essential condition of either version of national ideology, insofar as he is constructed as the quintessential Western Peasant as archetypal national subject, which constitutes the fundamental premise of both Catholic *bourgeois* nationalism and Protestant Ascendancy nationalism. In each configuration the young farmer Michael is transformed into a fantasy object onto which the political desires of each competing faction are transferred; he is elevated from 'a' peasant of historical specificity into 'the' Peasant of transcendent universality and the brute facts of Michael's subaltern status are elided in his transformation into the sublime object of national ideology.

The Anglo-Irish attempt to forge a sentimental connection failed for several reasons, the most significant of which was an inability to neutralise the power of Catholicism and familism,[32] two ideologies which effectively structured the lived reality of the Irish peasantry who 'constituted the mass'[33] of the people-nation. In sharp contrast, the various factions involved in the Irish Ireland attempt to forge a sentimental connection prevailed according to the degree by which they successfully embodied these ideologies in their representation of the people-nation. Irish Ireland advocate Arthur Griffith emphasised the highly charged relationship between dramatic and political representation in the cultural nationalism of the time: 'We look to the Irish National Theatre primarily as a means of regenerating the country. The Theatre is a powerful agent in the building of a nation.'[34] Adrian Frazier notes that, 'Irish history during this period provides an instance of a literary movement leading to a social and industrial movement for self-reliance[...] The great number of theatrical societies, carried forward by the momentum of this many-sided social revolution, themselves served the valuable propaganda service of representing on stage an ideal, spiritual and militant version of that revolution as already achieved. Its slogan was *Today, on the stage; tomorrow, on the streets.*'[35] If journalists like Arthur Griffith and D.P. Moran[36] were the ideologists who preached this precept of Irish Ireland nationalism, then dramatists like Thomas MacDonagh and Padraic Pearse were the idealists who practised it during the 1916 Easter Rising, and their resolve is epitomised in John Fitzmaurice's declaration in MacDonagh's *Pagans* (1915):

> JOHN: [...] A man who is a mere author is nothing. If there is anything good in anything I have written, it is the potentiality of adventure in me—the power to do something better than write. My writings have only been the prelude to my other work...I am going to live the things that I before imagined.[37]

John's words indicate the importance of the fantasmatic element in driving the Easter Rebels toward their patriotic self-sacrifice, particularly what one would describe as the *objet petit á* in Lacanian parlance, and how it manifested itself in Catholic Nationalist metaphysics as Christ, the crucifixion, Ireland and the afterlife, which formed the symbolic premise of the insurgents' activities. The dramatic evocation of these fantasmatic elements reaches its apogee in Pearse's *The Singer* (1917), where the protagonist MacDara declares: 'One man can free a people as one Man redeemed the world. I will take no pike, I will go into the battle with bare hands. I will stand up before the Gall as Christ hung naked before men on the tree!'[38]

What is striking in this play is that the organic-intellectual figure, MacDara, is in fact a peasant, specifically a 'poor man of the mountains [...] pale like a man that lived in cities, but with the dress and the speech of a mountainy man'.[39] MacDara is something of an oxymoronic character, being simultaneously the ' poor man of the mountains' and an intellectual who taught 'Irish and Latin and Greek in a school' and 'wrote a few poems [which] were printed in a paper.'[40] There is no evidence in the play to suggest that MacDara underwent class transition or received formal education other than the statement, 'I went to the school and taught in it for a year,'[41] which surely indicates that MacDara's attendance was in a teaching rather than a learning capacity. What is significant then is that MacDara is an intellectual with leadership potential who emerges from and represents the people-nation:

> MACDARA: I have lived with the homeless and with the breadless. Oh, Maoilsheachlainn, the poor, the poor! [...] In the pleasant country places I have seen them, but oftener in the dark, unquiet streets of the city. [...] The people, Maoilsheachlainn, the dumb, suffering people; reviled and outcast, yet pure and splendid and faithful. In them I saw, or seemed to see again, the Face of God.[42]

The equivalence of poverty with purity evokes the paradoxical phenomenon of the sublime subaltern whose traumatic qualities are crystallised in the fantasy object of MacDara:

> CUIMIN: [...] in the Joyce country they think it is some great hero that has come back again to lead the people against the Gall, or maybe an angel, or the Son of Mary Himself that has come down on the earth.[43]

The multiple idiosyncrasies of Western peasant, wandering bard, teacher, leader and Messianic hero are unified in MacDara and it is the sheer concentration of disparate qualities into one figure that makes MacDara such a powerful object cause of national desire within Irish Ireland ideology:

> MACDARA: The fifteen were too many. Old men, you did not do your work well enough. You should have kept all back but one. One man can free a people as one Man redeemed the world.[44]

A major tactical strength of Pearse's play was the deployment of Catholic symbolism in forging a sentimental connection with an overwhelmingly Catholic populace. Catholicism and familism constituted the ethical foundation of the Irish people-nation, which was successfully embraced by Irish Ireland ideologists and became the social praxis of Catholic *bourgeois* nationalism in its hegemonic ascension in the post-1922 Free State.

MacDara's function as fantasy object can be further explained in reference to Gramsci's study of Machiavelli's *The Prince*. According to Gramsci the figure of the Prince 'represents plastically and "anthropomorphically" the symbol of the "collective will".[...] in terms of the qualities, characteristics, duties and requirements of a concrete individual.[...] and gives political passions a more concrete form.'[45] Gramsci suggests that Machiavelli's *Prince* could be studied as an 'historical exemplification' of :

> a political ideology expressed neither in the form of a cold utopia nor as learned theorising, but rather by a creation of concrete phantasy which acts on a dispersed and shattered people to arouse and organise its collective will. The utopian character of *The Prince* lies in the fact that the Prince had no real historical existence; he did not present himself immediately and objectively to the Italian people, but was a pure theoretical abstraction—a symbol of the leader and ideal *condottiere*.[46]

Gramsci argues that '[t]he modern prince, the myth-prince, cannot be a real person, a concrete individual. It can only be an organism, a complex element of society in which a collective will, which has already been recognised and has to some extent asserted itself in action, begins to take concrete form.'[47] There is a striking similarity between Gramsci's formulation of the modern prince as a 'concrete phantasy' which has no 'real historical existence' yet gives 'political passions a more concrete form,' and Lacan's formulation of the *objet petit á* as an impossible fragment of the Real which has no corporeal existence other than its form as an empty signifier that materialises the void of desire. Apropos *The Singer*, Pearse almost seems to anticipate Gramsci's theoretical formulation as MacDara is a 'modern prince' before the fact in his materialisation of the national-popular collective will. MacDara's function as the paradoxical sublime subaltern—the 'poor man of the mountains' whose purity in poverty elevates him to the status of national object cause of desire—is the ultimate transmogrification of the peasant within Irish Ireland ideology and as such is ultimately problematical.

The Singer's status as the work of a patriot and national icon necessarily demands care and respect in any critical evaluation. Nevertheless as Robert Hogan and Richard Burnham suggest '[f]ortunately, it is not really necessary to regard the play as a sacred cow. Although it is very like Yeats' once-revered *Cathleen ní Houlihan* in its sentiment, it is also like Maud Gonne's *Dawn* and even like Constance Markievicz's *The Invincible Mother*. The Gonne and Markievicz plays are as impeccably and implacably republican, and yet hardly an Irishman [sic] has ever heard of, much less read, either of them.'[48] MacDara's oxymoronic status as the sublime subaltern depends on the contradictory fusion of Western peasant and national leader, where class and colonial subjection are conflated in MacDara's transcendent, Messianic death. The trauma of class disparity and economic hardship which MacDara registers is neutralised in its sublimation as an expression of divinity and 'the Face of God.' The equivalence of poverty with purity as 'reviled and outcast, yet pure and splendid and faithful,'[49] ultimately serves to elide the traumatic facts of poverty through a symbolic transformation that offers cold comfort to 'the dumb, suffering people' whose yearning for economic redemption persists long after national emancipation has occurred.

Where Yeats invested his Peasants with aristocratic qualities to support his vision of Protestant Ascendancy Anglo-Irish Ireland, Pearse invested his Peasants with the qualities of a Messianic leader in order to buttress his utopian vision of a sovereign, Catholic, Nationalist Irish Ireland. The peasant as sublime object of Irish Ireland ideology functioned as the nexus for national desire and as a vinculum that sutured the Symbolic order of the Catholic Nationalist people-nation, while simultaneously disavowing the trauma of class disparity in the cause of national unity. The struggle of a colonised people 'to live the things that [they] before imagined' in achieving national sovereignty, went hand-in-hand with the struggle for land tenure and peasant proprietorship to the extent 'that the one issue became effectively a metaphor for the other.'[50] The conflation of nationalism and *embourgeoisement* served to obfuscate the constitutive principle of Irish state formation—namely the subordination of the interests of subaltern groups such as cottiers and landless labourers consequent to the rise of strong farmers, graziers and traders on the tide of Catholic *bourgeois* nationalism.   The paradoxical symptom of the peasant as sublime subaltern thus emerged within Irish Ireland ideology precisely in order to mediate the trauma of social subordination intrinsic to nation state formation, and underwent its most public scrutiny and critical contestation in the drama produced during the 1900s up to the establishment of the Free State in 1922.

NOTES

1.   D.P. Moran, *The Philosophy of Lush Ireland* (Dublin, 1905), ch. 6, cited in F.S.L. Lyons, *Culture and Anarchy in Ireland 1880-1939,* Oxford 1980, 61.

2.   See 'Irish Ireland versus Anglo-Irish Ireland', in F.S.L. Lyons, *op.cit.,* 57-83.

3.   David Cairns and Shaun Richards, *Writing Ireland: Colonialism, Nationalism and Culture,* Manchester 1988, 71.

4.   *Ibid.,* 77.

5.   See Robert Kilroy, *The Playboy Riots*, Dublin 1971; Robert Hogan and James Kilroy, *The Modern Irish Drama, vol. 3: The Abbey Theatre: The Years of Synge, 1905-1909*, Dublin 1978; and David Cairns and Shaun Richards, 'Reading a riot: The "reading formation" of Synge's Abbey audience', *Literature and History*, 13 (1987), 219-31.

6.   David Lloyd, 'Discussion Outside History: Irish New Histories and the "Subalternity Effect"', *Subaltern Studies,* Vol. 9 (1996), 261-280.

7. Colin Graham, 'Subalternity and Gender: problems of post-colonial Irishness', *Journal of Gender Studies,* 5:3 (1996), 363-373.

8. David Lloyd, *Nationalism and minor literature: James Clarence Mangan and the emergence of Irish cultural nationalism*, Berkely 1987, 10.

9. Lloyd, 'Discussion Outside History', *op.cit.*, 267.

10. See Antonio Gramsci, *Selections from the Prison Notebooks*, London 1971, 52-55.

11. Lloyd, 'Discussion outside history', *op.cit.*, 266.

12. Graham, 'Subalternity and Gender', *op.cit.*, 365.

13. Ranajit Guha, *Subaltern Studies,* Vol. 1 (1982), 7.

14. Ranajit Guha, *Elementary Aspects of Peasant Insurgency in Colonial India,* Delhi 1992, 4.

15. Gayatri Chakravorty Spivak, 'Subaltern Studies: Deconstructing Historiography', in *In Other Worlds: Essays in Cultural Politics,* London 1988, 202.

16. Gayatri Chakravorty Spivak, 'Can the subaltern speak?', in Cary Nelson and Lawrence Grossberg, eds, *Marxism and the Interpretation of Cultures,* London 1988, 284.

17. *Ibid.*, 294.

18. Graham, 'Subalternity and Gender', *op.cit.*, 370.

19. *Ibid.*, 372-3.

20. See Jacques Lacan, *Ecrits: a selection*, London 1995, 11, and Jacques Lacan, *The Four Fundamental Concepts of Psychoanalysis*, London 1994, 282.

21. Juliet Mitchell and Jacqueline Rose, eds, *Feminine Sexuality: Jacques Lacan and the Ecole Freudienne*, trans. Jacqueline Rose, New York 1985, 31.

22. See Sigmund Freud, *Introductory Lectures on Psychoanalysis*, London 1991, 380-382.

23. Slavoj Žižek , *The Sublime Object of Ideology*, London 1989, 69.

24. *Ibid.*, 45.

25. See W.B. Yeats, *The Land of Heart's Desire* (1894) in *Collected Plays*, London 1982.

26. Lloyd, *Nationalism and Minor Literature, op.cit.*, 10.

27. W.B. Yeats, *Cathleen ni Houlihan*, in *Collected Plays*, London 1982, 88.

28. *Ibid.*, 75.

29. See Rosalind Clark, *The Great Queens: Irish Goddesses from the Morrigan to Cathleen ní Houlihan*, Gerrards Cross 1991.

30. Samuel Ferguson, 'A Dialogue Between the Head and Heart of an Irish Protestant', in *Dublin University Magazine* (Nov. 1883), 467, cited in Cairns and Richards, *Writing Ireland, op.cit.*, 29.

31. Standish O'Grady, *History of Ireland Volume 1: Heroic Period,* (Dublin 1878); reprinted New York 1970.
32. The term 'familism' was developed by the American anthropologists Arensberg and Kimball to describe the practices used by farming families in County Clare to consolidate and expand landholdings and transmit family wealth to subsequent generations. See Conrad M. Arensberg and Solon T. Kimball, *Family and Community in Ireland*, Cambridge (Mass.) 1968.
33. Seamus Deane, *Celtic Revivals: Essays in Modern Irish Literature 1880-1980*, London and Boston 1985, 12.
34. Arthur Griffith, 'All-Ireland', *The United Irishman* (8 November 1902), 1, quoted in Robert Hogan and James Kilroy, *The Modern Irish Drama, vol. 2: Laying the Foundations 1902-1904*, Dublin and New Jersey 1976, 38.
35. Adrian Frazier, *Behind the Scenes: Yeats, Horniman, and the Struggle for the Abbey Theatre*, Berkeley 1990, 52.
36. *Ibid.*: 'The journalists worked to embarrass "shoneen" Irishmen into buying the caps, wearing   the boots, eating the jam, spreading the mustard, speaking the language, playing the games, and naming their children according to the customs of their country. For instance, the peckish D.P. Moran, editor of the *Leader*, posted himself outside Catholic churches in Dublin nationalists districts in order to report on "the truly National congregation" emerging with "their recreant skins" clothed in a foreign covering.[...] In the *United Irishman* Arthur Griffith exposed those Dublin businesses that advertised abroad for work that could be done by Irishmen.'
37. Thomas MacDonagh, *Pagans* (1915) in William J. Feeney, ed., *Lost Plays of the Irish Renaissance Volume II: Edward Martyn's Irish Theatre*, New York 1980, 53.
38. Padraic Pearse, *The Singer* (1917) in *Plays, Stories, Poems*, Dublin 1980, 44.
39. *Ibid.*, 16.
40. *Ibid.*, 29.
41. *Ibid.*, 29.
42. *Ibid.*, 35.
43. *Ibid.*, 17.
44. *Ibid.*, 43-44.
45. Gramsci, *op.cit.*, 125.
46. *Ibid.*, 126.
47. *Ibid.*, 129.
48. Robert Hogan and Richard Burnham, *The Modern Irish Drama, vol. 5: The Art of the Amateur, 1916-1920*, Dublin and New Jersey 1984, 189.

[50.] Philip Bull, *Land, Politics and Nationalism: a study of the Irish land question*, Dublin 1996, 4.

Joyce and Dividing Lines

ELLEN CAROL JONES

Borderlines

James Joyce's *Ulysses* demonstrates how culture is produced in the act of social survival and *as* an act of social and political survival. Stephen Dedalus, that 'embryo philosopher', argues in the 'Oxen of the Sun' episode for the power of the artist's word to invoke forgotten history and the 'nations of the dead', as Odysseus calls forth the unnumbered dead to learn their histories and, from Teirêsias's shade, to foretell his future: 'You have spoken of the past and its phantoms ... . Why think of them?' Stephen asks. 'If I call them into life across the waters of Lethe will not the poor ghosts troop to my call? Who supposes it? I, Bous Stephanoumenos, bullockbefriending bard, am lord and giver of their life'.[1] His claim echoes the Welsh Glendower's boast in Shakespeare's *The History of Henry the Fourth, Part One*, 'I can call spirits from the vasty deep', and Hotspur's ironic cut: 'Why, so can I, or so can any man; / But will they come when you do call for them?' (*I Henry IV*, III.i.52-54). Can the artist's word prove any more efficacious than a rebel's boast against an imperium that will 'rebuke' rebellion, that will not leave the field 'till all our own be won?' (*I Henry IV*, V.v.1, 44). How is the struggle for the historical and ethical right to signify played out in the colonial Ireland of Joyce's *Ulysses*?

The nationalism of a colonised people, David Lloyd points out:

> requires that its history be seen as a series of unnatural ruptures and discontinuities imposed by an alien power while its reconstruction must necessarily pass by way of deliberate artifice. Almost by definition, this anti-colonial nationalism lacks the basis for its representative claims and is forced to invent them. In this respect, nationalism can be said to require an aesthetic politics quite as much as a political aesthetics.[2]

However, as Joyce recognised, an opposition necessarily constructed within the very system it opposes is ambivalent: the system of power prevents the constitution of oppositional identity, yet is at the same time the very condition of its existence. The representational politics and aesthetics of nationalism, the identification of self with nation, are as false as the representations imposed by imperialism, and thus he, as have other anti-colonial artists, conceived of 'a cultural politics which must work outside the terms of representation'.[3] 'We can't change the country. Let us change the subject', a 'crosstempered' Stephen suggests; and it is precisely in changing the subject of discourse, in challenging the strictures of representation, that Joyce attempts to change the country (U 16.1171). Discourses not only constitute what is speakable but are themselves bordered, bounded by a constitutive outside, by the unspeakable, the unsignifiable.[4] In such a cultural politics, translation—of language, of bodies—the metaphor for the historical necessity of the colonised to bear witness, itself bears witness to what cannot be signified, to silence, to the incommensurable.

Joyce substitutes Stephen's dream of mastery, his postcreation, with negotiation, a retroactive negotiation of the past which, through that negotiation, imagines a future liberated from historical determinism. His writing, as 'a retrospective arrangement, a mirror within a mirror' (U 14.1044), relocates the past, reactivates it, reinscribes it, resignifies it. Homi Bhabha argues that negotiation 'commits our understanding of the past, and our reinterpretation of the future, to an ethics of "survival" that allows us *to work through the present*. And such a working through, or working out, frees us from the determinism of historical inevitability—repetition *without a difference*'.[5]

Repeating English cultural history with a difference, recapitulating ontology with political economy, Joyce displaces the metaphysical and epistemological assumptions of that history. History, particularly the history of modernity, is comprehended by Joyce's text as language, representation, discourse, knowledge, power—the violence of the will to power. Writing in *Ulysses* is performative, interrogative, transformative: an uncanny repetition that projects a past, that initiates a differential history that will not return to the power of the same: 'history repeating itself with a difference' (*U* 16.1525-1526).[6] Rewriting history in *Ulysses*, and, specifically, literary history in 'Oxen of the Sun', reveals subjectivity as split—as repetition rather than origin. In this double movement, the materiality of consciousness, language, confronts what itself cannot be articulated: the unconscious both of history and of Joyce's text; the repressed and alien other; the untranslatable supplementary space of the other, beyond representation. The return of the repressed, of the subordinate, of the forgotten, as punctuation of the script of metropolitan history, forces a retelling, a re-citing and a re-siting of historical and cultural knowledge.[7]

How is the unrepresentable seen as the space of cultural difference? In what ways does Joyce's writing institute a postcolonial contra-modernity? That is, in what ways does Joyce construct a contra-modernity contingent to, bordering on, discontinuous with, in contention with the modernity of Western European imperial powers? Bhabha argues that the site of rebellion, and the subject of insurgent subaltern agency, is that of cultural hybridity (*Location*, 6, 206). How does Joyce use the cultural hybridity of Irish borderline conditions to translate—reinscribe and thus reclaim—the social imaginary of both the metropolis and modernity?[8] In what ways does *Ulysses* in particular counter the narrative thrust of Western European bourgeois nationalism to refine the Irish into modernity?[9] Narratives of national identity traditionally subsume the female 'symbolically into the national body politic as its boundary and metaphoric limit'.[10] The borders of race and gender circumscribe (and reinscribe) the imperialist—and nationalist—fantasy for borderless possession. What if one must live on the borderlines—of history and language, of race and gender? To live on the borderlines—what Jacques Derrida terms *sur-vivre*—is to inhabit the place of that splitting of the self, the shifting space of ambivalence in the structure of identification. To live on the borderlines is to be located in the elliptical space between the self and the other. This border then becomes a place of negotiation between incommensurable cultural differences.[11]

In an episode that posits history as text, and English and Anglo-Irish literary history as matrix for *Ulysses*, Joyce stages the extra-textual, the extra-linguistic, as the body of the mother (mater, matrix) as other. The body of the mother as other functions in *Ulysses* as remainder, as the traumatic element at the very centre of the symbolic order which cannot itself be symbolised, as the indeterminate or the unknowable around which the symbolic discourse of human history comes to be constituted. Transgression, border crossing, takes place, takes its place, across the reproductive space of a woman's body. And as unsublimatable body, as remainder, the mother survives—lives on—for the subject as a constitutive loss; it is on that inaugural loss of the mother that any being, meaning, language, or desire are founded. Enveloping the discourse of the fathers—the patrilineal discourse of (literary) history—by the womb of the mother, Joyce posits the maternal body as the border that frames the subject, the border that forms the subject. 'Oxen of the Sun' serves as Joyce's 'hymen minim' (*U* 14.349).[12]

Translation

To apprehend differences, 'even radical and incommensurable ones, in economic, political, and cultural terms', and their 'embodiment in ethnicity, gender and sexuality', is to apprehend how identities are constructed in transit, as process.[13] To inscribe incommensurable cultural differences is to perform a paradoxical act of cultural translation, confronting the language of translation with its uncanny double: the untranslatable, the alien, the other. The writing of cultural difference lies, Bhabha claims, in the staging of the colonial or sexual signifier in 'the narrative uncertainty of culture's in-between: between sign and signifier, neither one nor the other, neither sexuality nor race, neither, simply, memory nor desire' (*Location*,127). As Stephen Heath has noted, 'Joyce's writing resists the movement of Hegelian idealism and the sublimation of oppositions; its force is the "inhabiting" of oppositions that opens not onto a sublimation but, demonstrating limits, onto, as it were, an *excess* that is the unmasterable foundation of the movement of oppositions, their "wake". It is a question here not of the fusion of a new identity but of an illimitation, of a reference to multiplicity'.[14] Transitory and in transit, writing traces an elsewhere, an other, an opening onto an excess or *dé-bordement*, an overrunning of boundaries, that leads to unforeseen, unknown possibilities. It is that act of translation, that middle passage, that movement *between*, that Joyce stages in 'Oxen of the Sun', estranging the languages of a totalising imperial and colonial culture through parody, pastiche, and citation, reinscribing history through the writing of difference. To write the politics of difference is to reorient the axis of power and knowledge. What he dramatises in this hybrid writing is the political and cultural remainder of imperial history or patriarchal canons; a remainder that resists assimilation into the totalising narratives of modernity, narratives whose concealed but central logic is imperialism. Through this remainder, this 'unthought' of both politics and the psyche, Joyce reveals how a minority culture can construct political and personal agency. Such a transgressive agency negotiates its own authority through a process of iterative re-inscription and 'incommensurable, insurgent relinking'; it negotiates and translates cultural identities in a 'discontinuous intertextual temporality of cultural difference' (*Location*, 185). Indeed, as Bhabha reminds us, it is the 'inter'— 'the cutting edge of translation and negotiation, the *in-between* space—that carries the burden of the meaning of culture'. This liminal site of enunciation, of translation, this site where minority agency can be created through negotiation among incommensurable positions, provides a place from which to speak 'both of, and as, the minority, the exilic, the marginal and the emergent' (*Location*, 38, 149).

'My action', Joyce claims in a 1906 letter to Stanislaus Joyce, 'is a virtual intellectual strike'.[15] His revolutionary act of writing anticipates the future through repeating history differently, thus redeeming the past retroactively. Writing marginalises the monumentality of history in *Ulysses*— a history that is, indeed, troped as writing in the 'Oxen of the Sun' episode. If, as Bhabha claims, the force of writing—its metaphoricity and its rhetorical discourse—is a productive matrix which defines the 'social' and makes it available as an objective of and for action (*Location*, 23), then writing can be apprehended as an act of resistance, defiance, insurgency.

How does cultural translation as a tropic movement transform the heliotropics of a dominant culture, the heliopolitics of imperialism? The 'heliotropics' of a dominant culture would be that which returns to itself, replicates itself under the law of the same: the circle of heliotrope is a specular circle, 'a return to itself without loss of meaning', an interiorising turn that is the philosophical desire to master the division between origin and self.[16] Translation as wandering, errancy, exile, decanonises the 'original', fragments it, reinscribes it. Translation as migrancy travesties the metaphysics of authenticity or origins: 'For the nomadic experience of language, wandering without a fixed home, dwelling at the crossroads of the world, bearing our sense of being and difference, is no longer the expression of a unique tradition or history'; migrancy suggests a dwelling at the crossroads: in language, in histories, in identities constantly subject to mutation.[17] Translating the canon of British and Anglo-Irish Ascendancy literary styles into pastiche, Joyce questions assumptions of cultural supremacy and priority. And he also questions the demand for the mythical uncontaminated space of an authentic 'native' culture, a demand that 'perpetuates the imperial gesture through a seemingly opposed modality'.[18] Repeating literary history with a difference, restaging the past into the present, reproducing 'origin', Joyce calls into question the possibility of an originary identity, estranges the received tradition of a national narrative, mocks modernity's linear narrative of progress. In such an insurgent repetition, both the past and the present are displaced, disjunct, estranged. In this doubling of modernity, he opens up a space for political revision and initiation.

Taking the place of that tradition, Joyce's new literary history reconfigures the national narrative from a minority perspective, re-members a national narrative through a willed act of 'forgetting' its origins. Writing as repetition, reinscription, reproduction translates what *Stephen Hero* terms the 'chaos of unremembered writing' by dismembering and re-membering it— 'redismembers' it, as *Finnegans Wake* suggests.[19] 'Redismembering'—or what Joyce terms, elsewhere in the *Wake*, 'tabularasing'—reveals origin as a myth of annulled supplementarity and a myth of erasure, a repetition that exposes the minus in the origin. This re-membered narrative positions itself on the 'borderline of history and language, on the limits of race and gender', in an attempt to write the other (see Bhabha, *Location* 155, 170).

Transgression

How can the other be written? Subjectivity is constructed through language, through others' words and through the word of the other: 'I'm in words, made of words, others' words', claims the protagonist of Beckett's *The Unnamable*.[20] How can cultural and political identity be constructed, and how can it be interpreted? 'Can you rede (since We and Thou had it out already) its world?', the *Wake* asks, and posits the telling as a retelling; the construction, a reconstruction (*FW* 18.18-19). It is a loss and a finding, a 'meandertale, aloss and again', a tale of migrancy and irretrievable or impossible origins. And it is an illicit reproduction: 'It is the same told of all. Many. Miscegenations on miscegenations. Tieckle. They lived und laughed ant loved end left. Forsin'. The writing on the wall (mene, tekel, upharsin) foretells a doom that is constructed as past: 'Thy thingdome is given to the Meades and Porsons' (*FW* 18.18-22). For the colonised, re-membering sutures the dismembered past to make sense of the trauma of the present. Etienne Balibar, analysing how cultural identity *as* national identity could be constructed in relation to the Lacanian real, or that which resists symbolisation, asks: what *transgression* threatens the symbolic order, what transgression makes 'the limits of that order apparent in a way that is unbearable for the passion of identity: Is it betrayal, crime, heresy, unbelief? Or is it rather abnormality, monstrosity, deviance, representable "difference"? And why has a whole literature continually—whether to stigmatize it or to valorize the paradox—sought to *translate* one of these forms into the other?'[21] How does Joyce stage cultural identity *as* national identity through the transgressions of 'Oxen of the Sun'?

Conscious heresy, Richard Brown points out, is a 'curiously hybrid mode of rebellion':

> not an ignorance nor a rejection of orthodoxy but, like Joyce's idea of Wilde's art, a deliberate kind of sinning. It is a mode of thinking which, rather than presuming to forge new ground from first principles, offers a deliberately perverse or provocative revision of an established view or system: its rebellion couched in the very terms to which it objects.[22]

As radical revisions and re-readings, as translations of belief, heresies 'seem especially emblematic of a fiction built out of revisions and re-readings of earlier fictions, one whose attitudes are expressed as a "reading" of past literature such as Joyce's seems to be'.[23] The reading he stages is a labour of reading at the borders of knowledge, at the uttermost boundaries of the symbolic.[24] In 'Oxen of the Sun' Joyce produces such a radical revision of culture's role in the production of national identity by troping the trope of history itself. By decentering history, he intersects the knowledge/power axis of the center—and its economic, political, and cultural traffic—with the space of the subaltern, the periphery.[25] Subversion, subalternity, emerge from acts of displacement, from decentering strategies of signification (*Location,* 145). 'English'—as language, literature, history, national identity—becomes a palimpsest of traces of doubtful origin. Joyce's heretical re-writing opens up the space of the other in the languages of excess, transgression, transmutation.

Joyce provides double interpretations for the crime of 'Oxen': first, as 'fraud', in the formal sense of betrayal, of breaking a vow. On the level of narrative, 'Le Fécondateur' Mulligan, Ireland's 'gay betrayer', appears to have betrayed, 'skunked', his friends: 'But on young Malachi they waited for that he promised to have come and such as intended to no goodness said how he had broke his avow' (*U* 14.778; 1.405; 14.1538, 195-197). Betrayal is universalised: betrayal by the first mother causes the fall of man: 'our grandam, which we are linked up with by successive anastomosis of navelcords sold us all, seed, breed and generation, for a penny pippin', Stephen claims (*U* 14.299-301). And betrayal is writ into the very act of colonisation, figured as prohibited 'act of sexual congress'(*U* 14.1306)—that is, as an act of sex that transgresses the word, the law—as fornication, as abomination:

> Remember, Erin, thy generations and thy days of old, how thou settedst little by me and by my word and broughtedst in a stranger to my gates to commit fornication in my sight and to wax fat and kick like Jeshurum. Therefore hast thou sinned against my light and hast made me, thy lord, to be the slave of servants. Return, return, Clan Milly: forget me not, O Milesian. Why hast thou done this abomination before me that thou didst spurn me for a merchant of jalaps and didst deny me to the Roman and to the Indian of dark speech with whom thy daughters did lie luxuriously?(*U* 14.367-375)

The congress is also commercial; this passage echoes and satirises not only the songs of Tommy Moore and Moses but also Douglas Hyde's 1892 warning in 'The Necessity for De-Anglicising Ireland' against the Irish hastening to adopt, 'pell-mell, and indiscriminately, everything that is English, simply because it *is* English' and hence 'neglecting what is Irish'.[26] Thus the representative of colonial justification, appropriation, and usurpation in *Ulysses* is appropriately Haines, whose 'old fellow made his tin by selling jalap to Zulus or some bloody swindle or other', and who rationalises that 'history is to blame': 'My hell, and Ireland's, is in this life. It is what I tried to obliterate my crime'(*U* 1.156-157, 649; 14.1016, 1021-1022). 'Oxen' links heresy with sexual and national betrayal. The pastiche of Jonathan Swift's *Tale of a Tub* plays on the 1155 papal bull, *Laudabiliter*, through which Nicholas Breakspear, Pope Adrian IV, the only English 'sovereign pontiff'(*U* 14.280), granted the overlordship of Ireland to Henry II of England, by linking colonial gelding with sexual conquering: 'farmer Nicholas that was a eunuch' may have had the bull gelded 'by a college of doctors who were no better off than himself' before sending him to Ireland, but he also 'taught him a trick worth two of the other so that maid, wife, abbess and widow to this day affirm that they would rather any time of the month whisper in his ear in the dark of a cowhouse or get a lick on the nape from his long holy tongue than lie with the finest strapping young ravisher in the four fields of all Ireland'(*U* 14.589-599). The annunciatory intercourse of auricular confession appears to replace genital congress, the Pasiphaën 'copulation between women and the males of brutes'(*U* 14.993). Stephen claims that the device Daedalus constructed for Pasiphaë to satisfy her desire is, in fact, a confessional: 'Queens lay with prize bulls. Remember Pasiphae for whose lust my grandoldgrossfather made the first confessionbox' (*U* 15.3865-3867).[27] The phallus is indeed the transcendental signifier, 'Through yerd [penis] our lord, Amen':

> By this time the father of the faithful (for so they called him) was grown so heavy that he could scarce walk to pasture. To remedy which our cozening dames and damsels brought him his fodder in their apronlaps and as soon as his belly was full he would rear up on his hind quarters to show their ladyships a mystery and roar and bellow out of him in bulls' language and they all after him. (*U* 14.1527, 604-609)

It is the Pasiphaën nature of the 'earthly mother' to be 'but a dam to bear beastly', and thus she 'should die by canon for so saith he that holdeth the fisherman's seal', Stephen insists (*U* 14.249-251). Her trespass demands that she be 'trespassed out of this world' (*U* 14.206). Yet the unholy alliance of the 'imperial British state', 'the holy Roman catholic and apostolic church' and 'a third ... who wants me for odd jobs' produces a progeny as monstrous—and as captive—as any Minotaur: the subjugated Irish (*U* 1.643-644, 641).

Joyce's second interpretation for the crime of 'Oxen' entails another meaning for 'fraud': contraception—famously, 'the crime committed against fecundity by sterilizing the act of coition'.[28] As

Stephen asks of '[c]opulation without population', 'what of those Godpossibled souls that we nightly impossibilise, which is the sin against the Holy Ghost, Very God, Lord and Giver of Life?'(*U* 14.1422, 225-227). [29] In an episode titled after the sterile oxen of the sun-god Helios forbidden to Odysseus and his men, the very act of coition is sterilised by the guts of oxen: condoms, 'Killchild', were made of oxgut. Thus, although 'Carnal Concupiscence' is what the 'party of debauchees' in the 'Manse of Mothers', those worshippers of saint Foutinus, 'most lusted after'—'O lust our refuge and our strength'—they do not fear 'that foul plague Allpox and the monsters' because 'Preservative had given them a stout shield of oxengut'—what the *Wake* terms 'immaculate contraceptives for the populace'(*FW* 45.14)—and therefore 'they might take no hurt neither from Offspring that was that wicked devil by virtue of this same shield which was named Killchild' (*U* 14.803, 1520, 454-467). To murder their goods with whores, or to practise the gentle art of self-abuse, is to disobey the imperialist command of the 'god Bringforth', written in 'the book Law', to replenish the earth and subdue it (*U* 14.276, 436, 443). Tellingly, Joyce parodies historians of the Roman imperium to articulate this mandate in the beginning of the episode:

> Universally that person's acumen is esteemed very little perceptive concerning whatsoever matters are being held as most profitably by mortals with sapience endowed to be studied who is ignorant of that which the most in doctrine erudite and certainly by reason of that in them high mind's ornament deserving of veneration constantly maintain when by general consent they affirm that other circumstances being equal by no exterior splendour is the prosperity of a nation more efficaciously asserted than by the measure of how far forward may have progressed the tribute of its solicitude for that proliferent continuance which of evils the original if it be absent when fortunately present constitutes the certain sign of omnipollent nature's incorrupted benefaction. (*U* 14.7-17)

Copulation without population subverts the law of the father, the
paternal power of 'yerd our lord', by refusing to replenish the
earth through progeny or to subdue it through colonial plantation:

> Wherein, O wretched company, were ye all deceived for
> that was the voice of the god that was in a very grievous
> rage that he would presently lift his arm up and spill their
> souls for their abuses and their spillings done by them
> contrariwise to his word which forth to bring brenningly
> biddeth. (*U* 14.470-473)

Yet, paradoxically, it is the very fecundity of the repressed that
'Oxen of the Sun' foregrounds, a fecundity that transgresses the
bounds of racial difference. Theories of race in nineteenth-century
and early twentieth-century Britain focused on sexuality: in the
British empire, 'sexuality was the spearhead of racial contact'; the
metaphor of conquest and penetration calls attention to the
violence of that 'contact' as well as to the prohibited progeny of
that congress.[30] The hybrid progeny of miscegenation embodies
the very perversions of colonial desire, as in the analysis by the
speaker in Thomas Carlyle's 'The Nigger Question' (1849) of
how the 'unhappy wedlock of Philanthropic Liberalism and the
Dismal Science', that is, the anti-slavery lobby and an economic
and social science based on 'supply and demand'

> led by any sacred cause of Black Emancipation, or the like,
> to fall in love and make a wedding of it, - will give birth to
> progenies and prodigies; dark extensive moon-calves,
> unnameable abortions, wide-coiled monstrosities, such as
> the world has not seen hitherto![31]

The fertility of the colonised is potentially revolutionary precisely
because its hybrid progeny contests the identitarian politics of the
imperial state, a politics grounded in the privileging of the same.
   A claim such as Carlyle's that a 'connubial communion'(*U*
14.355) of British social and economic forces, led by black
emancipation, will give birth to 'dark extensive moon-calves,
unnameable abortions, wide-coiled monstrosities' assumes that
'species' of humans are distinct; the offspring of miscegenation,

minotaurian. Until the mid-nineteenth century, the fertility or sterility of offspring of parents of different races was thought to determine whether or not the human race consisted of distinct species. In his *Physics*, Aristotle reproduces Empedocles's argument that random coupling in the first phase of creation produced monsters such as the sterile oxman: 'Thus in the original combinations the "ox-progeny" if they failed to reach a determinate end must have arisen through the corruption of some principle corresponding to what is now the seed [origin]'.[32] The first recorded use of the term 'miscegenation' was the 1864 treatise, *Miscegenation: The Theory of the Blending of the Races, applied to the American White Man and Negro*; 'hybrid' appeared as early as Ben Jonson's 1630 *The New Inn, or the Light Heart*: 'She's wild Irish born, sir, and a hybride'.[33] Miscegenation was also believed, by nineteenth-century race theorists such as J.A. Gobineau, Louis Agassiz, and Carl Vogt, to produce mongrels, corruptions of the originals, degenerate and degraded, what Buck Mulligan (Hyg. et Eug. Doc.) sees as the 'fallingoff in the calibre of the race' (*U* 14.1243, 1250), resulting in a 'raceless chaos'. Tellingly, the catalogue of abnormalities, monstrous births, and misbirths in 'Oxen'—'all the cases of human nativity which Aristotle has classified in his masterpiece with chromolithographic illustrations'—is 'eviscerated' by a 'strife of tongues', a linguistic disemboweling that parallels the vivisecting of the fetishised female body in the illustrations of *Aristotles Master-piece, or the Secrets of Generation Displayed in All Parts Thereof* (*U* 14.975-977, 956, 952).[34] Paradoxically, as Robert Young points out, these 'raceless masses' which 'attain no new species through hybridization threaten to erase the discriminations of difference':

> the naming of human mixture as 'degeneracy' both asserts the norm and subverts it, undoing its terms of distinction, and opening up the prospect of the evanescence of 'race' as such. Here, therefore, at the heart of racial theory, in its most sinister, offensive move, hybridity also maps out its most anxious, vulnerable site: a fulcrum at its edge and centre where its dialectics of injustice, hatred and oppression can find themselves effaced and expunged.[35]

Hybridity also inscribes sexual reproduction, the sexual division of labour, within the mode of colonial reproduction. The Carlylean pastiche of 'Oxen' exhorts Theodore Purefoy to '[t]oil on, labour like a very bandog and let scholarment and all Malthusiasts go hang': 'In her lay a Godframed Godgiven preformed possibility which thou hast fructified with thy modicum of man's work'; 'Thou sawest thy America, thy lifetask, and didst charge to cover like the transpontine bison' (*U* 14.1412-1415, 1430-1431).[36] Labour here produces reproduction. Indeed, the father's 'labour' replicates the process 'whereby maternity was so far from all accident possibility removed' (*U* 14.45-46). Not only chance is erased. Jean-Joseph Goux points out that 'the position of labor within the capitalist "act of production" reproduces in its specific domain the position of female reproductive labor within paterialist reproduction. The value produced (children, goods) is a lost positivity, a "surplus" that becomes estranged from the producer. The relation between mother and offspring, under the father's control, is like that between worker and product under capitalist domination. There is an *inversion of fertilities*'. But rather than read this alienation as '*creation as emasculation*', as Karl Marx does, Goux suggests that, 'as both father and capital play the role of intermediary, the illusion of the Immaculate Conception is in substance reiterated by the dominate ideology of capitalist economic relations—*the capitalist relation as immaculate production*'.[37] The children's game of *Finnegans Wake* reveals the consequences of the hope that, for the '"fertilization" of matter and the consequent generation of the product', pure ideality—consisting of monetary value—could replace real labour upon matter. Here, the subtraction of desire results in the erasure of the mater, the material: 'Think of a maiden, Presentacion. Double her, Annupciacion. Take your first thoughts away from her, Immacolacion' (Goux 233; *FW* 528.19-21).

Transcription

Vico argues in *The New Science* that, for the first theological poets, thunder, the word of the father god, inaugurates civilisation—the birth of the nation, the birth of shame and the introduction of matrimony, the birth of metaphysics, the birth of language—thus ending the reign of the races that had 'lapsed into a state of bestiality' and consolidating 'the cyclopean paternal power of the first fathers'.[38] As with the 'reverberation of the thunder the cloudburst pours its torrent', in the final words of the pastiche of John Ruskin in 'Oxen of the Sun', 'so and not otherwise was the transformation, violent and instantaneous, upon the utterance of the word': 'Burke's! outflings my lord Stephen, giving the cry', and thus begins the pastiche of Thomas Carlyle on the uttered word, the birth of a language that is itself 'burked'—suppressed; refused publication; erased; murdered by suffocation, leaving no mark, no trace, of violence (U 14. 1388 – 1391).[39]

But what the utterance of the word—what the Carlylean pastiche describing the exit of the men from the 'antechamber of birth', the Purefoy afterbirth—breeds is vocalic babel, linguistic chaos, verbal hybrids: what Joyce notoriously described as 'a frightful jumble of pidgin English, nigger English, Cockney, Irish, Bowery slang and broken doggeral'.[40] The 'pregnant word' errs and is errant (U 14.259). Such hybrid language breaches boundaries; stages itself as same and other in a double-voicing; unmasks and contests authorial intent through undecidable oscillation; politicises cultural differences through dialogic contestation, a double-languaging.[41] Such a language effects what Bhabha terms a 'hybrid moment of political change': the re-articulation, translation, transformation of authority, the staging of 'elements that are *neither the One ... nor the Other ... but something else besides,* which contests the terms and territories of both', opening up a 'third space', the space of interrogation and intervention.[42] Such border disputes call into question the authority of imperial history. As a figure for cultural difference itself, hybridity, a kind of 'retrogressive metamorphosis' (U 14.390), Young claims, 'becomes a third term which can never in fact *be* third because, as a monstrous inversion, a miscreated perversion of its progenitors, it exhausts the differences between them'.[43]

The end product of English and Anglo-Irish literary history, then, is a 'redismembering' of that history through the hybrid languages of the dispossessed, the migrant, the diasporic. These hybrid, liminal languages—these border tongues[44]—reveal the impossibility of a culture's containedness, its limits, and the boundary 'in-between', the uncanny space of the subaltern. The trying on ('Just you try it on', evangel Alexander J Christ Dowie exhorts 'you triple extract of infamy!'[*U* 14.1591, 1583-1584]) of text-style translates, transcribes the word. *Ulysses* itself, that 'chaffering allincluding most farraginous chronicle', is a mixture, a hybrid (*U* 14.1412). Its script of heterogeneous traces makes strange the familiar; its chronicle of linguistic, cultural, social diasporas estranges the possibility of origins. A monstrous birth, indeed.

NOTES

1. Homer, *The Odyssey*, trans. Robert Fitzgerald, New York 1963, 11.36. James Joyce, *Ulysses*, ed. Hans Walter Gabler, New York 1986, 14.1295, 1112-1116. (Further references are to this edition and are given in the text).

2. David Lloyd, *Anomalous States: Irish Writing and the Post-Colonial Moment*, Durham 1993, 89.

3. *Ibid.* , 89.

4. Judith Butler, 'Subjection, Resistance, Resignification: Between Freud and Foucault', in John Rajchman, ed., *The Identity in Question*, New York 1995, 238.

5. Homi K. Bhabha, 'Culture's In-Between', *Artforum* 32.1 (September 1993), 212.

6. See Homi K. Bhabha, *The Location of Culture*, London 1994, 172, 237. (Further references are to this edition are given in the text).

7. Iain Chambers, *Migrancy, Culture, Identity*, London 1994, 3.

8. See Bhabha, *Location*, 6. In *Postnationalist Ireland: Politics, Culture, Philosophy*, London 1997, Richard Kearney, as Joyce famously argued in his 1907 Triestine lecture, 'Ireland, Island of Saints and Sages', argues for the political necessity of the Irish and the British to perceive themselves as 'mongrel islanders' (188).

9. David Lloyd, 'Nationalisms against the State', in Lisa Lowe and David Lloyd, eds, *The Politics of Culture in the Shadow of Capital*, Durham 1997, 177.

10. Anne McClintock, *Imperial Leather: Race, Gender and Sexuality in the Colonial Contest*, New York 1995, 354.

11. Bhabha, *Location*, 170, See Jacques Derrida, 'Living On: Border Lines', in Harold Bloom, *et al.*, *Deconstruction and Criticism*, New York 1984, 75-176. On intractability and incommensurability, see Jean-François

Lyotard, *The Differend: Phrases in Dispute*, 1983, trans. Georges Van Den Abbeele, Minneapolis 1988.

12. In 'The Double Session' Jacques Derrida analyses how the hymen in Mallarmé's text produces the effect of a medium, that which envelops opposing terms simultaneously, that which, as the in-between, 'takes place' in the 'inter-', in the 'spacing between desire and fulfillment, between perpetration and its recollection'. (*Dissemination*, trans. Barbara Johnson, Chicago 1981, 212.) For a discussion of Joyce's writing of the mother as the sexual other that remains the fantasy of a certain cultural space or knowledge that is in Joyce forever the horizon, the unfolding, the boundary of difference, see Ellen Carol Jones, 'Textual Mater: Writing the Mother in Joyce', in Susan Stanford Friedman, ed., *Joyce: The Return of the Repressed*, Ithaca 1993, 257-282.

13. Chambers, *op. cit.*, 82

14. Stephen Heath, 'Ambiviolences: Notes for Reading Joyce', in Derek Attridge and Daniel Ferrer, eds, *Post-structuralist Joyce: Essays from the French*, Cambridge 1984, 68, 107.

15. James Joyce, *Selected Letters of James Joyce*, ed. Richard Ellmann, New York 1975, 125.

16. Jacques Derrida, 'White Mythology: Metaphor in the Text of Philosophy', *Margins of Philosophy*, trans. Alan Bass, Chicago 1982, 268. See also Derrida, 'Violence and Metaphysics: An Essay on the Thought of Emmanuel Levinas', *Writing and Difference*, trans. Alan Bass, Chicago 1978, 79-153.

17. Chambers, *op. cit.*, 4-5. Such a concept—based on forced diasporas, migrations, exiles, internments of the colonised, decolonised, and nonprivileged—rejects the claim for the nomadic imperial subject of postmodern cosmopolitanism, as promoted by Jean-François Lyotard in *The Postmodern Condition: A Report on Knowledge*, trans. Geoff Bennington and Brian Massumi, Minneapolis 1984. Kumkum Sangari critiques the failure to recognise the political dissymmetries between these positions in 'The Politics of the Possible', in Abdul R. JanMohamed and David Lloyd, eds, *The Nature and Context of Minority Discourse*, New York 1990, 216-245.

18. Chambers, *op. cit.*, 72-73. For the necessity of resistance to such siren calls of inversion and reproduction of hegemonic power, see Frantz Fanon, *The Wretched of the Earth*, trans. Constance Farrington, New York 1963, and Benedict Anderson, *Imagined Communities: Reflections on the Origin and Spread of Nationalism*, 1983, rev. ed. London 1991; and, in the context of Irish culture, see, for example, Declan Kiberd, *Inventing Ireland: The Literature of the Modern Nation*, Cambridge, Mass. 1995, and Luke Gibbons, *Transformations in Irish Culture*, Cork 1996.

19. James Joyce, *Stephen Hero*, ed. John J. Slocum and Herbert Cahoon, New York 1963, 78. James Joyce, *Finnegans Wake*, New York 1939, 8.6. (Further references are to these editions and are given in the text).

20. Samuel Beckett, *The Unnamable*, London 1959, 390.

21. Etienne Balibar, 'Culture and Identity (Working Notes)', trans. J. Swenson, in John Rajchman, ed., *The Identity in Question*, New York 1995, 190.

22. Richard Brown, *James Joyce and Sexuality*, Cambridge 1985, 161-162.

23. *Ibid.*, 162.

24. See Jean-Michel Rey, 'Freud's Writing on Writing', in Shoshana Felman, ed., *Literature and Psychoanalysis: The Question of Reading: Otherwise*, 1977 , Baltimore 1982, 301-328.

25. Chambers, *op. cit.*, 84.

26. Douglas Hyde, 'The Necessity for De-Anglicising Ireland', 1892, in *The Field Day Anthology of Irish Writing*, 3 vols., gen. ed. Seamus Deane, Derry 1991, *II*, 527.

27. In his 1704 satire of Roman Catholicism in *A Tale of a Tub*, Jonathan Swift details as one of the inventions erected by Lord Peter (who signs himself as a 'man's man, EMPEROR PETER') the whispering-office. His (papal) bulls, 'whose race was by great fortune preserved in a lineal descent from those that guarded the *golden fleece*', appear to have degenerated: 'Though some who pretended to observe them curiously, doubted the breed had not been kept entirely chaste, because they had degenerated from their ancestors in some qualities, and had acquired others very extraordinary, but a foreign mixture' (Jonathan Swift, '*A Tale of a Tub' and Other Works*, ed. Angus Ross and David Woolley, Oxford 1986, 51, 53).

28. Joyce, *Selected Letters, op. cit.*, 251.

29. In the schema for *Ulysses* which Joyce sent to Carlo Linati on 21 September 1920 (printed as an appendix to Richard Ellmann's *Ulysses on the Liffey*, London 1972, and compared to the schema Joyce lent to Valery Larbaud in 1921, eventually published in Stuart Gilbert's 1934 *James Joyce's 'Ulysses'*), the word 'frodi' ('frauds') is listed as a symbol; 'fraud' is listed as 'crime' in the 'Correspondences' section of the Gorman-Gilbert plan. On the intervention of Joyce's work in the debates on population control, see Mary Lowe-Evans, *Crimes Against Fecundity: Joyce and Population Control*, Syracuse 1989. Intratextual echoes link heredity with heresy when Stephen's argument that the pregnancy of 'our mighty mother and mother most venerable' was '*Entweder* transubstantiality *oder* consubstantiality but in no case subsubstantiality' reproduces the heresies he recalls in 'Proteus'(*U* 14.307-308, 1.656-660).

30. Ronald Hyam, *Empire and Sexuality: The British Experience*, Manchester 1990, 211.

31. Thomas Carlyle, 'The Nigger Question' (1849), *Critical and Miscellaneous Essays*, 5 vols., London 1899, *IV*, 354.

32. Aristotle, *Physics* 2:8. See also *On the Generation of Animals* 1:1. Cited in Don Gifford with Robert J. Seidman, *'Ulysses' Annotated*, 2nd rev. ed., Berkeley 1988, 420.

33.   Ben Jonson, *The New Inn, or the Light Heart* (1630), quoted in the *Oxford English Dictionary*. Noted by Robert J.C. Young, *Colonial Desire: Hybridity in Theory, Culture and Race*, London 1995, 184, n.15. Young expertly analyses the permutations of this term in nineteenth-century scientific, social, political, and cultural theories. As Young points out, the debates about theories of race in the nineteenth century, 'by settling on the possibility or impossibility of hybridity, focussed explicitly on the issue of sexuality and the issue of sexual unions between whites and blacks. Theories of race were thus also covert theories of desire'(9).

34.   Molly Bloom thinks of these illustrations as Bloom is 'tucked up in bed like those babies in the Aristocrats Masterpiece he brought me another time as if we hadnt enough of that in real life without some old Aristocrat or whatever his name is disgusting you more with those rotten pictures children with two heads and no legs thats the kind of villainy theyre always dreaming about with not another thing in their empty heads ...'(*U* 18.1238-1241). For reproductions of illustrations published in later editions of the 1684 *Aristotle's Master-piece, or the Secrets of Generation Displayed in All Parts Thereof*, see Stephen E. Soud, 'Blood-Red Wombs and Monstrous Births: *Aristotle's Masterpiece* and *Ulysses*', *James Joyce Quarterly* 32.2 (1995): 195-208.

35.   Young, *op. cit.*, 19.

36.   Seamus Heaney's 'Act of Union' analyses within the context of the coercions of the 1800 Irish Act of Union and of heterosexual congress the 'imperially / Male' gestures of John Donne's Elegie 19, 'Going to Bed' ('Act of Union', *North* [1975]).

37.   Jean-Joseph Goux, *Symbolic Economies: After Marx and Freud*, trans. Jennifer Curtiss Gage, Ithaca 1990, 233.

38.   Giambattista Vico, *The New Science*, 3rd. ed. (1744), trans. Thomas Goddard Bergin and Max Harold Fisch, Ithaca 1984, *I.ii. xxlii.*195/*IIiii.i.*.517.

39.   The word derives from W. Burke, who was hanged in 1829 in Edinburgh for committing murders by suffocation, leaving no marks of violence. The pub Stephen names, 'Burke's of Denzille and Holles', was owned by John Burke, tea and wine merchant, at 17 Holles Street, Dublin (*U* 14.1399). Mark Osteen notes this derivation in 'Cribs in the Countinghouse: Plagiarism, Proliferation, and Labor in "Oxen of the Sun"', where he argues that by paralleling intertextual and political economies, 'Oxen' 'ultimately illustrates how Joyce privileges artistic labor—an Irish labor of excess that emerges from debt—over both the female labor of childbearing and the male labor of physical and financial begetting' (*Joyce in the Hibernian Metropolis: Essays*, ed. Morris Beja and David Norris, Columbus 1996, 237).

40.   Letter of 13 March 1920, in James Joyce, *Letters of James Joyce*, Vol. 1, ed. Stuart Gilbert, New York 1966, 139-140.

41.   M.M. Bakhtin positions hybridity between stylisation and parody. Hybridisation, he asserts, is 'a mixture of two social languages within the

limits of a single utterance, an encounter, within the arena of an utterance, between two different linguistic consciousnesses, separated from one another by an epoch, by social differentiation or by some other factor'. He distinguishes between 'mute and opaque' unconscious hybrids—various languages co-existing within the boundaries of a single dialect, a single national language—and intentional, conscious hybrids—double-voiced, double-accented, double-languaged (*The Dialogic Imagination: Four Essays*, ed. Michael Holquist, trans. Caryl Emerson and Michael Holquist, Austin 1981, 358).

42. Bhabha, *Location*, 28. If 'the act of cultural translation (both as representation and as reproduction) denies the essentialism of a prior given original or originary culture', then for Bhabha, 'all forms of culture are continually in a process of hybridity. But for me the importance of hybridity is not to be able to trace two original moments from which a third emerges, rather hybridity to me is the "third space" which enables other positions to emerge. This third space displaces the histories that constitute it, and sets up new structures of authority, new political initiatives ' (Homi K. Bhabha, 'The Third Space', in Jonathan Rutherford, ed., *Identity, Community, Culture, Difference*, London 1990, 211).

43. Young, *op. cit.*, 23.

44. Gloria Anzaldúa, 'How to Tame a Wild Tongue', in R. Ferguson, M. Gever, Trinth T. Minh-ha and Cornel West, eds, *Out There: Marginalization and Contemporary Cultures*, Cambridge 1990, 203-211.

This essay appeared in a slightly different version as 'Border Disputes' in *James Joyce and the Difference of Language*, ed. Laurent Milesi (Cambridge University Press 2003, pp. 142-160). The author and the editor wish to acknowledge Cambridge University Press for their permission to reprint in this volume.

Joycean Hypertext: Technology and The Word In *Finnegans Wake*

LOUIS ARMAND

Anticipating the increased significance of hypertext in James Joyce scholarship, Jacques Derrida, in his essay on *Finnegans Wake*, invokes the term 'Joyceware', suggesting that we might approach Joyce's writing as 'a hypermnesiac machine', 'capable of integrating all the variables, all the quantitative and qualitative factors', 'because you can say nothing that is not programmed on this 1000th generation computer—*Ulysses* or *Finnegans Wake*'.[1] The idea of Joyce's text as a type of complex language machine has also been treated, among many others, by Jean-Michel Rabaté.[2] In his essay entitled 'Lapsus ex machina', Rabaté examines *Finnegans Wake* as a 'system which can be described as a word machine, or a complex machination of meanings', a 'perverse semic machine' which 'has the ability to distort the classical semiological relation between "production" and "information", by disarticulating the sequence of encoding and decoding'.[3]

Like Derrida, Rabaté envisages a machine in which production is driven by an internal division—memory or desire—which opens a place of potentially limitless substitutions; a movement which finds itself programmed in advance by the irreducibility of the machine's own internal paradox. This paradox is pervasive, but it might be said to be most fully accommodated in the 'purpose' of the machine to supersede itself. As Rabaté suggests, this paradox functions as a 'lapsus' and points to the way in which a programmatic discourse would 'attempt to fill the blank space of desire left hollow by—or in—the machine'.[4] The desiring machine, miming the totalising movement

of an exegesis, or exe-genesis, approaches a topological relation
to itself similar to that of the Cantorean paradox of the set of all
sets.

By its own definition, this universal set can never be self-
similar since—being a set, and being the set of all sets—it must
of necessity contain itself and be contained by itself, at the same
time as exceeding itself, *ad infinitum*. In the absence of any limiting or stabilising 'identity', the set of all sets simply prolifer-
ates at its boundaries; a type of desiring machine caught in an
inflationary process of self-projection and manufacture. This
idea can be applied in a less exclusive manner to genetic processes of coding and decoding in which a programmatic identity
takes the place of an originary identity, and in which the genetic
code can be viewed as structurally anteceding itself within a sequence of metonymic substitutions.

In *Finnegans Wake* a parallel might be drawn between the
structure of genetic DNA, for example, and the figures HCE and
ALP, which henceforth could be thought of as taking on the role
of complementary genetic strands. Moreover, if we credit Derrida's view of *Finnegans Wake* as a 'hypermnesiac machine',
we might consider HCE and ALP as also describing the co-
ordinates of something like a genetic memory. (Joyce himself
described the *Wake* as a kind of Viconian machine, a 'vicocyc-
lometer', in which infinite repetition and renewal would be programmed within a finite sequence of historical conceits.)

One of the recurring features of *Finnegans Wake* is the problem of formal articulation in the structuring of identity posed
precisely by these 'figures', ALP and HCE—nominally 'Anna
Livia Plurabelle' and 'Humphrey Chimpdon Earwicker':

> Now [...]concerning the genesis of **Harold** or **Humphrey**
> **Chimpden's** occupational agnomen (we are back in the
> presurnames prodromarith period, of course just when
> enos chalked halltraps) [...] . **Hag Chivychas Eve**, in pre-
> fall paradise.[5] (Emphasis in bold type added.)

Identity here is presented through the repetition of the 'initial' letters HCE, not in terms of an autonomous singularity, or even as a moment of transition, but rather as a type of matrix or acrostic, contingent upon the relations affected between all of 'its' parts (a form of Joycean entelechy which recalls, among other things, the dependence of semantic content in de Saussure's linguistic model upon the differential relation of individual phonemes).

In this way the 'identity' of HCE is signified by the dissemination of these three letters throughout the text of *Finnegans Wake*, rather than by a single motif or figure as such, even though the pattern of this dispersal—HCE—is itself characterised by virtually infinite permutations and combinations (its elemental possibilities suggested, for example, in the pseudomolecular compound H_2CE_3 [*FW* 95.12]). This is further characterised in a play upon the idea of a textual genetics and the filial relationship of the author to the body of writing which bears his 'name'—whether Harold, Humphery, or, as in the passage cited below, the 'compound' Haromphery:

> The great fact emerges that [...] all holographs so far exhumed initialled by Haromphery bear the sigla H.C.E. [...] which gave him as sense of those normative letters the nickname Here Comes Everybody (*FW* 32.12-18).

As with the idea of a genetic blue-print, these holographs, initialled by their dead author, enter into a process of dissociation and dissimulation, not merely through the normative function of the sigla (which interchangeably signify both author and holograph, and which are interchangeable from one holograph to another), but also through the process of interpretation (eg. archaeology, paleontology, exhumation) and metamorphosis (eg. the substitution of a cognomen or nickname which is both singular and universally inclusive: 'Here Comes Everybody').

Recalling the figure of Adam in the *Book of Genesis*, the eponymous 'Haromphery' could be seen as engendering a species of signifiers in whose genetic code he is ultimately sub-

sumed and for which he exists as a mere inference, or at least as
the trace of a prior possibility of substitution (or metonymic
filiation), a cybernetic programme whose schematic signature
would be, in this case, the 'normative letters' HCE.

In their book, *Anti-Oedipus*, Gilles Deleuze and Félix Guattari
identify such a schematic in terms of a type of discursive em-
placement, or 'transverse'. Regarding the structurality of this
transverse, they write:

> the whole itself is a product, produced as nothing more
> than a part alongside other parts, which it neither unifies
> nor totalises, though it has an effect on these other parts
> simply because it establishes aberrant paths of communi-
> cation between noncommunicating vessels, transverse
> unities between elements within their own particular
> boundaries.[6]

Recalling the episode in *Finnegans Wake* by which Shem the
Penman writes over the entire surface of his body with his own
excrement,[7] the idea of 'transverse communications', as a rhetorical shift between metonymy and synecdoche, suggests a type
of self-reflexive textual process that also resembles the 'mor-
phological circumformation' (*FW* 599.17) of a hypertext programme. In his book *Dissemination*, Derrida describes such a
structure in terms of a similar 'apparatus' which would seem to
operate 'in two absolutely different places at once, even if these
were only separated by a veil',[8] an idea he further elaborates
upon in his essay 'Two Words for Joyce':

> Paradoxical logic of this relationship between two texts,
> two programmes or two literary 'softwares': whatever the
> difference between them, even if [...] it is immense and
> incommensurable, the 'second' text, the one which, fa-
> tally, refers to the other, quotes it, exploits it, parasites it
> and deciphers it, is no doubt the minute parcel *detached*
> from the other, the metonymic dwarf, the jester of the
> great anterior text [...] and yet it is also another set, quite

other, bigger, and more powerful than the all-powerful which it drags off and reinscribes elsewhere in order to defy its ascendancy. Each writing is at once the detached fragment of a software more powerful than the other, a part larger than the whole of which it is a part.[9]

The topological structure of the relationship Derrida describes here, between two textual programmes (one 'analytical'; the other, the analytical 'object') has its analogy in *Finnegans Wake* in the function of Anna Livia's letter as a 'metonymic dwarf' of the *Wake* as a whole. As this letter becomes more and more a part of the textual apparatus that surrounds it, and less distinguishable from its own exegesis, it begins to take on a mythological aura as the site of endless co-ordinates for an impossible *rendez-vous* with itself. Like ALP and HCE, this 'letter' serves as a kind of topological, or tropological 'space'—a point of 'continuity' which at the same time marks out a chain of 'discontinuities', or what Rabaté terms the 'disarticulation' of a sequence of encoding and decoding.

This paradox can be seen as describing a basic characteristic of such 'genetic' processes as translation and transcription which abound in *Finnegans Wake*, and which also describe a type of textual 'filiation'. It remains a commonplace assumption, for instance, that the *Wake*'s triads (ALP and HCE) describe a polymorphous, or 'genetic' network of possible identities (fictional, historical, autobiographical), which, however fragmented or divergent they may at first appear, can nevertheless be reduced to a set of normative predicates: what Roland Barthes calls a 'narrative ... unveiling of truth' which 'is a staging of the (absent, hidden, or hypostatised) father' (Joyce or HCE, for example), and which 'would explain the solidarity of [the text's] narrative forms' and of its supposed 'familial structures'.[10] This idea presents HCE and ALP as archetypal, or 'universal' parental figures who somehow engender all of the *Wake*'s various narratological forms, providing Joyce's text with a kind of architectonics. Each of these triads is thus regarded as acting like a genetic 'master key' whose permutations and com-

binations are supposed to follow underlyingly coherent, if superficially random, evolutionary patterns, and which, despite appearing to mark an 'aleatory scattering of semes',[11] nevertheless
remain gathered about a central identity or originary 'code'
which through a rigorous genealogical project might be fixed
and determined.

But while this genealogical impulse may provide a 'motivation' for a particular reading of the text, it remains that this impulse describes a structural outcome that its own process renders
illusory. We might say, in fact, that this 'motivation' remains
the condition of such a reading *throughout*, without there being
any actual approach to the possibility of closure, or of a final
decoding of the genealogical or genetic sequence, no matter how
much information is accumulated, or how much data is uncov-
ered. Reading in this sense would remain always in an 'initial'
state—a motivation or machination 'of' the textual programme.

This notion of a reading suspended in an 'initial state', or of a
genealogy '*in utero*', points towards another aspect of the textual pro-gramme: its literal or etymological sense of 'before the
word', the 'letter' or before 'writing', which might also suggest
one of the ways in which *Finnegans Wake* 'calls for' reading, as
something which Derrida describes as being precisely what we
have not yet *begun* to read. In this sense we might also say that
Finnegans Wake 'solicits' (i.e. motivates, machinates, or 'shakes
up') the textual apparatus, situating 'reading' at the limits of a
type of auto-production, or re-production, which would also take
the form of a hypertext 'machine'. As Geoffrey Bennington
suggests:

> Such a machine would suspend reading in an open sys-
> tem, neither finite nor infinite [...] and would thus also re-
> tain the memory of the traversals tried out [...] by all its
> readers, these being so many texts to plug back into the
> general network [...] . But this machine is already in
> place, it is the 'already' itself. We are inscribed in it in
> advance, promise of the hazardous memory in the mon-
> strous to-come.[12]

What is important in *Finnegans Wake* is how this 'machine' metaphor derives not from a particular thematics, nor from the numerous possible references to technological phenomena to be found in the *Wake*, but from a particular technological function that emerges from the *Wake*'s langage itself. As Jacques Aubert, in his essay 'riverrun,' has argued, the lexicography of *Finnegans Wake* implies a movement towards a re-constitution of formal syntactic and grammatical structures, and thus towards a possible semantic system. For Aubert, such an approach is both deductive and inductive, but it nevertheless requires the assumption that, in order to be 'readable', a text must first be constituted in relation to an horizon of expectations, and to the necessity of a prior linguistic code (even if this code is characterised by the *lack* of a system).[13]   According to Nicholas Abraham and Maria Torok, however, the mechanism which in fact initiates reading is not affected in terms of a prior code but rather by what they describe as the 'lexical contiguity of various meanings of the same word', or of the same compound.[14]

In Joyce's paranomasian text, this contiguity operates not only on the lexical scale, but also on a tropic and schematic scale—a structural shift orientated, as we have already seen, by such 'co-ordinates' as HCE and ALP. These co-ordinates would also be seen as describing simultaneous relations across all of these scales, and so bringing about transverse communications between otherwise non-communicating textual elements, causing them to intersect (with varying probabilities) like a boundless acrostic (or 'croststyx' [*FW* 206.04]) machine—what Joyce calls a 'polyhedron of all scripture' or 'proteiform graph' (*FW* 107.08).

The idea of a co-ordinate, or a system of co-ordinates, which operates within nominal limits of variability, also implies a type of archive or memory apparatus (a data retrieval system), again suggestive of Derrida's 'hypermnesiac machine'[15]—and in the case of the 'acronyms' HCE and ALP we are also reminded of the structure of the various mnemonic formulae, or *loci memoriae*, employed both in classical rhetoric and in contemporary

school rooms (viz. the 'Nightlessons' or 'Triv and Quad' epi-
sodes of the *Wake*). The point being that 'identity' in *Finnegans
Wake*, as a kind of 'genetic memory', is programmatic rather
than 'encoded', as what Rabaté refers to as the '*machination* of
meaning'.

Through its various processes of meaning formation and de-
formation, this Wakean programmatics can be seen as bringing
forth virtually infinite series of texts, causing them to 'intersect'
according to the co-ordinates HCE and ALP, and not only these
but numerous others also. At most we might say that ALP and
HCE indicate 'a certain schematic idea of one another and of the
place where contact could be made'.[16] They would catalyse and
orientate a drawing together of signifying 'events' that only signify in regards to the promise of some future 'advent'—such as
the idea that *Finnegans Wake* might become 'readable' at that
point at which all the semantic and linguistic ambiguities are
resolved, and at which the great palimpsest is separated out into
discrete units. ALP and HCE might then describe what Derrida
has called an 'interminable list of all the so called undecidable
quasi-concepts that [are] so many aporetic places or dislocations'.[17]

This 'interminable list' could be thought of as traversing another kind of narrative space, something like a simulacrum *index
rerum* cutting across the totality of Joyce's 'encyclopaedic' text.
We might then say that HCE and ALP *describe* a network of
'transverse communications' (*within* the Wakean textual machine) between differing moments of an implied desire for
signifying unity, 'to fill the blank space of desire left hollow
by—or in—the machine' itself. Each movement towards a
signified concept would thus be put back to work as so many
topological features within this solipsistic 'grand continuum'
(*FW* 472.30), marking out a chain of dis-placement and substitution whose apparent 'genealogy' describes, in the form of a
reductio ad absurdum, the 'programmatic' mediation of a set of
textual co-ordinates whose relatedness is otherwise nominal:
viz. HCE or ALP.

This does *not* mean, however, that in *Finnegans Wake* these 'onanymous letters', HCE and ALP, will have *taken the place* of a genealogy or of an identity as such—and the elevation of these triads in Joyce studies, to something like an analytical paradigm, remains symptomatic of a genealogical or hermeneutical drive towards recuperating significatory and structural play for identity and epistemological certitude. Instead we can see that what gives rise to concepts of identity in *Finnegans Wake* is not the proximity of its signifiers to some prior code, but rather a process of recurrence or repetition, whose 'open totality' might resemble something like a signifying memory, a *hetero-genetic* memory that would remain unfixed and whose apparent limits— topological or tropological—would indeed describe 'aberrant paths of communication' between otherwise 'noncommunicating vessels' and 'transverse unities between elements within their own particular boundaries'.[18] And if these triads appear at first to function together as a 'genetic key' that might unlock the *Wake*'s hypertextual labyrinth, it would only be in the sense that they *assume the coherence of a structure* which, as Derrida says, they nevertheless 'in advance, deconstruct from within'.[19]

NOTES

[1.] Jacques Derrida, 'Two Words for Joyce' in Derek Attridge and Daniel Ferrer, eds, *Post-structuralist Joyce: Essays from the French*, Cambridge 1984, 147-148.

[2.] Cf. Jean-Michel Rabaté, 'Pour une cryptogénetique de l'idiolecte Joycien' in Claud Jacquet, ed., *Genèse de Babel: Joyce et la création*, Paris 1985. Cf. also Jean-Michel Rabaté, 'Le Nœued Gordien de «Pénélope»' in Claude Jacquet, ed., *James Joyce «Scribble» 1 genèse des textes*, Paris 1988.

[3.] Jean-Michel Rabaté, 'Lapsus ex machina' in Attridge and Ferrer, eds, *op.cit.*, 79.

[4.] *Ibid.*, 79.

[5.] James Joyce, *Finnegans Wake*, New York 1939, 30.01-15.(Further references to *Finnegans Wake* are to this edition and are given in the text in brackets).

6. Gilles Deleuze and Félix Guattari, *Anti-Oedipus: Capitalism and Schizophrenia*, trans. R. Hurley, M. Seem, and H. R. Lane, New York 1977, 43.

7. Towards the end of Book I, Shem is described as 'produc[ing]': 'nichthemerically from his unheavenly body a no uncertain quantity of obscene matter not protected by copriright in the United States of Ourania or bedeed and bedood and bedang and bedung to him, with his double dye, brought to blood heat, gallic acid on iron ore, through the bowels of his misery, flashly, nastily, appropriately, this Esuan Menschavik and the first till last alchemist wrote over every square inch of the only foolscap available, his own body, till by its corrosive sublimation one continuous present tense integumented slowly unfolded in all marryvoising moodmoulded cyclewheeling history.' (*FW* 185.29; 186.02)

8. Jacques Derrida, *Dissemination*, trans. Barbara Johnson, Baltimore 1981, 221.

9. Derrida, 'Two Words for Joyce,' *op. cit.*, 148.

10. Roland Barthes, *The Pleasure of the Text*, trans. Richard Miller, New York 1975, 10.

11. Claudette Sartilliot, *Citation and Modernity: Derrida, Joyce and Brecht*, Norman, Oklahoma 1993, 49.

12. Geoffrey Bennington, 'Derridabase' in *Jacques Derrida*, trans. Geoffrey Bennington, Chicago 1993, 315-6.

13. Jacques Aubert, 'riverrun', in Attridge and Ferrer, eds, *opo cito* 69-77.

14. Nicholas Abraham and Maria Torok, *Cryptonymie: le Verbier de l'homme aux loups*, Paris 1976, 118.

15. Derrida, 'Two Words for Joyce', *op. cit.*, 147.

16. Jacques Derrida, 'My chances/*Mes Chances*: a Rendezvous with some Epicurean Stereophonies' in J.H. Smith and W. Kerrigan, ed., *Taking Chances: Derrida, Psychoanalysis and Literature*, Baltimore 1984, 3-4.

17. Jacques Derrida, *Aporias*, trans. Thomas Dutoit, Stanford 1993, 15.

18. Deleuze and Guattari, *op. cit.*, 43.

19. Jacques Derrida, *Mémoirs for Paul de Man*, trans. Cecile Lindsay, Jonathan Culler and Eduardo Cadava, New York 1986, 72.

'Appallingly Funny': John Banville's *The Broken Jug*

JOHN KENNY

'Outside of here it's death.'
>Samuel Beckett, *Endgame*

Ample sport for source hunters has been provided by the often intense intertextual crossovers between John Banville's work and that of a host of writers from national traditions other than his own. In terms of literature in English, Banville has sidestepped any potential British models and has consistently referred to two Americans, Henry James and Wallace Stevens, as his principal aesthetic exemplars. Influences from mainland Europe have been more numerous in his selected literary heredity however. Banville's interest in major European historical figures was well flagged with the first two books of his Tetralogy, *Doctor Copernicus* (1976) and *Kepler* (1981), but, other than this foundational biographical interest, his attention to certain strands of European literature and thought has been a matter of a complex, and often quiet, stylistic and thematic assimilation.

While Banville has been consistently influenced by French precursors since his dealings with Proust in his second novel,

Birchwood (1973), his major models, both in terms of specific works and general aesthetics, have been writers in German from a variety of periods. The fascination with the Faust myth that characterises all of his work has been gleaned primarily from Goethe and Thomas Mann. Though Kafka has been an especially quiet presence, his Josef K. lies behind the sense of absurdism of all the later Banville narrators. Hugo von Hofmannsthal is quoted directly in *The Newton Letter* (1982). Goethe's Werther, Robert Musil's Moosbrugger and Büchner's Woyzeck are all members of Freddie Montgomery's literary family tree in the *Book of Evidence* (1989), *Ghosts* (1993) and *Athena* (1995). Rilke has been a ghostly presence in the novels from the beginning; and, in more recent years, Banville has developed an interest in the thought of Nietzsche that surpasses perhaps even his enduring affection for James and Stevens.

In some cases, these German presences are closely paralleled by Banville. The thematics and even the characterisation of *The Newton Letter*, for instance, are heavily indebted to Goethe's novel, *Elective Affinities* (1809).[1] Only once, however, has he translated a German work—or indeed any work—more or less directly into his own English. *The Broken Jug*, his version of Heinrich von Kleist's dramatic comedy, *Der zerbrochne Krug* (1803-6, perf. 1808), had its première at Dublin's Peacock Theatre on 1 June, 1994 (the play had been previewed on 26 May). Directed by Ben Barnes, the play received an enthusiastic critical reception. While Banville has made some forays into the area of screen drama, *The Broken Jug* remains his single excursion onto the stage.[2]

Despite this singularity, the play has received scant critical attention. General studies of Irish drama may be justified in passing over the play since it is a derivative work as such and is not a component part of a dramatic *oeuvre*. Even the Banville experts however, do not seem to consider *The Broken Jug* important and the only considerably detailed study of the play published so far is in French.[3] Certainly, in the context of Banville's career as a whole, the play is a minor work, and Banville has said that the adaptation was 'a kind of *jeu d'esprit* ... I wrote it very quickly ... it was great fun to do ... it wasn't an entirely serious venture'.[4] No doubt many would welcome any kind of light relief in the midst of the serious ironies of Banville's fiction; and even the author himself seems to have found the collaborative nature of the dramatic genre somewhat liberating.[5] *The Broken Jug* should nevertheless be a component part of Banville studies since behind its comedy it perseveres with some of Banville's concerns with specifically Irish subjects, as figured in *The Newton Letter* and, especially, in *Birchwood*, whose themes and modal strategies would bear close comparison with the play. Indeed, it might be suspected that it is this cultural specificity of *The Broken Jug* that makes it unattractive to critics more concerned with Banville's undeniably more pervasive transcendental or deracinated aesthetic preoccupations.

While Kleist has inspired some approximate imitations, with, most famously, his 'Kolhaus' legend informing E.L. Doctorow's *Ragtime* (1975), he has not been a popular subject for stage adaptations in English, and he is not a particularly familiar model in Irish writing. *The Broken Jug* can nevertheless be seen as part of a substantial move in Irish theatre towards adaptations of classic European drama. The adaptors are usually poets and playwrights, and the predominant focus has been on Classical, Russian and French originals, making the case of Banville's German exemplar all the more notable.[6]

Kleist (1777-1811) has been a vital presence in Banville from the beginning of his career, though he has surfaced visibly only once or twice. Suggesting that Kleist is 'probably the greatest German dramatist', Banville, when asked just before his play opened about when he became aware of this classically inclined German Romantic, revealed a close personal attachment: 'I honestly can't remember. Now it seems I can't remember a time when I wasn't aware of him. I feel I have known about him all my life.'[7] Before *The Broken Jug*, Kleist's influence was patent, though unacknowledged, in *Mefisto* (1986). In this novel, the first section of which is titled 'Marionettes', Banville provides what amounts to a thematic elaboration on some ideas contained in a little-remarked essay of Kleist's, 'On the Marionette Theatre' (1810), an essay that is, Banville argues, 'one of the key works on modernist aesthetics at least a hundred years before its time'.[8] (Significantly, this small Kleist piece was a vital influence on some other of Banville's German exemplars: Rilke, Hofmannsthal and Mann.) A divagation on Banville's sophisticated employment of Kleist's theory of puppets is for another time. For the present, discussion will be confined to *The Broken Jug* and to the curiosity that for this one straightforward adaptation of an admired European masterpiece, Banville chose a definitive Irish setting.

In a review in 1988 of one of the standard translations of the major Kleist plays, that by Martin Greenberg, Banville commended *Der zerbrochne Krug* as 'that most unexpected of things, a genuinely funny German farce', and he included the parenthetical plea: 'By the way, when will some enterprising theatre director commission an Irish adaptation of this splendidly apposite romp?'[9] As far back as the early eighties, Banville had suggested to Garry Hynes—an established director with The Druid Theatre, Galway, and now famously associated with Martin MacDonagh's drama—that she gets an Irish writer to adapt this play. Hynes eventually commissioned the adaptation when she became artistic director of the Abbey, Banville having by then decided that the only way to get Kleist onto the Irish stage was to do it himself. The peculiar appositeness of Kleist's original which he had in mind was revealed when the Peacock Theatre audiences discovered that, as adapted localised setting for the comedy, he had chosen the deadly serious year of 1846 and the Great Irish Famine.

The motivation behind the unexpected conjunction of the mode of high farce with the subject matter of Ireland's traditionally most tragic moment of history is explainable by reference to Banville's perception of Kleistian *ambiguity*, a quality he admires in literature and a quality which characterises his own work. Banville could be describing his own literary mode when he commends Kleist for his idiosyncratic combination of farce and moral seriousness, of the unresolved antinomies of plain comedy and tragedy: 'Kleist saw with unwavering clarity that at the heart of things there is always ambiguity. At the height of his tragedies there will suddenly break out for a moment (but *what* a moment!) a kind of helpless laughter, a Nietzschean whoop, which can have an extraordinary effect.' Conversely, Banville sees an ostensible comedy like *Der zerbrochne Krug* as deeply, if intermittently, emotive since, 'in the midst of the farce, with its inevitable cruelty, there come moments of tenderness and regret, when a sort of sigh is heard behind the action, and we glimpse the sadness of things'.[10] It would seem then, that the subject of the Famine would have received more or less equal treatment from Banville regardless of combinative mode, tragedy with a whoop, or comedy with a sigh. In any case, Kleist's brand of comedy was chosen by him because the essential world view he wanted to communicate was not, in his own distinction, 'isn't life quirky, funny and wonderful?', but 'isn't life appalling and appallingly funny?'[11]

While Kleist's original play contains some intricate plotting, his basic scenario, set in early nineteenth-century Utrecht in Holland, is quickly given. Two autochthonously named characters, a lecherous fool of a provincial judge, Adam, and an innocent but self-righteous young girl, Eve, are involved in a court hearing that investigates an alleged assault on Eve the previous evening. Romping but frequently cruel chicanery ensues concerning the likelihood of a broken hymen, or at least of compromised virtue, symbolised by a valuable jug seemingly shattered by Eve's fleeing assailant. Litigation for damages is instigated against Eve's suitor, Ruprecht, by Eve's mother, Frau Martha, proprietor of the precious pitcher. The situation comedy develops from the fact that all this takes place in front of Walter, a visiting Inspector of Courts and, principally, from the dawning realisation that Judge Adam himself, rather than Ruprecht, is the guilty party.

Advertising his adaptation as 'after' Kleist, Banville, as clarified by the published script, largely retains the original story structure, though he commingles and alters some scenes to provide two acts whereas in Kleist there are simply twelve straight scenes.[12] Kleist's characterisation is also closely followed, though Banville has invented a minor, but impressive character called Ball, who is the visiting inspector's servant. In choosing his Irish setting he invokes Brian Friel's archetypal townland, Ballybeg, and the action takes place in an equally toponymical

'Ballybog', which, going by details in the play, can be located
somewhere near Sligo town. (Banville has his usual fun with
proper nouns, and another town called 'Boghill' is included as
variant.) The dialogue Banville gives his characters more or less
retains the straight accent of Kleist's own classical German. The
play is largely in the form of blank verse, with the occasional
rhyming couplet, particularly at the end of scenes. Though idio-
matic phrases are used occasionally, Banville's West-of-
Irelanders do not speak in any consistent approximation of nineteenth-century brogue. While one reviewer saw in the opening
night's performance a 'touch of the Boucicaults', the touch is
more generally hammy than stage-Irish, and Judge Adam's she-
nanigans owe as much to the frenetic nature of Kleist's original
as to any intention Banville might have had to create some kind
of Myles-na-gCopaleen.[13]

   While the author of the first extended critique of the adaptation suggested that Rüdiger Imhof had translated the play for
Banville, this would seem to be misguided speculation since,
while Imhof provided a useful biopic, entitled 'Kleist, The
Tragic Comedian', for the programme notes, there is no acknowledgement of any involvement by him in the actual writing
of the adaptation.[14] Though Banville has picked up some of the
language over years of attention to German literature, it is likely
that he consulted the Greenberg translations. Commending the
translator's 'wonderful introductory essay' to his 'handsome
volume', he commented that 'Mr Greenberg has, insofar as I am
capable of judging, done a fine job of translating these subtle
and intricate dramas.'[15] It should be pointed out however, that
there is no acknowledgement of any sources in either the programme notes or the published play, the inference being that
Banville's is primarily an independent translation.

   Banville's new temporal setting of the play is the vital date of
August 1846, the point at which the Irish Famine entered its
most devastating period. Banville has allowed that the Famine is
'the most important event in modern Irish history'.[16] His way of
reflecting this importance however, influenced by Kleist's contrapuntal style, is highly individualised. Kleist's great talent, at
least as Banville reads him, was that he was able to 'contain in

very beautifully crafted and classical rigorous drama the absolute hysteria of his character and of his time'. This elemental,
dialectic sense of a chaotic world controlled through sheer style
is central to Banville's view of the function of art generally and
thus he chose, as a suitable challenge to his version of Kleist's
style, the topic of an Irish period of 'absolute hysteria'. The
'hectic quality and the frenzy' of *Der zerbrochne Krug*, he said,
'seemed to me to suit the Ireland of that particular time when a
catastrophe was taking place'.[17] As if to prove Artaud's thesis in
his lecture 'The Theatre and the Plague' (1933), that the mass
death of plague is an effective image of social and artistic liberation, Banville disregards the pathos usually attendant on dealings with the Famine and enacts his own version of a theatre of
cruelty by backgrounding the gross actuality of the Famine victims themselves. He especially liked, he said, 'the idea of having
everyone in the play busy ignoring the fact that there's a famine
going on'.[18]

A calculated trivialisation of Ireland in 1846 depends principally on the blitheness of Judge Adam, in Banville's manifestation a gombeen man who, from a position of relative luxury and
in order to elevate himself, spends much time denouncing his
impoverished tenants. (Kleist's Adam is eminently suitable to
Banville's purposes here since, in the original, he has been involved in the abolition of his people's tithe rights.) Operating in
a court that has a dilapidated sleazy air (the Peacock's production set, designed by Joe Vanek with lighting by Rupert Murray,
consisted of a greyish, filthy, stable-like room), and accompanied by his wily clerk, Lynch, Adam's function in the context of
the Famine theme is to determinedly ignore the emptiness of the
government meal depots and the general horrors going on
around him. Though Judge Adam's type was infamously unlike-
able in nineteenth-century Ireland, Banville, in accord with his
general predilection for morally dubious characters, allows that
his sympathies in the play lie with this 'likable old rogue'.[19] Despite his perfidious deeds, the comedy of the play depends too
heavily on this rogue for there to be any doubt of his primary
position over the other characters, all of which are either wiser
or more truthful than he ever manages to be. His clowning

power is especially highlighted by the fact that he overshadows
Eve, though she is essentially the victim of the play. From the
first scene, where he appears '*dishevelled and hungover*' with a
damaged head and leg, to the last, where he is finally disgraced,
he is unremittingly hilarious: he moans that he is threatened with
'the runs' and with vomiting; he gets his superior's name wrong
and nods off during the supervised court hearing; and even in
encroaching adversity he is busy entertaining himself with
asides.

As a serious counterpoint to Judge Adam and by way of fa-
cilitating specific cultural commentary, Banville observes the
well-worn convention of having an Englishman visit the colonial land only to become progressively puzzled at native behaviour. In this case, the visitor is the Lord Lieutenant's inspector
of courts, Sir Walter Peel. While Sir Walter is the hand of centralised authority and displays impatience with local customs,
particularly when these are exaggerated by Judge Adam, he is as
ostensibly benign as in Kleist: 'The Lord Lieutenant's wishes
here are plain: / That laws shall be fairly administered, / Trans-
gressors punished, and the realm protected. / Too often English
rule is seen as harsh, / Ignoring local custom, local rights ... .'[20]
The presence of this conventional character provides for some
ludicrous distinctions between Ireland and England by Judge
Adam, who, with his sham version of patriotism, ignores Sir
Walter's conciliation and provides this enlightenment:

The fact is, sir, we do things different here. / We have peculiar
statutes in these parts / That are not written down, nevertheless /
Are tried and true, and come to us direct / From old traditions
we in Ballybog / Hold dear. Perhaps in London all is modern, /
The old ways all forgot, the past ignored. / We are an ancient
civilisation, sir; / We had our Brehon Laws when you in England / Still lived in caves and smeared yourselves with woad. /
... The trouble is, when you come over here, / You Englishmen
I mean, you do not see / That things are different here to over
there, / And try to push your customs down our
throats—(I.vii.41)

Judge Adam's constant reiteration of the fact that Sir Walter is a representative of the civilised centre now engaged in dealings with the essentially different periphery, though itself a convention when an archetypal visiting Englishman is involved, is largely a self-serving strategy. It also becomes clear however, that his actual grasp on due process is somewhat tenuous. Some of his funnier moments on the bench are those where he grapples with legal jargon:

JUDGE ADAM The matter now to hand, / The questions of procedure and of law, / Of *nolle prosequi* and *habeas corpus* / Compel me to adjourn the court until — [...] The Statute Book, you see, / Declares — in section quarto, I believe, / Or is it quinto? — that when jugs are broken, / When jugs, or heads, or anything like that / Get smashed, then daughters cannot testify / In cases where the mother is the plaintiff.'
SIR WALTER (*Aside to* JUDGE ADAM) What nonsense, sir, is this? What Statute Book?
JUDGE ADAM Don't mind me, sir, it's just that they expect / A little bit of Latin now and then, / And talk of statutes, all that sort of thing: / The kind of hocus pocus that they hear in church (I.vii.44, 54).

The law is portrayed as assuredly an ass through Judge Adam's simultaneous conviction that the health of Britain depends on him: 'I know I'm just a country magistrate, / But on such chaps as me the empire stands, / For we're the backbone, or the feet, at least, / Upholding little laws, and keeping guard, / And watching out for native restiveness'(II, i, 57).

Despite his initial good intentions, Sir Walter is less steadfast than in Kleist. His ignorance of the ways of his districts is discreetly indicated in the fact that he doesn't know what the rundale system of agriculture is or that poteen is illegal. Even before he is further afflicted by Judge Adam's plying him with requisitioned poteen, he veers towards outright distraction: 'I don't believe I'm hearing what I hear ... Dear Lord, my head! / This godforsaken place will drive me mad ... I do not want to hear talk of religion! / I've heard of nothing else since I arrived'

(I, vii, 46, 48, 54). So affected is he by Judge Adam's manufactured mayhem that he almost succumbs to the farce of the court himself, eventually taking to the poteen with gusto and allowing his hauteur to drop in favour of speaking '*Roguishly*'. Though he recovers his resolve in order to see the case of the broken jug through, in an exasperated comment towards the end he provides a summary that is a standard for the archetypal visiting Englishman that he is: 'What a benighted country!'(II.ii.75).

The pattern of the play generally is for the interaction of Adam and Sir Walter comically to uncover certain truths. The particularities of historical personalities are called into play when Judge Adam, with his self-proclaimed Tory rectitude, joyfully assumes at one point that Sir Walter is a Tory when in fact he is a Whig. He tells a joke at the expense of the leader of the Whigs, Lord John Russell, but Sir Walter immediately reveals that he is actually a cousin of Russell's. These erroneous suppositions and apparent ignorance of English politics are purposeful in relation to Banville's specific setting of the action in August of 1846. For his Sir Walter, Banville clearly has in mind Sir Robert Peel, Chief Secretary for Ireland from 1812 to 1818, and Tory Prime Minister for his second period during the years 1841 to 1846. (Sir Walter is referred to in the play by Daniel O'Connell's doubly punning epithet for Sir Robert, 'Orange Peel'.) Peel lost power in June 1846 at the very time when the failure of the impending potato crop would be total; the succeeding Whig administration, under Russell, retreated from Peel's relief policies thus exacerbating the ensuing crisis. The changeover of power in the months following June was somewhat complex, with Peel being regularly consulted on issues of Famine policy. Thus, there is an empirical precedent for the commingling of Tory and Whig, Peel and Russell, in Judge Adam's mind. Taking place on the cusp of this political changeover, the play's action serves as a neat synthesis of the complicated and often confused attitudes of both British administrations to Irish policy during the Famine years.[21]

Banville's more obvious and impressive use of Irish historical specifics is figured in Eve's mother, Martha Reck, whose character is inseparable from her family heirloom, the now broken jug. Along with implicitly symbolising the taking of her daughter's virginity, her jug, in Banville's version, operates as a symbolic re-enactment of the course of Irish history. Instead of the shattered scenes from Dutch history depicted on Frau Martha's jug, Banville provides for Martha Reck an Irish historical inventory. 'This isn't some old pisspot or spittoon', she emphasises for the court, and proceeds, in the longest monologue in the play, with what Judge Adam calls her 'history lessons':

The fairest thing I owned is kicked and smashed. / ... A beauteous and historic thing it was, / It told old Ireland's history, all in scenes. / See here, where there's now nothing but a hole, / The Firbolgs and the Tuatha Dé Danann / Were shown in mighty battle on the plain, / And there Cuchulainn swung his hurley stick: / Those are his legs, that's all that's left of him. / There's Brian Boru, at prayer before Clontarf; / you see him kneeling?—That's his backside, see? / Though even that has suffered a hard knock. / There's good Queen Maeve, and Granuaile O'Malley, / And poor Kathleen Ní Houlihan herself; / You see them where they stand, the three of them, / Bawling their eyes out over Ireland's fate? / They're legless now, and Maeve has lost her head, / And Granuaile's two elbows are broke off. / Dermot MacMurrough, look, and Strongbow too, / And Dermot's daughter, what's-her-name, that one. / Strongbow looks like he's going to fall down: / His sword is gone that he was leaning on. / The walls of Limerick, look, the siege of Derry, / The glorious victory at the river Boyne—/ Our country's history, broken up in bits! (I.vii.42-3)

Through this burlesque panorama of historical icons from both nationalist and unionist/colonial sides, much more plaintive as a passage than in Kleist, Banville disallows any easy political allegiances to be gleaned from the play. Class conflict—a subtheme Kleist included in the play but which many commentators prefer to ignore—is an area touched on by Banville in his delineation of the quarrel between Martha Reck and the accused, Robert Temple. Though no definitive information is provided, Martha argues to the court that Robert is a lowly nationalist rebel and that he is courting her daughter only to get his hands on Reck land. This is, as Judge Adam has it, a conflict between 'Prods and papists' and the matter of intermarriage gives the play a momentary frisson. Banville has no truck with a documentary realism that might develop such a topic however. Many of his characters are heightened stereotypes and the positions they hold cannot be taken quite seriously. The figure most patently treated ironically is Robert, who attempts to defend his case. A young 'spalpeen' who speaks '*loftily*', with '*orator's pose*' and often in rhyming couplets, he is a cardboard cut-out medium for nationalist soundbites, evident the moment he begins to give his details to the court: 'My name is Robert Temple, of this town; / I am a tenant farmer, with my father, / On land that woman's people stole from us— ... I mean the native Irish; / The Recks were planted on us by King Billy / When Jamesy ran away after the Boyne.' Sir Walter immediately voices one of the more stereotypical complaints levelled at the Irish in matters such as this: '(*Aside*) Dear God, more history!' Ridiculing Robert for fantasising he is Robert Emmet, Judge Adam also gets an expected cut in at clichéd patriotic cant: 'Yes yes, enough! / We know you are descended from high kings, and all the rest of it ...' (I, vii, 47)[22]. Any potentiality for serious political clashes is thus deflated (Eve, in any case, confirms that Robert's intentions towards her may mainly involve land hunger), and, although Robert is notably defiant of Sir Walter at the end, shouting 'Be damned to that! ... Go back to England, you, you damned stuffed shirt!', this is more a matter of personal indignation than ideological statement (II.ii.80-1).

Parodic characterisation apart, the one element that bears the brunt of serious satire is the court system itself. As happened with the first German performances of *Der zerbrochne Krug*, the target of the play is easily overlooked.[23] One of the more frequent complaints levelled at Kleist's original is that it contains no analysis by Judge Adam of his own flaws; but it is important to note that the play's ambiguity would have been seriously damaged by the inclusion of any kind of Shakespearian self-reflection on moral downfall. Nevertheless, while Banville has toned down even the few more overt measure-for-measure passages of the original, he does retain a vital early scene, so singular as to be almost incongruous, in which Judge Adam relates a prophetic dream wherein he condemns himself to death.(I.iv) More important than this brief resort to the idea of transcendental justice is the very practical criticism the play discreetly levels at the law. Martin Greenberg, in the introduction to his translations, noted that one of Kleist's chief themes is the judicial system's eagerness to cover up its own crimes and blindness.[24] Kleist's discrete moral critique of the law makes for some suitable commentary in Banville's version on a British colonial court system operating at a time in Ireland when criminal cases increased greatly in frequency due to the depredations of hunger. An official above all intent on the protection of officialdom, Sir Walter juggles the eventual realisation of Judge Adam's incompetence with an insistence on visible proprieties. (In the programme notes, Imhof points out that, in German, Walter means 'upholder'.) While he wishes to discover the truth of Martha Reck's allegations, he aims to do this while quietly saving face for a rigid system manned by the cupidity and imbecility of the Judge:

SIR WALTER (*Aside to* JUDGE ADAM) If you have something that you wish to say, / I beg you, for the honour of the court, / To say it now, before things go too far. ... (*Sotto voce*) Judge Adam, I advise you, close this case. ... (*Sotto voce*) Have you no shame, sir, joking here like this? / I swear, I'd see you hunted from the bench, / Were it not for the honour of the court. ... Dismiss the court, and save what face you can.(II.ii.73, 78-9)

Even when Judge Adam has been clearly found out in his misdemeanours and Robert and Eve try to attack him, Sir Walter is still insistent on the proprieties:

Silence in court! ... have you no wit at all? It is the *judge* that you are shouting at. ... (*Sotto voce*) Be quiet, now, this is a court of law; / I cannot allow anarchy to rule. / The man's a rogue, but

also he's a *judge*; / It is the *bench* that we must recognise, and
not the man (II.ii.80).

Thus Sir Walter, instead of resolving the issue on the spot, insists that Robert and Eve acquiesce to being publicly con-
demned by 'the state's authority' and then apply for guaranteed
bail and go about appealing the case. Public disgrace of the
court and *ad hoc* procedures must, in Sir Walter's mind, be
avoided at all costs. Yet even when Sir Walter promises Lynch
at the end that he will be given administrative charge, the audience knows that matters judicial will hardly improve since this
court clerk is portrayed all along as equally duplicitous, though
far superior in toadying skills, to Judge Adam.

   The double edge of Kleist's sense of ambiguity, and of Banville's extension of it to Irish concerns, extends to the very comedy of the play itself, a comedy that does not guarantee its own
purity. One of the great powers of theatre generally is the capacity to suggest the reality of a world that lies outside the stage
bounds, a power taken to its extreme in a figure like Beckett's
Godot whose presence in his play depends exclusively on his
accentuated absence. Chris Morash, who has done extensive
work on the figuration of the Famine in Irish writing, sees much
of the impact of Famine plays to be reliant on just this combination of devised on-stage presences and, more especially, off-
stage absences. 'At every moment,' he has suggested, 'each of
these states is ripe with the potential for transformation into the
other. In the space where they meet, when the potential for the
invisible offstage to be transformed into visible onstage is at its
most tangible, the theatre does its work'.[25] It is via this basic
dialectic that Banville's noncommittal dealings with the Famine
theme have their impact.

   One of the few still moments of the play occurs when Sir
Walter, having just appeared on stage, refers directly to the
source of the town's hunger. Though Judge Adam's determined
inattentiveness here to even the most mundane of realities is one
of the inaugural contributions to the play's general air of comic
puzzlement, the effect is eerie:

JUDGE ADAM The weather is unseasonal, of course; / The rain has not let up for seven weeks.
SIR WALTER Bad for the crops?
JUDGE ADAM The crops?
SIR WALTER Potato crops.
JUDGE ADAM Potatoes! Ah, potatoes. Yes. The spuds.
          Pause.
SIR WALTER I'm told this rainy weather brings on blight.
          Pause. (I.v.27)

Judge Adam then quickly changes the subject by inquiring after Sir Walter's sprained hand and potatoes are not mentioned again. Amidst the frenetic pace, well established at even this early point, the 'pauses' here are tremendous silences into which any potential serious analysis of the causes of the Famine thereafter disappears.

Though the ugly realities outside of the courtroom are conversationally ignored in the second act, the presence of famine is persistently alluded to in the first. It is the outsiders, Sir Walter and Ball, who remark on the skeletal appearance of the Board of Works employees and on how the Ballybog people appear to be eating grass and roots. An increasingly confused exchange of perspectives takes place:

BALL That's what they tell me, squire: / While all around him starved, he filled his pockets—
JUDGE ADAM Who starved? We have no hunger around here. / Our folk are fit as fiddles, and well-fed. / We have no hunger here. ...
BALL I must have been imagining it, then; / I swore I saw them dying in the streets.
JUDGE ADAM I tell you, stuff and nonsense! Lies, all lies! It's everywhere the same; these cunning brutes / Put on a show whenever strangers come; / All sham, and nothing more.
          ...
SIR WALTER Those people, judge, it seems to me, are starving.

JUDGE ADAM Don't mind them, it's an act they're putting on.
/ They're up to every trick, believe you me. / They put on rags,
and borrow sickly babes, / And make consumptives get up from
their beds/ And then come here to make a show of me ...
(I.ii.19; I.v.29)

The background appearances of Judge Adam's starving people,
occasional though they are, might be seen to damage the sub-
tlety of the play, a potential flaw of the adapted setting that was
noted by one reviewer of the Peacock performances.[26] The his-
trionics of these background characters, however, are very much
a bluntly bathetic set-up on Banville's behalf. The programme
notes included this emotive excerpt on the Famine from Thomas
Gallagher's book, *Paddy's Lament* (1982):

> No one living in Ireland at the time who saw the rotting
> fields and caught their stench, who saw and heard the
> people wailing, had to be told that for the majority of
> its population all the great and simple purposes of exis-
> tence were soon to be forgotten in the oncoming strug-
> gle with death. A famine unprecedented in the history
> of the Western world, a chapter in human misery to
> harrow the human heart, was about to start, and even
> the little children could see its quick, sure approach in
> the nakedly fearful eyes and faces of their parents. A
> terrible sense of danger and dread descended on the
> land like the thick fog that covered the countryside on
> the fatal night, the fog that people in Ireland still speak
> of as the 'potato fog'.[27]

This was, presumably, intended as a hyperbolical inclusion that
would lure the audience into misplaced expectations of seriousness, since Gallagher's tone, hardly creditable to Banville's
broadly revisionist sensibilities, is virtually ridiculed by the fact
that it is entirely absent from the play proper. The bleakly humorous effect of Judge Adam's 'cunning brutes' depends on the
audience being allowed only intermittently to view or hear of
the world outside of the courtroom while the stage is largely

kept sanitised. The distinction between the off-stage and the on-stage worlds is maintained from the beginning and this ensures that the few points at which they meet are all the more resonant:

SIR WALTER Those people at the door, they seem so …
JUDGE ADAM Eh?
SIR WALTER (*pointing off*) Those people, there—they look like skeletons.
JUDGE ADAM What people, where? I don't see anyone. …
        Exit JUDGE ADAM.
JUDGE ADAM (*Off*) Get off to hell, the lot of you—get off! / By God, I'll burn the roofs over your heads / If you don't keep away from my courthouse!
…
BALL (*At window*) There's fifty of them lined up at the door.
JUDGE ADAM (*Goes to the window*) What? Let me see. Those scroungers back again! …
BALL (*Still at the window*) They faint convincingly, I'll say that for them: / That young one with the baby just went down.
From outside, faintly, come the wails of women and curses of men as LYNCH *disperses the crowd;* JUDGE ADAM *speaks loudly to cover the noise.* (I.v.26-30)

In Act two, the evidence of Famine similarly remains outside the room of action, impinging only on Judge Adam's sham sense of propriety. This is Banville's stage instruction at the very opening of Act II: '*throughout the scene, the faces of hungry people come and go at the window, and* JUDGE ADAM *in dumbshow keeps trying to wave them away, while diverting* SIR WALTER'S *attention.*'(II.i.56) The contrast between inside and outside is at its most appallingly funny point here since, while the hungry faces come and go, the two principals are '*seated at a small table, eating*'.

    As is reflected in Banville's own interpretation of Kleist generally, comedy does not necessarily prohibit seriousness of treatment or effect. Much as Banville admits that throughout the play, 'I was half-blushing and half-laughing myself silly, thinking "this is absolutely disgraceful" … it was pure carnival, pure burlesque', the effect is all the more sensational when, as in *Birchwood*, actual events that are accepted as tragic become grotesque under the whims of farce.[28] As a play that might, in context, be almost described as unnatural, *The Broken Jug* could be beneficially read in the context of other contemporary dramatic treatments of the Famine, such as Eoghan Harris's *Souper Sullivan* (1985) or Joe O'Byrne's *The Last Potato* (1994). *The Broken Jug* is an especially vital point of comparison with the most revered Famine play, Tom Murphy's *Famine* (1968), in that it is the modal opposite of the tragic-epic style that play established as the one most suitable for the treatment of a national tragedy. Banville's play is in ways more incendiary since, in a variation on the principal effect of Banville's late work, it remains so provocatively ambiguous on vital moral issues. Martha Reck's case of her 'country's history, broken up in bits', has collapsed unattended. As her supplication in the play's closing line has it: 'Here, wait now, what about my broken jug ...?'

NOTES

1. For an extensive discussion of Banville's borrowings from Goethe's novel, see Gordon J.A. Burgess,'An Irish *Die Wahlverwandtschaften*', *German Life and Letters*, 45:2 (April 1992), 140-57. For further   discussion of Goethe, and also of Hofmannsthal's importance to *The Newton Letter*, see Rüdiger Imhof, 'German Influences on John Banville and Aidan Higgins', in Wolfgang Zach and Heinz Kosok, eds, *Literary Interrealtions: Ireland, England and the World*, vol. 2, *'Comparison and Impact'*, Tübingen 1987, 335-47.

2. In the time since this paper was presented, Banville has staged *God's Gift*, his version of Kleist's *Amphitryon* (perf. 1807). The play was premièred at the Dublin Theatre Festival in October 2000 by the Barabbas theatre company. In order to retain the original sense and context of the paper, discussion of *God's Gift* has not been incorporated here. Banville's first signifi-

cant involvement with screen drama was his adaptation of *The Newton Letter* (1982) as *Reflections*, dir. Kevin Billington, Court House Films for Channel 4 Productions, in assoc. with Bord Scannán na hÉireann/RTÉ, 1983. His original screenplay, *Seachange*, dir. Thaddeus O'Sullivan, was filmed for RTÉ's 'Two Lives' series in 1994. He has recently moved into cinema work with his adaptation of Elizabeth Bowen's *The Last September* (1929), dir. Deborah Warner, Scala Thunder Productions, 1999. Banville also adapted *Birchwood* for screen in 1986 in collaboration with Thaddeus O'Sullivan and Andrew Patmann. O'Sullivan, in correspondence with the present author, recollects that some scenes were shot but that the project was abandoned due to lack of funding. See 'Extracts from the *Birchwood* Screenplay', *the Irish Review*, 1 (1986), 65-73.

3. See Françoise Canon-Roger, 'Ruptures en Représentation: *The Broken Jug* de John Banville', *Études Irlandaises*, 21:2 (1996), 125-36. In his expanded edition of *John Banville: A Critical Introduction* (1997), Rüdiger Imhof confined mention of the adaptation to a bibliographic entry. Joseph McMinn, in his revised and expanded edition of his book on Banville, allots the play only a brief two page summary discussion. See Joseph McMinn, *The Supreme Fictions of John Banville*, Manchester 1999, 157-9.

4. Mike Murphy, 'Interview with John Banville', *The Arts Show*, RTÉ radio, 8 Feb. 1995.

5. Of his respite from the renowned control he exercises in his fiction, Banville, admitting to being a little 'stage-struck', said: 'It has been fascinating to me to watch what happens to a text when real live flesh and blood people animate it. I started out with the full knowledge that this text would be taken away from me and people would do things to it. I don't believe in the Beckett attitude that the text is absolutely sacrosanct ... I think that's death in the theatre.' See Jocelyn Clarke, 'A Man Who Finds Life Appallingly Funny', *The Sunday Tribune*, 29 May 1994, sec. B, 8.

6. In 1981, two versions of Chekov were staged, Brian Friel's *Three Sisters* and Thomas Kilroy's *The Seagull*; Derek Mahon has concentrated on the French tradition, adapting Molière's *The School for Husbands* as *High Time* (1985) and also staging a version of *The School for Wives* (1986); Tom Paulin attended to Sophocles and Aeschylus respectively for his plays *The Riot Act* (1984) and *Seize the Fire* (1990); Seamus Heaney also used Sophocles for his *The Cure at Troy* (1990); Frank McGuinness provided more Chekov with his *Three Sisters* (1990), and he has also adapted Brecht and Ibsen.

7. Eileen Battersby, 'Comedy in a Time of Famine', *the Irish Times*, 24 May 1994 , 10.

8. John Banville, 'Good Goods in Small Parcels', *the Irish Times*, 11 Mar. 1995, 'Weekend', 9.

9. 'The Helpless Laughter of a Tragedian',*the Irish Times*, 3 Dec. 1988, 'Weekend', 9. The edition in question is *Heinrich von Kleist: Five Plays*, New Haven 1988. I use Greenberg for my own comparisons here.

10. *Ibid.*, 9.

11. Clarke, Jocelyn *op. cit.* Banville isolated this passage from Greenberg's introduction as 'a good description' of the Kleist effect: 'To read Kleist is to be constantly surprised, constantly taken aback. Sometimes the surprise has a questionable source; but it is always interesting ... Kleist is like somebody who jumps up behind you when you are looking ahead, ahead of you when you look behind. This is alarming but also something of a joke.' See 'The Helpless Laughter of a Tragedian', 9.

12. The adaptation was simultaneously published in hardback and paperback to coincide with the first performances, and all references are to this edition: John Banville, *The Broken Jug (after Heinrich von Kleist)*, Oldcastle, Co. Meath 1994. The first staging of *Der zerbrochne Krug* at the Weimar theatre in March 1908 occasioned a famous disagreement between Goethe and Kleist. Goethe, unsure of the play's merits particularly in terms of structure and plotting, commented that Kleist's was 'yet another play written for a theatre that does not yet exist' and insisted on dividing the play into three acts. Going by contemporary accounts, the original performances were badly produced and badly received affairs. Kleist, influenced more by critics than by Goethe, eventually shortened the twelfth and final scene considerably and, though he published both endings, his shortened version is generally regarded as the standard text. For a discussion of the production wrangle and a commentary on the longer variant of scene twelve, see   Seán Allan, *The Plays of Heinrich von Kleist: Ideals and Illusions*, Cambridge 1996, 79-81.

13. See Gerry Colgan, 'A Touch of the Boucicaults', *Irish Times*, 2 June 19-94, 12.

14. Canon-Roger writes: 'C'est Rüdiger Imhof qui a traduit la pièce de Kleist pour Banville'. *Op. cit.*, 126.

15. 'The Helpless Laughter of a Tragedian', 9. Banville continued with this precise assessment of the quality of Greenberg's translations: 'He decided to concentrate, so he tells us, more on the sentence than the line, feeling that it is better to communicate the dash and flow of the action than to attempt the (probably impossible) task of rendering the verse as verse. The result is a vigorous, muscular free poetry which, foi all its forceful striding, manages to catch the shimmer of Kleist's singular imagination.'

16. Battersby, *op. cit.*, 10.

17. Clarke, *op. cit.*, 8.

18. Battersby, *op. cit.*, 10.

19. Battersby, *op. cit*, Eamon Morrisey's performance as Judge Adam was central to the success of the Peacock run. Fintan O'Toole commented: '[Morrisey] brings a persona of melancholia triumphantly to bear on Judge Adam. [He] has a way of playing dishevelment that presents it, not as a mere absence of order, but as a positive vocation in life, one that requires dedication and determination if a high quality of chaos is to be maintained.'

See Fintan O'Toole, 'Vigour Meets Rigour', *the Irish Times*, 7 June 1994, 10.

20. *The Broken Jug*, I, v, 28. Further references to the adaptation are given in the text, and are in the same format: Act, scene, page no.

21. The standard work on Peel's career during this period is Norman Gash, *Sir Robert Peel: The Life of Sir Robert Peel after 1830*, rev. ed., London 1986.

22. Robert Tracy's review of the play noted that Pat Kinevane, who played Robert, posed 'like a waxwork of Robert Emmet'. See 'The Broken Lights of Irish Myth', *Irish Literary Supplement*, 14: 2 (Fall 1995), 18.

23. For a discussion of developments in analysis of the serious aspects of the play, see Seán Allan, *op. cit.*, 81f.

24. Greenberg, *op. cit.*, *xxxviii*.

25. 'Sinking Down into the Dark: The Famine on Stage', *Bullán*, 3: 1 (1997), 76. Though Morash does mention *The Broken Jug* in a note, the temporal compass of his discussion ends at 1968 with Tom Murphy's *Famine*. Morash's title here is taken from Banville's *Birchwood*.

26. The single complaint Fintan O'Toole made in his admiring review was that Banville had used 'hammy shadow-figures and groans to signify a calamity that would be much more powerfully evoked by much more subtle means'. *Op. cit.*, 10.

27. Thomas Gallagher, *Paddy's Lament: Ireland 1846-1847, Prelude to Hatred*, Dublin 1994, 8.

28. Joe Jackson, 'Hitler, Stalin, Bob Dylan, Roddy Doyle ... and Me', *Hot Press*, 18: 19 (5 Oct. 1994), 15.

(Con)Fusing Borders: The Politics of Place in Bernard Mac Laverty[1]

MARISOL MORALES LADRÓN

At the end of Brian Friel's *Translations*, the hedge-schoolmaster, Hugh, comments that 'confusion is not an ignoble condition.'[2] In a talk given at the University of Alcalá (Madrid) in 1999, the Northern Irish writer Bernard Mac Laverty echoed Friel's words to refer to the way the socio-political reality of Northern Ireland has to be apprehended, adding that 'if you are not confused you don't fully understand'. The evolution of Mac Laverty's literary production in the last two decades attests to this precise vision of the Troubles, which is becoming more and more commonly accepted. From an examination of stagnant and simplistic clear-cut divisions of identities, as they emerge in his collections of short stories—*Secrets* (1977), *A Time to Dance* (1982) and *The Great Profundo* (1987)—and in his two novels, *Lamb* (1980) and *Cal* (1983), Mac Laverty's recent fiction has moved to a more fluent and relative attitude towards sectarianism and the given clash between the two cultures. This is evident in some of the stories and sketches that comprise *Walking the Dog* (1994) and, even more to the point here, in his penultimate novel *Grace Notes*, shortlisted for the Booker Prize in 1997. Both works play with the (con)fusion of borders concerning distinct political sections of society and the historical dis-

crepancies between Britain and Ireland, and they succeed in deconstructing traditional stereotypes that have perpetuated a
somewhat reductive view of the conflict. Bearing all this in
mind, the purpose of my study is to analyse the building-up of
Mac Laverty's literary creation in the context of his exploration
of the Troubles, which has run parallel to the historical changes
of the conflict itself.[3]

In his article '"Within Two Shadows": The Troubles in
Northern Ireland', Richard Deutsch suggests that the literary
production of the seventies was characterised by its mimetic
search for verisimilitude in the description of a 'polarised northern society ... indulg[ing] in a dichotomy which already existed
in the mental patterns of their ancestors: a closed society with its
two cultures'.[4] The eighties, however, according to Joe
McMinn, brought two kinds of novels: those interested in pursuing a kind of 'documentary realism', which found expression
mainly in the form of the popular thriller; and the novels that
used the Troubles as a 'background for romance', in which one
could find 'a threat to privacy and individualism'.[5] Other critics,
like Eve Patten or Gerry Smyth,[6] have added other types to this
classification, suggesting that Troubles literature has actually
become 'one of the region's few growth industries'.[7] It was not
until the nineties that a less angry and muted vision of the strife
emerged in a new kind of fiction that incorporates, on the one
hand, some sort of hope brought by the various cease-fire attempts and, on the other, a more parodic and ironic interpretation of the conflict itself. In this vein, Laura Pelaschiar comments in her article, 'Transforming Belfast: the Evolving Role of
the City in Northern Irish Fiction', that in the last three decades
the literature of Northern Ireland, especially that which is set in
the city of Belfast, has undergone a significant evolution with
regard to the perception of the political contention, moving from
the stagnant and clear-cut divisions that characterised earlier
discourses to a more open and plural view of the sectarian divide: 'Belfast is thus the only Irish metropolis which has been
redeemed from its role as the essence of the modern nightmare
and which has attained the status of a postmodern urban centre,
with all the *pros* and the *cons* that that entails.'[8]

Although not all of Mac Laverty's writings can be categorised as 'Troubles' literature, his novels and most of his short stories are set in Northern Ireland in an atmosphere of violence, fear, oppression and bigotry that is inseparable from the socio-economic and political realities of the place. The development of his literary career, I shall argue, encompasses all the changes that the several discourses on the Troubles have met over the last thirty years, and his fiction has finally grown into an acceptance of a more plural and tolerant notion of duality, as an inclusive rather than as a narrow term. My argument is that Mac Laverty, together with other 'prodigal novelists'—if I may use a phrase coined by Eve Patten—like Glenn Patterson or Robert McLiam Wilson, has recently become more interested in exploring troublesome dichotomies and in deconstructing the (Northern) Irish identity across the divide than in offering a reductive, sensationalist and moral view of the conflict.[9]

Mac Laverty was born in Belfast, a city that inspired him first and foremost when he started writing and was invited to join the informal meetings of the 'Belfast Group' organised by Philip Hobsbaum in the early sixties. This was a gathering of young Irish writers that included Seamus Heaney, Michael and Edna Longley, Stewart Parker, Michael McLaverty, Derek Mahon, Paul Muldoon, James Simmons and Medbh McGuckian, among others, all of whom were eager to share their literary viewpoints and to comment on their individual achievements. Since then, and with a few exceptions, Mac Laverty's novels and short stories, although published while he was living abroad, have been set in Ireland and have explored Irish issues. In 1975 he received an Honours Degree in English from Queen's University Belfast, moving shortly afterwards to Scotland where he taught English at various schools in Edinburgh and Glasgow till 1978. He then took another teaching job in the Isle of Islay—off the coast of Scotland—which he eventually left in 1981 in order to devote all his time to writing, settling his permanent residence in Scotland. From his self-imposed exile, Mac Laverty has certainly benefited from a distance that has allowed him to adopt a detached perspective in his writing. More significant, however, is the way he has been highly acclaimed by Irish and Scottish academic critics and general readers alike, as evidenced by the number of literary prizes he has received.[10]

Mac Laverty began to write at the age of nineteen as something to do, in his own words, 'after the dot disappeared on the TV set.'[11] In 1975, the Northern Arts Council awarded him a bursary for his stories, many of which had appeared in various literary journals and anthologies. Two years later, *Secrets and other Stories* was published, for which he received the Scottish Arts Council Book Award. Using a style reminiscencent of William Trevor, his main concern lies in the representation of everyday reality through the exploration of diverse individuals, from children to university students, unemployed people, or old couples close to death. Dialogue, the reproduction of idiolects that particularise characters, together with his ability to convey a condensed message combining realism and drama with humour are his most distinctive traits. Not surprisingly, Mac Laverty has encountered no difficulties in adapting many of his short stories for television and radio, as he did with 'Secrets', the most significant of this homonymous collection.

With the publication of his first novel, *Lamb* (1980), he received the Scottish Arts Council Book Award and was runner-up for the Guardian Fiction Award. Although the story is 'obliquely related to the Troubles',[12] the fine blending of politics and religion can only find expression in the oppressive and destructive atmosphere of a remote and desolate place in Northern Ireland. *Lamb* focuses on the life of an epileptic twelve-year old, Owen Kane, in a Brothers' school; a kind of bleak reformatory, where the physical and emotional coldness of the institution emphasises the loveless relationship between the Christian Brothers and the children. With the financial support of his father's will, Michael Lamb —in truth, Brother Sebastian— decides to break the rules of the place and flee to England with the child, in an attempt to keep him away from the physical abuse of the principal, Brother Benedict, the bullying from other children, a cruel mother and a brutally destructive life.

Playing the role of an adoptive father, Lamb tries to give Owen everything he lacks. The child explains to him that the onset of an attack is the most pleasurable experience that he has ever had. As he runs out of money and England turns out not to be the right place for a vulnerable and easily influenced child, Lamb cannot find any hope for him either in Northern Ireland or anywhere else. Concluding that the only escape from such a dreadful life is death, he exchanges Owen's medicine for aspirin and makes a decision out of love: to bring Owen's suffering to an end by provoking his death from an epileptic attack. In a dramatic and extremely moving ending, when the fit comes, Lamb drowns Owen in the sea. The impossibility of finding a way out from the oppression exercised by the power of religion and of politics serves as a means to reflect the stagnant reality of a place characterised by endemic violence and fear.[13] As the narrator resumes: 'Owen was dead. He had killed him to love him.'[14] Although *Lamb* is not a Troubles novel, '(t)he culture which has produced this psychopathology is heavily implicated in the Troubles of the North, since the brother in charge of the Borstal, Benedict, is a Republican with strong links to the IRA.'[15] The novel finally comes to imply that in this environment there is no possibility of a successful challenge to the threat of authority represented by politics and religion alike. For Mac Laverty himself, *Lamb* 'was an image of what was happening in Ireland; that there were certain violent people and organisations who claimed to love Ireland but in fact were destroying it. This man says he loves the boy and yet he kills him'.[16]

This novel was followed by the publication of another collection of ten short stories, *A Time to Dance* (1982), which also received the Scottish Arts Council Book Award. Continuing the line of *Secrets*, characterisation becomes stronger than plot and 'comedy acquires layers of seriousness'.[17] To the ingredients of realism and humour, Mac Laverty here adds an element of surprise in an attempt to shock the reader into the unexpected unfolding of the stories.[18] Most of them have a final humorous twist, like 'Language, Truth and Lockjaw', and there are other very short ones, like 'Father and Son' or 'The Beginning of Sin', with grey Trevorian endings.[19] Among all the narratives that make up the collection, perhaps only 'My Dear Palestrina'—dealing with the relationship between a talented boy and his music teacher, and rich in symbolic overtones—could be said to touch very subtly upon the political background of the Troubles through Catholic Northern Irish bigotry and the oppression of a provincial society that pulls the boy and his teacher apart.

Mac Laverty's second novel, *Cal* (1983), has been classified both as a domestic romance across-the-divide and as a gripping political thriller. The setting is rather vague, since the story takes place at various locations surrounding a nameless country town, but it can easily be placed in Northern Ireland in the late 1970s. *Cal* explores the topical sectarian conflict of Northern Ireland, in which an impossible and tragic love story is set against the bitter backdrop of the Troubles and comes to symbolise the impossibility of union between the two Irelands.[20] Furthermore, *Cal* can be read as a 'Catholic study of guilt, expiation, and the desire for confession, forgiveness and absolution'.[21] In the novel, Cal is a young working-class Catholic, unemployed and motherless, who lives in a neighbourhood surrounded by Protestant families. In a milieu of fear and violence, Cal is given no choice other than to become an active participant in the tribal war between Catholics and Protestants. As the driver of a car in an IRA terrorist act, he becomes an accomplice in the murder of an RUC reserve officer policeman—Robert Morton—and in the serious wounding of his father. As the murder haunts him throughout the story, he meets the librarian Marcela (the widow of his victim), falls in love with her, manages to find a job on her in-laws' farm and ends by having a love affair with her. Cal is both the victim of the circumstances and an active participant in them, but he has no way of escaping from this Catch-22 situation. When he and his father are burned out of their home, he tries to break his ties with the IRA and to find a secure place in which he can feel free, but neither of these is possible. As a Catholic, his guilty conscience will drive him to alert the security forces to a firebomb which his mate Crilly has planted in the library. The reader leaves him at the end of the novel, trying thus to redeem himself from his 'sin', waiting passively to be caught by the police—and the last lines tell us that he 'finds himself grateful that at last someone was going to beat him to within an inch of his life.'[22] *Cal* is, therefore, a clear example of the mimetic narrative referred to previously, which uses documentary realism to represent the dynamics of the Troubles during the seventies and eighties.

Shortly after *Cal* was published, Michael Gorra praised it in the *New York Times* as 'a most moving novel whose emotional impact is grounded in a complete avoidance of sentimentality … . In its full imaginative consideration of an apparently intractable political problem, *Cal* will become the *Passage to India* of the Troubles.'[23] However, following Patten's classification of the novels of the Troubles, *Lamb* and *Cal* could more appropriately be said to belong to a 'series of slim novels set against the violence of the seventies and early eighties [that] established a determinist formula which repeatedly located a well-meaning individual within a debilitating and ultimately damaging political context.'[24] The two novels explore the impossibility of finding a middle way between becoming an accomplice of the 'war' and preserving innocence.[25]

Mac Laverty's third story collection, *The Great Profundo* (1987), continues to explore some of his more recurrent themes, primarily the father-son relationship and family matters. In one of them, 'Some Surrender', there is a slight manifestation of bigotry in the Unionist father, but there is no further exploration of the Troubles.[26] The collection seems to mark the ending of the first stage in Mac Laverty's literary career, where his writing had served to reinforce what Patten has described as 'a compulsive literary stereotype—that of the Irish writer defiantly extracting the lyrical moment from tragic inevitability', failing to explore and represent a 'multi-textured and abstruse society'.[27] I shall argue then, that this is precisely the path he takes in what I regard as the second stage in his literary career. In *Walking the Dog* and *Grace Notes*—a further compilation of short stories and a novel, both products of the nineties—Mac Laverty plays with ambivalence as far as the 'reality' of the strife and of the narrative are concerned.

Walking the Dog (1994) is his most recent collection. In terms of themes and subject matter it resumes where *The Great Profundo* left off, although formally it is substantially fresher and more innovative. The settings of the stories include several places in Northern Ireland, where characters are threatened by

some sectarian upheavals—like the boy in 'A Silent Retreat'—
as well as Mediterranean resorts in Spain—in 'The Grandmas-
ter' and 'At the Beach'. Here, it is the reproduction of naturalis-
tic dialogues rather than description that makes the stories progress; and the reader is aware of Mac Laverty's mastery with
conversation, his ability to capture the nuances of language and
his effective utilisation of slang. Although most conversations
are apparently trivial their full meaning is always revealed in the
ending. The writer's aesthetics involve his dealing with the or-
dinariness of life, focusing on everyday detail and describing
very vivid, simple people.

Walking the Dog consists of nine stories, each of which is
preceded by a very short, funny and rather inexplicable vignette
that has an italicised title and starts with the Irish phrase 'Your
man', alluding to the author's *alter ego*. The condensed significance of these minimalist accounts adds meaning to the more
developed narratives that follow them and function as their
counterpoint. In this sense, one could say that it is a polyphonic
book that attempts to approach serious subjects from a comic or
even frivolous angle. The purpose, according to the author, was
to 'do something comic in between these bleak stories ... . They
are all about writing in some shape or form'.[28] Throughout the
collection, Mac Laverty plays with the expectations of the
reader, subverting accepted ideologies and challenging monolithic notions of identity by means of a final twist. The first vignette, suggestively entitled 'The Art of the Short Story', is
about self-conscious writing and the creation of fiction. However, the most outstanding story of the collection is 'Walking the
Dog', an exceptional example of a new mode of perceiving the
Troubles through which the traditional binary social, political,
cultural and religious dichotomies are subverted into an ironic
solution that accommodates the existing gaps among all of
them.[29]

'Walking the Dog' is about a Belfast man who takes his dog
for a walk and is suddenly kidnapped by two armed terrorists
identified as IRA men. With violence and insults, they force him
to enter their car. They then subject him to an absurd cross-
examination about his religious beliefs, to which the protagonist,

John Shields, answers by saying that he does not 'believe in any of that crap. I suppose I am nothing.'[30] In a humorous tone, they make him recite the alphabet, following the well-known belief that Catholics and Protestants pronounce the eighth letter differently due to separate schooling. Shields, clearly uninfluenced by bigotry and narrow nationalism —asserting that: 'In our house nobody believed in anything'(7)— cannot remember which is the correct one and says it both ways in an atttempt to convince them that he has no clear-cut beliefs. They also ask him to say a Hail Mary and, when the terrorists are convinced that he seems not to be 'interested in that kind of thing' (9), they finally dump him by the road. The reader suddenly comes to see that they were actually UDR men posing as members of the IRA, trying to find out whether he was a Fenian. The discovery of this final twist rests in an allusive reference to the symbolism of colours when, at one point, the terrorists stop the car at a traffic light that suggestively changes 'from orange to green' (10)[31]. The achievement of this story resides in the parodic treatment of questions of identity understood as a monolithic essence. The apparent unity that this concept has been made to embody is exposed as an unstable category capable of welcoming opposite sides as alternative facets of the same reality. The story ends on an ironic note: the man returns to his everyday life, while the reader witnesses him listening to 'the clinking of *the dog's identity disk* as it padded along beside him.'(12, my emphasis).

If *Walking the Dog* did inaugurate a new mode in the author's approach to the conflict, , *Grace Notes* (1997), conceived during the 1994 cease-fire, went further in the final hope with which the story finishes. Both accounts can be interpreted as a response to a question that Patten had posed in her article on Northern Ireland's prodigal novelists: '... is it possible to produce fresh images of the situation in a medium impoverished by cliché and overkill?'.[32] Whereas 'Walking the Dog' ends on an ambiguous note, fusing and confusing the traditional sectarian borders in its deconstruction of the very notion of a stable identity, *Grace Notes* offers a more optimistic view of the strife through the exploration of the universal and unifying symbol of music that also fuses and confuses the sound of the drums played by Prot-

estants in parades with the Catholic odour of the Latin mass recalled by the protagonist.

In terms of form, *Grace Notes* departs from the more traditional style of Mac Laverty's prose of the eighties, adding complexity to the devices and narrative techniques used while also
combining different voices in the narration. Divided into two
sections, it is set in various locations: Northern Ireland, Glasgow
and the island of Islay. Although the novel oscillates between
third and first person narration, the reader is always confronted
with Catherine's angle of vision, either through the rendering of
her own internal thoughts or by means of the narrator's use of
free indirect speech. The construction of the plot is thus based
on a fragmented discourse, formed by glimpses and recollections of her past, that progresses very slowly and displaces the
centre of the narrative into a richer, allusive musical dimension.

The novel starts with Catherine MacKenna, a young piano
composer, travelling home to Northern Ireland to attend her
father's funeral.[33] It is her first visit after five years, not so much
because she had left, but because: 'She just failed to come back
after her postgraduate year in Glasgow. One thing led to another
'(40). Through the continuous flashbacks to her childhood, the
reader forms an image of her as an estranged only child and as a
single mother who is suffering from an artistic block. After a
few days there, in an atmosphere of tension, painful remem-
brances and frequent bomb scares, she returns to Glasgow and to
her baby daughter, Anna. The first half of the novel ends with
Catherine hearing the good news that Anna has been able to
utter her first words. The second part steps back in time and
place, to her post as a music teacher on the remote island of Islay, and to an account of her destructive relationship with her
English boyfriend, Dave; to her pregnancy and to her consequent struggle with post-natal depression, and to her final over-
coming of all this. Unable to put up any longer with an alcoholic, aggressive partner who mistreats her physically and psychologically, Catherine leaves him and resumes her career as a
composer. Her inspiration eventually comes, forming a significant parallel with Anna's first steps, when suddenly Catherine
pre-hears music in her mind. The novel ends with the successful

radio broadcast of an instrumental symphony that she has created, commissioned by the BBC.[34]

This composition, in which she triumphantly manages to inte-
grate the rhythms of the huge Lambeg drums which Orangemen
have been playing for centuries with the harmony of a Catholic
Latin mass, bears the whole symbolic weight of the novel.[35] It is
at this point that the 'Grace Notes' of the title are echoed, having
being defined at the beginning of the novel as 'the notes within
the notes'(33) and, further on, as the 'notes which were neither
one thing nor the other' (133). At the start, the beating of the
drums during the Protestant marching season is seen by Catherine's Catholic father as a threatening and violent act:

> On the Twelfth they thump them so hard and so long they
> bleed their wrists. Against the rim. Sheer bloody bigotry
> ...   They practise out here above the town to let the
> Catholics know they're in charge. This is their way of
> saying the Prods rule the roost (8).

Being a child, Catherine experiences a mixture of threat and
excitement, and feels 'thrilled by the sound, [she] could distinguish the left hand's rhythm from the right' (8). The bigotry of
her father, however, representing as it does the narrow views of
an older generation, is something she must overcome in her
adult life before she can finally succeed in creating a music free
from national ideologies, combining the thunderous sound with
an unexpected result. As her friend Liz says of '*Vernicle*', the
audience 'really like it—I have no idea why ' (277).

Despite the obvious political symbolism of the integration of
both cultures into this single piece of music, Catherine seems to
be mainly concerned with the 'great sound' that it produces, and
with the intense feelings that the complicated rhythms evoke.
Her old music teacher, Miss Bingham, wisely tells her that the
press is not interested in that: 'All they want to get is a story
about cementing the divide, or bridging the sectarian gulf '(105).
And clearly, when the piece is performed at the end of the novel,
the narrator's focus is placed on how the 'whole church rever-
berates. The Lambegs have been stripped of their bigotry and

have become pure sound' (276). Mac Laverty himself has explained in an interview that:

> both *Lamb* and *Cal* reflect the negativity, the disappointment, the gloom of the situation in Northern Ireland. But *Grace Notes* came to be written during the cease-fire ... I'm not a gloomy person. I felt that this might be an opportunity to end the book with hope although it doesn't end on a kind of an unreasonable level of hope; it is a very attenuated hope.[36]

On a final note, the word that significantly closes the first part of the novel, '*Credo*',(138) parallels the closing '*Bravo*' (277), the two terms celebrating life in the creation of the music as much as in the (con)fusion of the two cultures that are attempting or pursuing some sort of reconciliation.

Throughout the novel Catherine apprehends the world in terms of its sound, as 'the world in sound—a kind of aural atlas' (36). In like manner, the reading process is made to resemble the playing of a piece of music, with variations of tempo and rhythm, which move from 'piano' and 'pianissimo' to the 'forte' and 'fortissimo' of its last lines (276)[37]. As an autobiographical novel, it comes as no surprise that Catherine—like her creator himself—prefers to live in Glasgow, a city that is described in the book as: 'Great. Like Belfast [but] without the killings' (44). For this reason, following Mac Laverty's own interpretation of his novel, the significance of Catherine's composition lies in the fact that 'she is a musician and can use the power of the drums musically once the bigotry is ... subtracted from them'.[38]

Grace Notes distances itself from Mac Laverty's early narrative in his treatment of female characters. These were usually one-dimensional figures, stereotypes of some sort—like Owen's cruel mother in *Lamb* and Marcella's simple characterisation in *Cal*—or non-existent; Cal is motherless, and both his father and Michael Lamb are depicted as rather maternal figures. *Grace Notes*, however, not only has a woman as its protagonist; it outlines a completely female world where male characters are either absent—the protagonist's father, has just died; she lives with a married girlfriend in Glasgow, whose husband is outside the scene—or are portrayed negatively; her drunkard boyfriend, for example, who soon disappears from the story. Throughout the novel, Catherine's warm recollections of her grandmother are linked to her mothering of a daughter and to her wish for Anna to become the mother of yet another daughter; all of which contributes to strengthen the female bonding that exists in the novel. *Grace Notes* is a brilliant examination of the female consciousness and the female world in its celebration of motherhood and creation; that is, in the giving birth to a baby and in her giving life to music. As the novel often suggests: 'Music was being conceived' (129); 'She is pregnant with it [music]' (134). Catherine MacKenna has to overcome the oppressive circumstances that surround her while she also tries to come to terms with different facets of her past: as a woman, because she is a single mother living with an aggressive and alcoholic man who beats her up; as a musician, since she is a piano composer trying to compose a Latin mass as she tries to find her place in a male-dominated profession; and as a daughter, having failed to come back home to see her father before his death, and not being understood by her own unsympathetic mother.

Dividing Mac Laverty's literary production into two different stages—his early writings of the late seventies and the eighties; and a more recent period, in which he has turned his attention to the exploration of unsolved troublesome dichotomies—helps to set his work alongside the evolution of the socio-political concerns of the Troubles themselves, with which it forms a parallel. If *Lamb* and *Cal* fulfilled the Ulster agenda of 'sex, violence and sectarianism',[39] *Grace Notes* incorporates the Troubles as a background in which politics stand as a metaphor for the social and emotional fragmentation of the 'troubled' people of Northern Ireland.[40] Both this novel and *Walking the Dog* amplify the range of Mac Laverty's literary exploration of the Troubles, moving from a central preoccupation with love, death, tragedy, violence and family matters, to an ambivalence in the treatment of some other relevant topics, such as politics, religion and individual freedom.[41] Religion and nationalism, the main concerns of *Lamb*, found ample representation in *Cal*. Individual freedom, or the fight against oppression and conformity, is the main topic of *Grace Notes*. Most of the characters of his early works were, therefore, lonely people struggling against an adverse fate. Religion and violence, the focal points of *Lamb* and *Cal*, find in his subsequent work a more subtle focus tinged with other more universal themes such as individual freedom or the fight against oppression and conformity. In the interview referred to above, Mac Laverty informed me that he was preparing another novel. *The Anatomy School* was published in 2001, and we will have to wait for further studies to see the path he is taking at present.

NOTES

1. The research carried out for the writing of this article has been financed by the 'Vicerrectorado de Investigación'—research project UAH2002/OS1—of the University of Alcalá (Madrid, Spain).
2. Brian Friel, *Translations*, London and Boston 1981, 67.
3. Apart from his four story collections and his four novels, Mac Laverty has also written and/or illustrated children's books, and has adapted many of his stories for radio and television.
4. Richard Deutsch, '"Within Two Shadows": The Troubles in Northern Ireland', in Patrick Rafroidi and Maurice Harmon, eds, *The Irish Novel in Our Time*, Lille 1975-76, 149.
5. Joe McMinn, 'Contemporary Novels on the Troubles', *Etudes Irlandaises*, 5 (1980), 113-14.
6. Patten talks about two trends in the fiction of Northern Ireland: the realist and documentary mode that functions as 'the most appropriate means of self-critique'; and the 'consensual (and usually apolitical) liberal humanist comment' (Eve Patten, 'Fiction in Conflict: Northern Ireland's Prodigal Novelists', in Ian A. Bell, ed., *Peripheral Visions: Images of Nationhood in Contemporary British Fiction*, Cardiff 1995, 131). Smyth classifies the Northern Irish novel into three kinds: the Troubles thriller, the national romance and the domestic novel. To these, and following Patten, he later adds the recent orientation taken by 'prodigal fic-

tion' (Gerry Smyth, *The Novel and the Nation: Studies in the New Irish Fiction*, London 1997, 114-17).

7. Patten, *op. cit.*, 128.

8. Laura Pelaschiar, 'Transforming Belfast: the Evolving Role of the City in Northern Irish Fiction', *Irish University Review*, 30 (Spring/Summer 2000), 130. In this survey, Pelaschiar follows Edna Longley's well-known article, 'The Writer and Belfast' (in Maurice Harmon, ed., *The Irish Writer and the City*, Gerrards Cross 1984, 65-89), in which Longley analyses the vision that poets and prose writers, such as Michael McLaverty, Brian Moore, Louis MacNeice, John Hewitt, Seamus Heaney and Derek Mahon, have put forward in their respective work.

9. Although Patten does not include Mac Laverty in her analysis of the 'prodigal novelists', my point is that his literary production in the nineties can be identified with that of a group of writers who have 'succeeded to some extent in countering or adjusting the sterile images produced by mainstream Northern Irish writers during the Troubles.... manag[ing] to combine strategies of irony and dislocation with fresh approaches to realism in order to contest established readings of their situation without imposing new stereotypes.' (Patten, *op. cit.*, 146).

10. Among a long list, he has been awarded the following prizes: the Pharic McLaren Award for Best Script with the adaptation of 'My Dear Palestrina' for radio and TV (1980); the RTÉ Jacob's Award for Best Play (1981); The Sunday Independent Award for Literature (1983); the Evening Standard Award for Best Screenplay (1984); the Screenplay Bronze Medal, Lucarno Film Festival (1987); the McVities Prize for the Scottish Writer of the Year (1988); the Irish Post Award (1989); and the Society of Authors Travelling Scholarship.

11. See the following web site for some of Mac Laverty's biographical details: http://www.englisch.schule.de/cal/Laverty.htm.

12. Neil Corcoran, *After Yeats and Joyce: Reading Modern Irish Literature*, Oxford and New York 1997, 155.

13. See Juan Francisco Elices Agudo, 'Deconstructing the Religious Authority through the Use of Animal Imagery in Bernard Mac Laverty's *Lamb*', in José Luis Caramés Lage and Carmen Escobedo de Tapia, eds., *El discurso artístico. literatura y poder*, vol. 1, Oviedo 2000, 173-80.

14. Bernard Mac Laverty, *Lamb*, London 1981, 152.

15. Corcoran, *op. cit.*, 155.

16. Marisol Morales Ladrón, '"Writing is a state of mind, not an achievement": an interview with Bernard Mac Laverty', *Atlantis*, 23.2 (December 2001), 208.

17. Arnold Saxton, 'An Introduction to the Stories of Bernard Mac Laverty', *Journal of the Short Story*, 8 (Spring 1987), 113.

18.   Again, not surprisingly, some of these stories were adapted for radio
      and television: 'My Dear Palestrina' won the Pharic MacLaren Special
      BBC Award and was runner-up for the Pye Radio Award; 'No Joke'
      was adapted for the radio; and both 'Phonefun Limited' and 'The Daily
      Woman' were made into television dramas.

19.   This one calls upon a central topic in Mac Laverty's writing, echoing
      his own autobiography since his own father died when he was only
      twelve. The experience of the paternal absence exerted such an enor-
      mous influence on his life that most protagonists in his work are either
      motherless or fatherless or both, and experience difficulties in trying to
      cope with the situation.

20.   I have analysed *Cal* elsewhere as a direct response to the Troubles. See
      my contribution 'La re-presentación del conflicto de Irlanda del Norte en
      Cal de Bernard Mac Laverty' ['The Re-presentation of the Northern Irish
      Conflict in Bernard Mac Laverty's *Cal*'], *Actas del XXIII Congreso de
      AEDEAN*, León 2002. See also Stephen Watt, 'The Politics of Bernard
      Mac Laverty's *Cal*', *Eire-Ireland*, 28.3 (1993), 130-46.

21.   Corcoran, *op. cit.*, 156.

22.   Bernard Mac Laverty, *Cal*, London 1984, 154. Further references are to
      this edition and are given in the text in brackets.

23.   Michael Gorra, 'Guilt and Penance in Northern Ireland', *The New York
      Times Book Review* (Sunday August 21, 1983), 1.

24.   *Ibid.*, 131.

25.   It is noteworthy that *Lamb* and *Cal* have been produced as major
      successful films, for which Mac Laverty himself wrote the screenplays.
      Lamb (1985) was directed by Colin Gregg and *Cal* (1984), which won
      the Evening Standard Film Award, was directed by Pat O'Connor. See
      my article 'Más allá de binarismos esencialistas: del texto literario al
      discurso fílmico en *Cal* de Bernard Mac Laverty' ['Beyond Essentialist
      Binarisms: from the Literary Text to the Filmic Discourse in Bernard Mac
      Laverty's *Cal*'], in José María Paz Gago and José Ángel Fernández Roca,
      eds., *Actas del IV Congreso Internacional de la Federación
      Latinoamericana de Semiótica*, A Coruña 2002, forthcoming.

26.   This story, together with 'The Break', also became a radio drama.

27.   Patten, *op. cit.*, 128.

28.   Morales, 'Interview', *op. cit.*, 204.

29.   Apart from this, another story set in the Northern Irish sectarian divide
      is 'A Silent Retreat', about a Catholic boy who has a vocation for
      priesthood and is confronted with a B-special policeman with whom he
      has a theological conversation and discovers that both share common
      doubts.

30.   Bernard Mac Laverty, *Walking the Dog*, London, 1995, 7. Further refer-
      ences are to this edition and are given in the text in brackets.

31. Colours are also very important in *Cal*, where, for instance, the protagonist recalls his disgust at the 'red and white cross of the Ulster flag with its red hand', or at the 'kerbstones [that] had been painted alternating red, white and blue'(9). Further references abound throughout the novel.

32. Patten, *op. cit.*, 129.

33. Although the name of the place is never mentioned, it can be recognised as a town in Co. Derry, since there are passing references to her convent school in Toomebridge. Bernard Mac Laverty, *Grace Notes*, London 1998, 7. Further references are to this edition and are given in the text in brackets.

34. It is also significant that, as the narrator explains: 'The concert was sponsored by the European Broadcasting Union and was being transmitted live to about twenty European countries'(259).

35. The Catholic overtones of its title, '*Vernicle*', are obvious. A '*Vernicle*' was a badge worn by pilgrims. As Catherine says, it 'is a Pilgrim's medal. Chaucer's Pardoner had one sewn on to his hat to show where he'd been'(104).

36. Morales, 'Interview', *op. cit.*, 206-207.

37. For instance, Mac Laverty plays with onomatopoeic words and the ambivalent meaning of homophones, such as 'Lynn C. Doyle /Linseed Oil' or 'Bar talk / Bartok'.

38. Morales, 'Interview', *op. cit.*, 207-208.

39. John Wilson Foster, *Forces and Themes in Ulster Fiction*, New Jersey: Rowman and Littlefield, 1974, 254.

40. As Mac Laverty has explained: 'I was trying to write from the age of 20 and by the time I was 29 the Troubles had "refreshed themselves". And if you're a writer, and you're paying attention and suddenly the world around you explodes into violence and hatred that's going to affect you as a writer and forever more. So Catherine comes back to mid-Ulster and picks up again on all those hatreds, the things that get in the way of things. Those hatreds are terrible and they are a part of the book which is in some way about the hurdles that block people's progress'. (Liam Carson, 'Bernard's Lonely Voice', available at: http://cgi-bin.iol.ie/andersonstown-news/1997.09.06/Bernard.html).

41. Saxton summarises Mac Laverty's themes in 'loneliness, isolation, [and] discontent', *op. cit.*, 116.

'Here it begins': Figuring Identities in

Dermot Healy's *A Goat's Song*

KIM WALLACE

Fiction has the power to remake reality. The text intentionally aims at a horizon of a new reality that we may call a world. It is the world of the text that intervenes in the world of action in order to give it a new configuration ... in order to transfigure it.[1]

Dermot Healy's *A Goat's Song*[2], published in 1994, is one of the few Southern novels to cross the border and address conflict in Northern Ireland and North/South relations. It exploits the transfigurative potential of fiction by juxtaposing the narratives of Protestants and Catholics, North and South, challenging the boundaries of Irish identity and attempting to determine parameters for reconciliation. The novel can be read as a personal tragedy of estrangement, as the particularity of the title suggests. But, in its use of the English translation of the Greek word, τραγῳδία, it appropriates a classical literary form, and suggests an engagement with communal experiences. *A Goat's Song* alerts the reader to the illusions, prejudices and gaps in understanding that make opposing versions of 'reality' and which inhibit reconciliation between, and within, communities in Ireland.[3] As Maurice Goldring remarks, 'Anything that destroys the tribal border is conducive to peace'.[4] Yet it can also be read as constructing a 'double-voiced' discourse.[5]   It transfigures the world of Ireland, but also examines the problematics of remaking 'reality', exploring the dialectic between the 'world of action' and the 'world of the text'.

Healy's novel questions the extent to which fiction can assimilate often disparate discourses yet transcend the limits they impose upon it.   Like Joyce's 'The Dead', *A Goat's Song* expresses a fear of paralysis within a present that is continually haunted by the spectre of the past.[6] However, unlike Joyce's Stephen Dedalus in *A Portrait of the Artist as a Young Man,* who is desperate to escape the 'nets' of 'nationality, language, religion',[7] Healy's characters attempt to reconcile conflicting polarities within Irish religious and political discourse. Fiction becomes a site of contest, and representations of the artistic consciousness demonstrate the potential for moving beyond the limitations of some of those historical, religious, political and social discourses that construct the 'extraliterary' consciousness.[8]

Whilst Healy's novel challenges divergent ideological positions, it also draws attention to the problematics of narrativity, of remaking 'reality'.   *A Goat's Song* is, paradoxically, bound by the limitations which language imposes on the consciousness, and cannot be freed from the culturally constructed images that it begins to question. It exemplifies Michel Foucault's suggestion that all discourse contains the beginnings of its own subversion and that such problems are intrinsic:

> we must make allowances for the complex and unstable process whereby discourse can be both an instrument, and an effect of power, but also a hindrance, a stumbling-block, a point of resistance and a starting point for an opposing strategy. Discourse transmits and produces power, it reinforces it, but also undermines and exposes it, renders it fragile and makes it possible to thwart it.[9]

Seamus Deane appears to recognise this precariousness when he argues that Irish literary and political discourse are concerned in 'structuring and destroying structures' and 'in modern Ireland, especially, art and politics have gone through matching phases of revolution and consolidation'.[10]

The positioning of the artist within culture is addressed in Paul Durcan's poem 'In Memory: The Miami Showband'.[11] The poem's speaker ironises perceptions of artistic responsibilities which insist upon a limiting politicisation of art:

> You must take one side
> Or the other, or you're but a fucking romantic.

In an essay entitled 'Passage to Utopia',[12] Durcan rejects sectarian polarisation and perceives Ireland as oscillating between 'two main poles—opposite poles—violence and utopia' (192). He sees artistic creation as a 'series of journeys' and maintains that 'my work as a poet has always been searching for the *other place*', a place of artistic distance—'The home away from home', a 'utopia' (192-3, italics in original). He further states that detachment 'enables us to be freer, no longer captive to our island. It also encourages us to struggle for peace in our first and literal home. You see things when you return from the journey that you had not seen before' (196). Similarly, in 'Stories from the Beginning of the Word', Dermot Healy discusses the dynamics of writing and, like Durcan, describes the artistic imagination in spatial terms. He conceives of a 'blur', a 'hazy space', an 'indistinct area'[13] which is crucial to the imaginative process. Thus, *A Goat's Song* can be read as a journey through the 'hazy space' of the literary consciousness, *and* a journey between and beyond Ireland's borders.

Reading Healy's novel within its Irish frame of reference, relations between Jack Ferris,[14] a writer whose alcoholism threatens his creativity, and his lover, Catherine Adams, are a microcosmic representation of polarised ideological positions. Ferris is descended from a Southern Irish, rural and Catholic tradition whilst Catherine's ancestry is Northern, urban and Protestant. Through Ferris's imagined narratives, the novel recovers Catherine's past,[15] the beginning of their relationship and their eventual estrangement in an examination of the sources of conflict between them; it begins and ends with their anticipated reconciliation.

Before tribal borders can be challenged, a multiplicity of intrusive narratives, represented in the novel through various images and peripheral characters, must be reconciled. For example, the fragmented, emblematic representations of Catholic orthodoxy found in a retreating 'plane from Knock airport' (19), the 'Sorry-looking priests'(11) and 'holy pictures'(76) suggest a decline in religious faith that contains an ambivalence which is also reflected in Ferris's attitude to Irish history. The 'Illustrated Sons of Ireland' found in 'a junk shop'(250) whose names form a litany which 'When you hear it all in one breath it's hard to take in. And then it means nothing. Nothing at all' (251). The iconisation of the participants in Ireland's struggle for emancipation contains fixity that is assimilated but loses humanity, meaning or relevance to the instabilities of contemporary realities. Thus, Healy's novel critiques those aspects of identity constructed through religion and history.

Despite a plethora of voices that constitute the exterior discourses through which identities are constructed, representations of the relationship between Ireland and Britain are minimal, yet encoded in the novel form; Irish experiences are mediated through the English language, the title employs a direct English translation of the Greek, and allusions to English literary discourse frame the novel. Its structure—four sections that are subsequently divided into various chapters and a narrative circularity which promises closure—invokes the conventions of classic realism.[16] However, a semblance of unity or reality is disrupted and undermined. The narrative strategy, reminiscent of English novelists such as Thomas Hardy, Charles Dickens and George Eliot, also evokes Dostoevsky's narrative mode in *Crime and Punishment*.[17] The subjective 'I' in Healy's novel is rendered absent by third person narration which gives the reader access to Catherine's past, yet it asserts a presence obliquely because the authority and scope of that narration is limited, often remaining within the bounds of Jack Ferris's perception, which is closely linked to the narrating subject. Ferris's role in the narrative, therefore, shifts 'from major to minor' (67), but apparent attempts at recovering, empathising with, and becoming Catherine are undercut by a sense of the masculine perception of the omnipresent narrator. Whilst a displacement of the speaking 'I' subverts the English novelistic paradigm, it is also an element of discontinuity that suggests the futility of conceiving of an autonomous subject when that subject is merely a composite of competing discourses.

The transformative potential of art offers ways of transgressing geographical, sectarian and gender divisions, creating a bridge between the polarities North/South, Catholic/Protestant, masculine/feminine. However, the novel suggests that if this potential is to be realised then the writer must engage with alternative story fields, which may involve a re-engagement with narratives of the past. For Jack Ferris, 'A link had snapped between him and the past. There was no use looking for it' (76). But it becomes an inescapable, fragmented presence that constantly impinges upon his consciousness. *A Goat's Song* rejects unified notions of identity as Ferris embodies a fragmentary multiplicity that he attempts to reconcile as the interrogation of past conflicts destabilises fixities:

> He woke to find a mirror-image of himself seated in a chair at the other end of the room. The other fellow did not look wise. Jack rose disheartened, only to find that he kept meeting after-images of himself in the small rooms of the cottage ....
>
> Was this death, he wondered, when the time came that he did not know in which of the images his consciousness rested?

> Scattered around the room were representations of himself .... To go anywhere was to assemble a train of disparate images and fragmentary moments that moved along with him. (404)

This series of replications 'continually trapped him in the present. There was nothing after' (275), enforcing limitations on the imagination:

> In triplicate he moved from the chair to the middle of the floor, to the door. ... Any movement increased his anxiety, and yet to remain still was even more terrifying for then the waiting made the horror in each image climax in his mind. The one mind was shattered into pieces. The pieces were stored in these ghosts that hovered around. (404)

Thus, any reconfiguration of identities requires a shift of consciousness that inevitably induces uncertainty, but which is preferable to a state of static singularity. The sense of alienation he experiences also leads to a perceived fragmentation of language as 'inside his head language no longer arrived grammatically, but surfaced as a series of bizarre signs'(60) that appear to construct their own sequence, effectively reordering and transforming 'reality'.

A resolution to the question posed by Ferris, 'How do you build from within as your identity falters?' (8), is offered through fictionality.

> Someone had been living through all of this on his behalf—a stranger. Now he had to create something from nothing. A man. He didn't know what expression he should wear. What politics he had. Or the architecture that surrounded him. Yet once, out of habit, he walked in his shoes. For her he must remake himself. But she had all the materials he needed to begin. (10)

The re-figuring of identity is presented as being dependent upon the perceived 'other', suggesting the interdependency of identities, and how subjectivity is only attainable through an individual's willingness to incorporate other consciousnesses. Such interdependency is dramatised by Healy in his play, *Mister Staines*, which was premiered at Trinity College, Dublin in September 1999, although it was conceived in 1989 around the time that *A Goat's Song* was written. The play represents the interplay between divergent ideological positions through off-stage voices that continually prompt and intrude upon the on-stage actors, and, like *A Goat's Song*, disrupts the idea of the autonomous subject.

Jack Ferris attempts to transcend his subject position and incorporate Catherine into his consciousness in order to effect reconciliation with her:

> Now he had to live on in a different world. To transcend.
> To enter a new story. She must be imagined. He opened a
> spiral-bound notebook and thought. Here it begins. (84)

He disavows 'nostalgia' and vows to recover her 'woman's past, her childhood, her jealousies, her other loves, her private moments—everything that was herself' (5). In *The Bend for Home*, the narrator suggests that 'nostalgia ... steals material from the same source as fiction then leaves the reality wanting'.[18] Fiction offers a means to extend the consciousness, and art is presented as a route to move beyond limited and limiting perceptions. *A Goat's Song* suggests how the artistic imagination with its capacity for defamiliarisation has the potential to effect a fusion of identities.

Ferris rejects a 're-reading of Irish history' and chooses instead to engage with Catherine's personal history in order to gain a different perspective on present realities. His attempts at sense-making begin with her paternal past as a means of recovering the multiple and communal narratives from which her own narrative is constructed. A shift in narration and location to Fermanagh (aptly, a Northern border county) creates a space where myths of identity are contested as Jonathan Adams, her father, a Northern Presbyterian, becomes the focus of narration.

Adams is a 'failed preacher'(99) whose anxieties about the capacity of language to mediate spiritual experience lead to a crisis of faith. Central to Adams's narrative is Matti Bonner, his Catholic employee and neighbour, whose suicide acts as a catalyst for Adams's obsessive compulsion to consolidate his Protestant identity. Through this event, the novel draws Catholics and Protestants into proximity with each other to expose and challenge signifiers of identity which are perpetuated within both communities. In an act of transgression, Matti Bonner 'hanged himself from a tree midway between the Catholic chapel and the Presbyterian Church' (87), suspended at the juncture of those communities to form a tripartite configuration that disrupts the Catholic/Protestant polarity.

Matti Bonner's positioning between the two communities is described, ironically, as signifying that 'Ecumenism was in the air, and the war had only just begun' (89). His transgression unifies Catholics and Protestants in the sense that they both begin to question the 'trappings'(89) that inhibit mutual perceptions. However, it also reinforces sectarian divides. At Bonner's funeral, the Presbyterian community observes Catholic rituals from the 'doorway' of the church and 'watched with fascination all that their forebears had forsworn take place on the altar'(89). This mystification deals in abstractions rather than the 'all' that is envisaged:

> Lighted candles. Chalices. Beads in prayer. Instead of supper that was a memorial, here was a feast that was a sacrifice. The ecumenical men looked on bemused at all the trappings, while others, like Jonathan Adams, watched with distaste the red gorge of the priest billow out like a frog's as he drank the wine. His fingers fumble with the

wafer. How he dusted his hands and knelt with a rustle and turned and blessed the congregation. (89)

The fragmented syntax, in which grammatical contiguity is displaced, erases connections, leaving only disjointed signifiers, 'bizarre signs' (60), that do not construct a coherent narrative. The communion rite and the distance of the 'ecumenical men' from such rituals reflect a narrow perception whilst suggesting a furtive veiling that compounds the distance between the communities.[19]

Matti Bonner begins to disrupt stereotypes and destabilise monolithic positions: 'His death modified the Protestant strut, the Catholic lurch' (89). Yet proximity of the perceived other also induces revulsion:

> ... it was into a deep compartment of the mind that they put Matti Bonner, a place where the existence of God has never been fully resolved, nor their own lives really authenticated. His death triggered off in their psyches questions about the meaning of the word *everlasting*, the meaning of *despair*, and the meaning of the concept of *redemption*. There could be no uplift of the spirit in burying a man who had died by his own hand opposite two churches on Thanksgiving Day. Even the earth that was thrown on his coffin was somehow transparent, made of nothing. And the prayers for the dead seemed the final blasphemy. (90, italics in original)

Signifiers are estranged from their signifieds as meanings are questioned and concrete realities fragment. Bonner is interred literally and psychologically, but despite his burial remains an influential presence that opens up a gap in the psyches of the two orthodoxies, suggesting the meaninglessness of their beliefs. In committing suicide, he inhabits the realms of taboo, subverting Catholic doctrine and challenging the validity of religion as a defining discourse of identity.

Religious discourse and ritual is presented as offering authenticity and meaning by engaging in processes of mystification and veilings that reinforce prejudices and inhibit reconciliation between and within communities. Whilst Bonner's suicide leads to a questioning of attitudes amongst the community, ultimately any questions are subjugated to the need to preserve myths of identity, as his death becomes subject to a renewed mythologising. Jonathan Adams perceives him as a 'vengeful spirit', and this fear only consolidates their estrangement: 'now the dead man was a complete stranger' (96). Bonner is further transformed by 'Catherine's lies' and her sister's 'imagination'(93) into a demonically potent figure:

> He was a small house with poor walls, a name, a Catholic yard, a white bleating goat, a way of walking, a way of talking with bothered outbursts, a bachelor with a missing digit on the right hand. Someone they could look down upon. Now he was an immense frightening figure in a state of eerie erection. (93)

In death, Bonner achieves a degree of power that he lacks whilst alive. Formerly he has been a fragmented presence, characterised by disjointed speech and physical incompleteness, reduced to a series of signifiers connected with place, name and religion. The 'white bleating goat' gives his character a tragic dimension that also links with the carnal that infuses the girls' dreams, but it is complicated by its 'bleating', which connects with the aesthetic and the sacrificial.[20] Like the figure of the writer, he occupies a transgressive space that is perceived by others as subversive, dangerous and destructive, but which has the potential for expanding perceptions of history, politics and religion beyond current disabling polarities, prejudices and limitations.

Jack Ferris occupies such a mediating position, and the possibilities of the literary are reinforced by Catherine when she writes letters to him during their separation:

> the act of writing itself negotiated a middle ground. All
> the ambiguities remained but had somehow softened. The
> writing down of certain words would strangely enough
> bring her across the void, as if they contained some power
> of healing. (345)[21]

This treatment of the potential of art is counterpointed by
anxieties about the capacities of literary discourse to represent
unfamiliar experiences, reconfigure identities and resist
politicisation. Healy's novel suggests how the literary
consciousness creates spaces in which polarities can be
questioned, but this 'dark gap' (273) displaces absolute
certainties, and destabilises linguistic fixities:

> He was no longer able to control the darkness. But
> *darkness* was too broad a word for what was
> overwhelming him, as was *overwhelming* the wrong word,
> as all words were the wrong words when they had not been
> lived in. (27)

This raises questions about authenticity, the limitations of
language and the capabilities of art to represent experiences that
have not been 'lived in'. Yet, 'lived' experience can induce
linguistic failure:

> He no longer had any language in which he might
> contemplate the world, but only stinging asides from his
> past with Catherine. His memory was impaired, and since
> memory depended on words, no words would come except
> those which had already been defiled. (70)

Ferris possesses language but it is desecrated, suspending him in
the present: 'It was present times he was addicted to' (69).
    The novel suggests that there is a danger of nihilism if the past
is rejected rather than assimilated and re-presented. Thus, Ferris
attempts to reconcile the 'old crew' of 'acrimonious, scolding,

shouting' selves returned to haunt him: 'these ghosts', waiting 'until by some act of faith, he could incorporate them into himself', as he feels to 'put them by' is to 'induce a worse sentiment—nothingness—in its place' (73).

The problematics of artistic autonomy and artistic engagement with the past are addressed through Ferris's recollection of a period spent in Belfast co-ordinating a writing group. He transgresses the codes of the North by ignoring sectarian divides and becoming a naïve reader of tribal signifiers. He abhors tribal borders, North and South:

> Jack thought of home as a place frozen in the wastes. He was being lifted and transported. He believed in miracles and hated those who did not. He hated those people for whom change was not only unthinkable, but unlucky. (280)

Ferris desires transcendence, which, potentially, art can offer, although it is often subject to a limiting politicisation,[22] as he discovers when his writing cooperative attempts to devise a play which has as its central character a Northern Catholic, Shamey Coyle.[23] A Northern Republican asks him to consider the political implications of being a writer: 'If you want to write a play about us, you'll have to start from the point of view of propaganda. For instance, do we need your play?', and 'If we liked it, it would be because it suits our point of view' (311). This is followed by a discussion about authenticity in which the signifier 'authentic'(311) indicates many signifieds despite its intimation of authoritative 'truth':

> Authentic for some people means blood and guts on a side street ... Authentic to me means being true to the Republican cause. If you were writing a play about another class of human beings things would take a different course. But here is where we are. People are

either true to their Republican or Loyalist traditions or they
are not. (311)

The Republican locates authenticity in political engagement—a
view which leads to polarisation—and relates sectarian politics to
history via the word 'traditions', asserting, 'You'd need a few
hundred years of history to get [Shamey Coyle] right' (311). He
appropriates history and experience as necessarily political and, in
suggesting that the experience must be lived to be authentic,
denies art or the imagination any power. The fatalism of 'this is
where we are' does not project a future but is reconciled with a
monological position. It constructs a polarity between
'Republican' and 'Loyalist', Paul Durcan's 'one side/Or the
other', which does not take account of ambivalence or mediating
positions.

The limitations and transformative possibilities of fiction are
further explored through the presentation of Jonathan Adams who
represents a Protestant community under threat, displaced and
disorientated.   Like Ferris, he experiences a dissolution of
meaning. He gives up a promising career in the Presbyterian
ministry[24] after his first sermon. The homily, '*to give some form
to that which cannot be uttered*'—which, ironically, is what
literary texts strive to achieve—proves to be an 'unfortunate
choice', and his proposed oratory is transformed into an
embarrassing silence as 'Meaning departed' (99).   Adams's
linguistic paralysis can be compared to Ferris's alcoholic
paralysis and is a consequence of a loss of subjectivity as he
becomes 'trapped in a set of thoughts which were denoted by the
pronoun I', but:

To say I implied a thinking subject, and yet he suddenly
realized: I know nothing of myself. To whom does this I
refer? He tried desperately to get hold of some valid point
of principle for his assertions, but a void opened. (99)[25]

His silence is derived from gaps in discourse that undermine fixed meanings as, like the Republican, he senses that authenticity needs to be guaranteed by experience.

Adams later comforts himself with the 'facts' that construct his 'Fenian Ledger'(108), which serve to authenticate his role as an RUC officer. Ironically, 'he did not read fiction' because:

> Fictions contained inaccuracies, untruths, generalizations, assumptions. The real world was a poor metaphor for what might happen in the hereafter, but at least it was more true than fiction.
> The language of the imagination offered licentious freedom. It acquired trappings, idols, delusions, false promises, too much madness. (114)

His character embodies a Presbyterian anxiety about the capacity of the human imagination to mediate spiritual experience, but the hierarchy of truth that he perceives is as illusory as the 'real world' that he contemplates.

Ironically, Adams's position is threatened when he becomes part of a fictionalising process during the Troubles and is filmed beating a demonstrator.[26] The cinematic present generates a narrative in which the absence of a personal dimension to a public conflict leads to crisis and his 'isolation' (124). Jonathan Adams 'had become a part of history'; he is consigned to become part of one particular historical chronicle yet is also decontextualised, estranged from his own personal history. Fiction challenges media constructions of the Troubles as Healy's novel re-imagines his past to produce an alternative narrative that also has its limitations:

> They were calling him a bigot, but he was a patriot. He was not by nature a violent man. The camera could not tell the history that led to that moment when he had become one of those statistics he despised. (122)

Adams's craving for stability is partly appeased when he moves
to the South, which provides him with a precarious security: 'The
peninsula, joined to the mainland only by the old bridge at
Belmullet, was so isolated that it made him feel secure' (140). He
tries to create 'his own private Republic'(166) by reconstructing
an oral tradition[27] and collecting stories of the 'departed world of
Protestantism' (161).[28] He naively believes that his 'own mind...
was an exact apolitical place guarded by sanity' (162), but his
attempts at cultural preservation are joined by political
engagement with the landscape as he undertakes a geographical
reterritorialisation of the South by 'drawing maps and marking in
the boundaries of the old landlords' houses' (163).

Adams's search for verification of identity through 'the early
Irish myths' leads him 'back inexorably, even contemptuously, to
events in contemporary Ireland'(174)[29] in a 'marvellous
reconciliation'(175) of present and past. His journey appears
meaningless, however, failing to offer a view of the future; and
myth as a means of reconnecting to the past appears to result in a
kind of static circularity.

Jack Ferris and Jonathan Adams can be read as embodiments of
an 'interplay between ideology and utopia'.[30] Adams's search
through myth is an attempt to conserve an ideological position.
Paul Ricoeur suggests that:

> At its three levels—distortion, legitimation,
> symbolization—ideology has one fundamental function: to
> pattern, to consolidate, to provide order to the course of
> action whether it preserves the power of a class, or ensures
> the duration of a system of authority, or patterns the stable
> functioning of a community, ideology has a function of
> conservation in both a good and bad sense of the word. It
> preserves, it conserves, in the sense of making firm the
> human order that could be shattered by natural or historical
> forces, by external or internal disturbances. All the
> pathology of ideology proceeds from this 'conservative'
> role of ideology. (318)

Ricoeur's emphasis upon the positive and negative functions of ideology helps to highlight the ambiguity of Adams's position. His attempt at consolidation amidst feelings of dislocation is also disabling in that it distorts his perception. In contrast, Jack Ferris embodies the 'subversive function'(322) of utopia, which Ricoeur defines as 'the imaginary project of another kind of society, of another reality, of another world' (319). Ricoeur suggests that, whilst ideology 'tends towards integration, repetition and mirroring of the given order', utopia 'tends towards disintegration because it is eccentric' (323). Ferris, unlike Adams, undertakes a journey of the consciousness in which alternative possibilities are explored. He is a nomadic character, engaged with an 'imaginary project' which contains the potential for change.[31]

Despite the limitations of myth, A *Goat's Song* invokes the story of 'The Salmon of Knowledge' in which images of transgression, transformation and transcendence become metaphors for the novel's concerns with the reconfiguration of identities through art. Adams's search for the 'definitive version'(194) of the story reveals many narratives, none of which is privileged. In one version, the hero enters the Tower of Babel which denotes 'home' and attempts '[t]o give some form to that which cannot be said' (201). The babble in the tower represents a myriad of voices within Irish discourse, speaking of 'the sanctity of life, of everlasting life, of violence and peace' (202), which converge to create 'chaos and pandemonium and total indifference'(201). A traveller (possibly Ferris the fictionist) becomes 'hypnotized by the pure disparity and common sense of the voices. Inside the perfect version of the story existed' (202). Paradoxically, an inclusive, irreconcilable 'disparity', which characterises political conflict in Northern Ireland, is presented as being 'pure', and dissonance begins to make 'perfect sense' (202). The traveller encounters a lark who 'protects by singing above what is not her home'(202) and 'like a poet, sings not of this place beneath but of over there hidden in the high grasses' (203). Ferris is both traveller and lark—displaced, detached, yet attempting to redefine home and to signpost those indefinable spaces which exist on the outer reaches of consciousness. The aesthetic, however, cannot be separated from carnality, and the traveller's journey culminates when he 'penetrates the copse' and 'is overcome by a form of sensual melancholia ... the quest had led back to her'(203). This sexual imagery signifies the relationship between Ferris and Catherine and their quest for reconciliation, yet also suggests an imaginative space that is linked with the spiritual but cannot be separated from the carnal. Although the aesthetic journey is only a temporary transcendence of the material, the destabilisation and displacement of artistic perception is presented as having the potential for subverting and transforming perceived realities.

A Goat's Song intimates that for reconciliation to be achieved there needs to be both a preservation and transformation of identity; a complex positioning that is represented by Adams and Ferris. Identity cannot be separated from how it is constructed; therefore to transform it is to threaten the basis of its construction and leads to a sense of fragmentation and discontinuity.

The novel's title, and Jack Ferris's precise explication of tragedy's historical and cultural significance—'I pen songs of the buck. Billy tunes', or 'Tragedies. Tragos—goat. Oide—song. From the Greek'(227)—in its separation and conjunction of the carnal and the aesthetic, foregrounds the limitations of art. Furthermore, ritualistic sacrifices of the goat to which the novel alludes, like Celtic mythology, displace Christian rituals which separate the spiritual and the sexual. The figure of the writer, embodied by Jack Ferris, becomes identified with the sacrificial victim, offering a means towards a displacement of communal violence by transforming conflict into cathartic reconciliation. However, as the potential for spiritual transformation is limited by carnality, so art is limited by the terms of its own construction. Thus, transgression of boundaries—to enjoy a 'rootless feeling'(321) and offering the possibility to 'break through the prejudice of the mind'(65)—has its limitations.

The point of transgression and transformation of the individual consciousness denoted by 'Here it begins'(84) can be read as an indicator of how *A Goat's Song* positions itself within a field of literary and extra-literary relations.   The novel 'begins' to negotiate boundaries of identity, and to allude to the transcendent possibilities of the artistic consciousness.   However, it also confronts the possibility that such a notion is, to some extent, a Romantic illusion.   Whilst Healy's novel aspires towards a depoliticisation of art, it is always conscious of its limitations. Bakhtin's attempts to define the problematical positioning of the modern novel within discourse encapsulate the limitations of narrative, which *A Goat's Song* explores:

> The literary-artistic consciousness of the modern novel, sensing itself on the border between two languages, one literary, the other extra-literary, each of which knows heteroglossia, also senses itself on the border of time; it is extraordinarily sensitive to time in language, it senses time's shifts, the ageing and renewing of language, the past and the future—and all in language.[32]

Dermot Healy's *A Goat's Song* can be read as an exploration within, and beyond, the geographical, sectarian, and historical borders that have been constructed within Ireland, North and South. Yet it is also an examination of the literary consciousness, revealing anxieties about the capacity of the literary to fulfil the imaginative function of reconfiguring identities. Thus, it remains 'sensitive' to the transitionary nature of Ireland's borders, and of language itself.

NOTES

[1.]   Paul Ricoeur, *From Text to Action: Essays in Hermeneutics II*, trans. Kathleen Blamey and John B. Thompson, London 1991, 10.

2.   Dermot Healy, *A Goat's Song*, London 1995, reprinted from 1994 edn., 84. Further references are to this edition and are included in the text in parentheses.

3.   The communities which are foregrounded in the text are Northern Protestant and Southern Catholic. The British/Irish relationship is never really developed, and the British influence on the Protestant mindset is dismissed as inducing a kind of apathetic somnambulance; 'people shuffled to and fro on the edge of Empire, waiting to be summoned'(328). The relationship between Ireland and Britain is a focal point in Healy's most recent novel, *Sudden Times*, London 1999.

4.   Maurice Goldring, *Pleasant the Scholar's Life: Irish Intellectuals and the Construction of the Nation State*, London 1993, 143.

5.   Mikhail Bakhtin, 'Discourse in the Novel' in Michael Holquist, ed., *The Dialogic Imagination: Four Essays by M.M. Bakhtin*, Austin 1998, reprinted from the 1981 edn., 259-422, 326.

6.   In Joyce's short story, Gretta is haunted by her past relationship with Michael Furey, which stifles her present relationship with Gabriel. Gabriel feels 'His own identity was fading into a grey impalpable world: the solid world itself, which these dead had one time reared and lived in, was dissolving and dwindling'. This internal haunting is possibly mirrored by an external haunting of the text itself by the past of the Famine. James Joyce, 'The Dead', *Dubliners*, London 1992, 202.

7.   James Joyce, *A Portrait of the Artist as a Young Man*, London 1975, reprinted from the 1960 edn., 203.

8.   Bakhtin, 'From the Prehistory of Novelistic Discourse' in Holquist, ed., *op. cit.*, 41-83, 67.

9.   Michel Foucault, *The History of Sexuality Volume I: An Introduction*, trans. Robert Hurley, London 1978, 100.

10.   Seamus Deane, 'The Artist and the Troubles' in T.P. Coogan, ed., *Ireland and the Arts*, London 1983, 42-50, 47.

11.   Paul Durcan, 'In Memory: The Miami Showband: Massacred 31 July 1975' in Frank Ormsby, ed., *A Rage for Order*, Belfast 1992, 202.

12.   Paul Durcan, 'Passage to Utopia' in Richard Kearney, ed., *Across the Frontiers: Ireland in the 1990s*, Dublin 1988, 192-196. Further references are to this edition and are included in the text in parentheses.

13.   Dermot Healy, 'Stories from the Beginning of the Word' in Judy Kravis, ed., *Teaching Literature: Writers and Teachers Talking*, Cork 1995, 157-164, 159.

14.   The name 'Ferris' contains a linguistic paradox that embodies the nature of his character, and the paradoxical positioning of artists within society. 'Ferris' invokes a rotating amusement wheel, spinning yet circular, returning, containing and framing. His character is often out of control,

yet is always constrained by external limits, which are primarily defined geographically, linguistically and psychologically.

15. This is debatable, given the narrative strategies employed within the novel. The first part of the novel is focalised through Jack Ferris and culminates in the assertion that he will recover and reimagine Catherine's past. However, the recovery of her past is not mediated through his consciousness, as anticipated, but is effected by a shift in focalisation to Catherine with the omniscient narrator still retaining a totalising, authoritative position.

16. In 'Stories from the Beginning of the Word', Healy refers to the influence of Dickens on his writing, suggesting that *A Tale of Two Cities* 'opened a whole world to me'. Healy, 'Stories from the Beginning of the Word in Kravis, ed., *Teaching Literature*, 159. He elaborated on this in an interview with me when he suggested that Dickens's novel provided insight into 'structure and form'. Dublin, 22 September 1999.

17. Omniscient narration in Dostoevsky's novel is counterpointed by a controlled focalisation process which evokes a sense of first person narration: 'We sometimes encounter people, even perfect strangers, who begin to interest us at first sight... Such was precisely the impression made on Raskolnikov by the guest who sat apart and looked like a retired official'. F. M. Dostoevsky, *Crime and Punishment*, trans. Richard Pevear and Larissa Volokhonsky, London 1992, 11.

18. Dermot Healy, *The Bend for Home*, London 1996, 25.

19. Similar distances are evoked in Seamus Heaney's 'The Other Side' in *Seamus Heaney, New Selected Poems 1966-1987*, London 1990, 28, as well as in John Hewitt's 'The Hill-Farm' in Frank Ormsby, ed., *The Collected Poems of John Hewitt*, Belfast 1991, 124-125. In Hewitt's poem the rosary is observed from 'outside its little ring of light' in the 'vast enclosing night' suggesting a sense of alienation yet undermining the power of Catholic ritual that 'light' intimates. The speaker in Heaney's poem represents his Protestant neighbour's single-mindedness in territorial terms: 'His brain was a whitewashed kitchen/hung with texts /swept tidy /as the body o' the kirk'.

20. Bonner's suicide positions him in the role of sacrificial victim, both revered and reviled by the community. René Girárd suggests that the 'purpose of the sacrifice is to restore harmony to the community' because it 'serves to protect the entire community from its own violence; it prompts the entire community to choose victims outside itself'. René Girárd, *Violence and the Sacred*, trans. Patrick Gregory, Baltimore 1977, reprinted from the 1972 edn., 8. He also states that 'ritual victims' tend to be marginalised, as 'the victim must be neither too familiar to the community nor too foreign to it'. (*Ibid.*, 271.)

21.   If read in a Northern Irish context, this can be linked to the construction of the Good Friday Agreement, which depends upon a careful choice of language. Fintan O'Toole suggests that the British and Irish governments 'have had to blunt the edges of some very sharp words. In a series of texts, accumulated over the past thirteen years, they have subtly reworked the familiar language of the conflict. They have, in a sense, been forced to act more like poets and novelists than like politicians, massaging fixed meanings so that they become supple and fluid; complicating the definitions of words so that they become open and ambiguous'. Fintan O'Toole, 'The Meanings of Union: Taking the Trouble out of the Troubles', *The New Yorker*, 27 April-4 May 1998, 54-62, 56.

22.   In 'The Artist and the Troubles', Seamus Deane suggests that artists are often reluctant to represent Northern Ireland's conflict because 'it can lead to a distortion of the works into a propaganda exercise'. Deane, 'The Artist and the Troubles' in Coogan, ed., *op.cit.*, 43. He also argues that 'A preoccupation with history does not necessarily involve a politicization of the artist in Ireland, the reverse is often true'. (*Ibid.*, 49.)

23.   Before the play is written, it has political implications. The name, 'Coyle', for instance, imbues it with a number of connotations. It relates to the word *coil*, meaning noise, which is derived from the Irish word, *goille*, meaning rage.

24.   Jonathan Adams evokes the character of Abraham Adams in Henry Fielding's *Joseph Andrews*. In Fielding's novel, Parson Adams is described as 'a man of good sense, good parts, and good nature, but was at the same time entirely ignorant of the ways of the world', and 'simplicity was his characteristic'. Henry Fielding, *Joseph Andrews*, London 1960, 23.

25.   In a wider sense, the narrative strategy adopted within the novel reflects this displacement of the speaking 'I' in eschewing first person narration in favour of third person, almost omniscient, narration although at times focalisation is so concentrated on one character that it becomes like an interior monologue.

26.   J.J. Lee suggests that in 1969 'The RUC was in danger of becoming involved as participants rather than arbiters' in conflict between the Catholic and Protestant communities. He describes an incident in August 1969 when 'The primitive police response' was 'captured on television'. J.J. Lee, *Ireland: 1912 – 1985*, Cambridge 1989, 428-429.

27.   Eavan Boland's poem 'The Oral Tradition' similarly suggests a refuge in song: 'the oral song/avid as superstition/layered like an amber in/the wreck of language/and the remnants of a nation', but also contains suggestions that art forms can become fossilised, embedded within ideas of tradition. Eavan Boland, *Selected Poems*, Manchester 1989, 76.

28. This Protestant appeal to the pre-Christian antiquities echoes the efforts of Yeats and others to circumvent the Catholic heritage of Ireland.

29. Similarly, the opening paragraph of Dickens's *A Tale of Two Cities* establishes the historical period as being 'so far like the present period'. Charles Dickens, *A Tale of Two Cities*, London 1973, reprinted from 1949 edn., 1.

30. Paul Ricoeur, *From Text to Action: Essays in Hermeneutics II*, trans. Kathleen Blamey and John B. Thompson, London 1991, 323. Further references are to this edition and are included in the text in parentheses.

31. Frank Kermode favours this fluidity of fiction against the consolidating, static nature of myth, offering a useful distinction between them which emphasises myth's fixity as opposed to the transformative potential of fiction: 'myths are the agents of stability; fictions the agents of change'. It is this 'stability' that Jonathan Adams craves, and 'change' which he resists and Ferris desires. Frank Kermode, *The Sense of an Ending: Studies in the Theory of Fiction*, Oxford 1967, 39.

32. Bakhtin, 'From the Prehistory of Novelistic Discourse' in Holquist, ed., *op.cit.*, 67.

Patrick McCabe: Transgression And Dysfunctional Irelands

CLARE WALLACE

Since the success of his novel, *The Butcher Boy*, and of the subsequent film adaptation by Neil Jordan, Patrick McCabe has proved himself to be a caustic and provocative voice in contemporary Irish fiction. His portrayals of 'dysfunctional Ireland in all its glories' have been notable, not so much for the originality of the material, (violence, sexual abuse, family breakdown and predatory priests have been the repeated focus of much Irish writing since the sixties) but because of McCabe's ability to arrest the reader with equal doses of horror and humour; to produce satire without superiority and empathy with dysfunction.[1] Although reviews of some of his latest work (*Breakfast on Pluto* [1998], *Mondo Desperado* [2000], and the series of stories recently broadcast by RTÉ radio, *Emerald Germs of Ireland* [2000]) have highlighted its humorous and parodic aspects, McCabe in a recent interview in the *Irish Times* has angrily rejected what he has interpreted as the insinuation that he is merely a 'funny' writer.[2] Clearly, he is determined that his writing be perceived as more than brinkmanship for its own sake. Indeed, if one surveys his fiction from *Carn* (1989) to the present he seems intent upon exploring transgressive territory, obsessively returning to the grotesque, the extreme and the uncanny in the familiar. Critical responses to McCabe's work have so far centred around *The Butcher Boy*. However the aim of this paper is to examine some of the properties and implications of transgression in the broader context of his three recent novels; *The Butcher Boy* (1992), *The Dead School* (1995) and *Breakfast on Pluto* (1998).[3]

If the concept of transgression is to be employed critically it is productive to return to the word's etymological root, meaning to cross or step over. Thus the term immediately encodes an invocation of a border, frame or order. Boundaries or limits are intrinsic to any notion of transgression. Similarly as Jacques Derrida in 'Living On: Border Lines' has demonstrated, the 'necessity of such an overrun, such a *débordement*' is inherent in the notion of borders, limits or frames.[4] Or as the clichéd version would have it, rules are made to be broken. Conversely, rules are also made to be kept and borders are dividing lines which imply a binary logic of either/or, outside/inside, other/self which is fundamental not only to a concept of transgression but also to identity.[5] Borders differentiate, separate, mark difference. And yet if the concept of border is approached via Derrida's trope of *différance* the binarism of the either/or it implies is revealed as constantly destabilised and uncertain. The sites of difference delineated by a border are then always already interconnected.

'Framed' in this manner, McCabe's writing in many ways seems to wander in what might be referred to as border spaces, literally in a geographical sense (the border counties of Ulster) but more often metaphorically (another form of crossing over) in terms of his characters' liminal worlds. If as Hélène Cixous suggests, 'writing [should] work[ing] in the in-between, inspecting the process of the same and other without which nothing can live', then it seems appropriate to regard McCabe's writing as both constructive and deconstructive in its engagement with transgression.[6] There are three aspects of this engagement I wish to address here: first the novels' textual strategies with regard to narrative; second, the multiplicity of texts involved in each book and their intertexture; and third, McCabe's treatment of sexual identity.

In an early interview in *Irish Studies Review*, McCabe speaks of his literary influences, citing his admiration for 'older Irish writers like Michael McLaverty or Benedict Kiely, in whom the strong narrative position is very positive' and for 'William Burroughs and the cut-ups and various postmodernist writers'.[7] The tension between these styles of writing emerges in McCabe's fiction as a kind of corrupted and digressional narrative. Each of the three novels in question is structured around narratives which are fragmentary, repetitive and often disjointed. A 'cut-up' style, which clearly owes much to cinematic narrative techniques, may be observed in all the texts; *The Butcher Boy* is broken into sections varying in length from a couple of lines to several pages; in *The Dead School* the sections are formalised into chapters bearing headings and *Breakfast on Pluto* is the only text explicitly divided into titled and numbered chapters, although this numbering clearly does not seem to imply a 'reasonable' or progressional sequentiality. In each novel McCabe employs textual strategies that might be said to approximate or correspond to the characters' deteriorating state of mental health. These strategies simulate transgression or crossing over between apparent reason or sanity and apparent madness where the 'imaginary' is privileged over the 'real'.[8] It is relevant here to note McCabe's interest in film which also informs his narrative stylistics. With regard to *The Butcher Boy*'s storyteller Francie Brady, he reminds us that 'He's (Francie) a cute hoor [...] It's an old Hitchcock trick, that one – where the audience is drawn in and is an accessory to what's being done. It's done in "Psycho" and "Vertigo"'.[9]   *The Butcher Boy*'s almost constant, polyphonic flow of commentary, self-correction, wit and mimicry veils the fact that the narrator rarely exists in dialogue with anyone other than himself, or rather his selves. *The Dead School*, is framed as a 'little tale' addressed to 'boys and girls' but soon proves itself to be neither. This 'little tale' is perhaps more appropriately described as a grim allegorical journey tracing the maturation of the independent Irish State. *Breakfast on Pluto* is apparently a confessional memoir of transvestite prostitute Patrick 'Pussy' Braden written for 'her' analyst, Dr.

Terence, who may or may not exist, about events which may or may not have happened in the manner in which Pussy relates them. This 'memoir' moves between Pussy's reflections on various highly camp outfits to flights of fancy involving true love, revenge upon the priest she believes to be her father, and terrorism, but is punctuated by brief accounts of violent sectarian murders which are narrated in a different voice. It remains uncertain as to whether these are doses of a harsh external 'reality' or are indeed yet another aspect of Pussy's repertoire of fantasy. The possibility for a clear bounded self for the character, and the possibility of a clear bounded narrative for the reader, are both undone.

These narrative strategies are transgressive in that they involve a distortion of the distinction between what is assumed to be real and what is assumed to be imaginary. This corruption of the either/or of fantasy or reality, reason or madness, infects the boundaries between past, present and future to produce a sense of time which, like a scratched record, sticks at certain points or jumps erratically back or forward. Francie Brady provides a striking illustration of this distortion. His understanding of time remains childlike, although as he states in the opening line he '(...) was a young lad twenty or thirty or forty years ago (...)'(*BB*,4) he never grows into adult time or behaviour. He remains arrested at a particular juncture returning to an imaginary utopian time—'They were the best days them days with Joe. They were the best days I ever knew, before ... Nugent and all this started'(*BB*,6). Francie's ideal time involves very precise divisions which simultaneously excise traumatic memories and events and draw attention to their lingering presence. In *The Dead School* tension between the pasts and the presents of the characters Raphael Bell and Malachy Dudgeon drives the narrative and also drives them over the brink of reason. Like Francie, both Raphael and Malachy become increasingly obsessed with pasts in which they seem to be arrested to the extent that the present seems hallucinatory. McCabe's 'Prelude' to *Breakfast on Pluto* also draws the reader into distorted time. It explicitly situates the 'fictional' Patrick Braden and his narrative in the 'factual' violent history of Ulster from the Battle of the Boyne in 1690 to the Belfast Good Friday Agreement of 1998. Yet if this enunciation of a very particular and violent history of borders is an attempt to stabilise or authenticate the narrative in time or place, 'history' is repeatedly transgressed by Pussy Braden who might as well be from Pluto and whose 'memoir' makes little distinction between the atrocities of 1970s and '80s fashion and the atrocities of sectarian violence.

Both *The Dead School* and *Breakfast on Pluto* are also framed by self-reflexive devices which gesture beyond their stories and yet are clearly also part of them. The devices are rhetorical and familiar—the omniscient narrative voice interjecting to guide the reader into the text. *The Dead School* begins with a chapter entitled 'Hello There' which opens 'Boys and Girls and I hope you are all well. The story I have for you this morning is all about two teachers and the things they got up to in the days gone by' (*DS*,1). The concluding chapter also opens with a reminder of this semi-pedagogical frame—'So there you are, that's the end of my story and what a sad end it turned out to be (...)' (*DS*,343). As mentioned above, *Breakfast on Pluto* is prefaced by McCabe with a précis of the political history of the place into which Mr Patrick Pussy Braden is born. While these devices highlight a crossing over from context to text, the implicit aspects of self-reflexivity in the narratives they introduce invite the reader to suspect the tenability of such a division. Again it might be asserted that McCabe explores a transgressive territory, this time between language play and language out of control. Francie Brady's narrative provides a masterful example. Francie continuously plays roles, adopts personae and accents, to the extent that real events and emotions are displaced, disarmed and anaesthetised. Yet in an episode toward the end of the novel Francie's efforts to force all language into this evasive play are thwarted, the fluidity of the spoken is frozen in the written word:

I went by Doctor Roche's house it was all painted up with big blue cardboard letters spread out on the grass: AVE MARIA WELCOME TO OUR TOWN. I was wondering

could I mix them up to make THIS IS DOCTOR ROCHE
THE BASTARD'S HOUSE, but I counted them and there
wasn't enough letters and anyway they were the wrong
ones. (*BB*, 194)

Similarly we might remark upon Malachy Dudgeon's fixation
with playing out the monologues of the male heroes of the
films 'Midnight Cowboy' and 'Chinatown'. In acting the
characters of Joe Buck or J.J. Gittes, Malachy apes a version of
masculinity to which he aspires but fails to master. Raphael is
also confronted by the slipperiness of the texts which have
'written' him. The books with which he attempts to recover
himself significantly range from the historical, *J.C. Beckett's
History of Ireland*, to the religious, *Catechism for Boys and
Girls* and *My Friend Our Lady*, but also include *Hall and
Knight's Algebra, A New English Primer* and a collection of
jotters and sum copies. The titles alone provide, in shorthand,
the script of forces and beliefs which have been instrumental in
the construction of Raphael's character. The disintegration of
his ordered world is confirmed when he can no longer see
(metaphorically or literally) the familiar texts which have
mapped his past:

> (...) just as he was about to start reading again the words
> went and swooshed off the page and round the room like
> wordy tornadoes curling all about him and trying to tease
> and make a cod of him. He tried to get hold of them, shake
> some sense into them, but it was like trying to wrestle
> smoke and anyway there was no point because the more he
> tried the more they tickled him and laughed at him
> (...)(*DS*,264).

Pussy Braden's memoir is also a smokescreen of language.
Through writing therapy, Pussy perfects her transgressive self
as pastiche and in fanatical outbursts writes and rewrites the
story of her conception. In each of these cases, language out of
control signals a degeneration in the character's capacity to
rationalise her world.

Thematically McCabe's writing also works in 'the in-between' advocated by Hélène Cixous. Common to all three novels is an exploration of the scar of family trauma, and of madness in an 'unreasonable' world of perverted or inefficient institutions, romanticised pasts and violent presents. McCabe enlists multiple dissonant texts and vocabularies and juxtaposes them so as to produce a warped, satirical perspective on the familiar. High and low, traditional and modern, local and international cultural fragments are jumbled, with the result that the boundaries between trivial and serious, public and private become uncertain. This equalisation of multivalent registers is, I would assert, the most outstanding aspect of McCabe's writing and is perhaps its most postmodern feature.

In a recent article in the *Irish University Review*, Roberta Gefter Wondrich addresses the metaphorical use of exile in contemporary Irish fiction, drawing attention to the dramatisation of '(...) the idea of transgression with regard to Ireland, itself a boundary, still to be fully known and appropriated, as well as demythologised'.[10] And yet, although in the novels being discussed here, the pig, the Irish 'mammy', the priest and the school master are all filtered through the lens of an alternative reality where the ghost of Kavanagh seems to stand shoulder to shoulder with 'Mr Baldy Khrushchev', McCabe places new mythologies *alongside* the old. While it would be foolhardy to claim that McCabe's Irelands are positive or healthy, this gesture might be read as constructive, not because the texts which disturb, or even remythologise Ireland are presented as superior, but rather because it does not attempt to reduce the poly-vocality of these texts.

The variety of cultural references and registers at work in *The Butcher Boy* have been the subject of sustained interest since the book's publication. However, McCabe's exploration of the boundaries and spaces between these elements is perhaps more stridently illustrated by *The Dead School* in which texts of a traditional nationalist Ireland are interwoven with those of a modern Ireland. While, as mentioned earlier, the novel is introduced as a little story, it seems appropriate to read it as a text ripe with allegorical potential. Raphael Bell's personal history is also a potted history of the Irish state and thus traverses the boundaries of the public and the private. It takes the form of a simplified Catholic nationalist ideology. Reared in the heart of a devout Catholic family, his early life is a composite of literary and historical texts and of stereotypes. His father, an archetypal figure indeed, triumphs in what bears an uncanny resemblance to Liam O'Flaherty's 'The Reaping Race'; he can 'charm the birds out of the trees' with his rendition of Charles Kickham's 'She Lived Beside the Anner' and dies a heroically violent death at the hands of the Black and Tans. Raphael too is the renaissance Irish citizen—a singer, a scholar, and a sportsman. He loves his mother, respects the Church, sings 'God Save Ireland' with pride. Even his marriage affirms this narrative of national identity by harmoniously erasing the border between Northern and Southern Ireland—his wife, Nessa, is a Northerner. The tale of his youth is a melange of familiar icons, symbols and events from a carefully romanticised national mythology. Raphael's world is one in which violation and tragedy are the consequences of British imperialism, where women are all but invisible, where it is sufficient to be 'firm but fair'. The codes, limits and boundaries in Raphael's Ireland are definable and reliable and significantly he is, as headmaster, the arbiter of justice in his own domain. Implicit to Raphael's history is, of course, that St Anthony's is his microcosmic empire. However, even as he polices the borders between order and chaos, a latent violence threatens his control. In an incident ripe with irony McCabe exploits the dissonance of register; Raphael the hero-headmaster, metes out discipline to an unruly bully whose 'crime' drives him into a white hot rage. McCabe allows the reader to discover the terrible crime, cause of such distress to Raphael, as follows:

'Did you take his marble?' he shouted at him again, their noses almost touching. 'Did you?' (...) Raphael felt as if his head was lifting off his body, lightweight drifting into air.(*DS*,110)

As a new Ireland transgresses Raphael's old one, his faith in the boundaries he has adhered to, the absolute logic of either/or, becomes unsustainable.

A new Ireland appears in another selection of multivalent texts. One of these is Malachy Dudgeon, whose history seems absolutely foreign to Raphael's but is in fact also a product of the bright simplified ideology of Catholic nationalism. Malachy's life is a blend of familiar elements – family breakdown, suicide, punks, alcohol and drug abuse, Hollywood films, pop music and rock gigs. As Tom Herron in a recent essay on McCabe and Tóibín has pointed out, Malachy is the anglicised form of Maolseachlainn, the name Raphael had intended to give his first-born but still-born son.[11] Malachy is the offspring of Raphael's Ireland but the differences between them are all too obvious and McCabe never lets the reader stray too far from the juxtaposition. Whereas Raphael's anthem might be 'Macushla' or 'She Lived Beside the Anner', for Malachy the dross pop song 'Chirpy Chirpy Cheep Cheep' becomes the signature tune of his tragedy. In contrast to Raphael, Malachy is spineless, powerless and directionless. Malachy's encounter with Raphael causes his world to implode. He fails to fix the boundaries between order and chaos either at school or at home, with tragic results. The death of one of his pupils and the departure of his girlfriend cause him to leave Ireland for England. This geographical crossing over initiates a complete breakdown of order as Malachy drops out of functional society and sinks into a haze of alcohol and drug abuse until he finally comes to his senses in a mental hospital.

Other texts impinging upon Raphael's also signify a disintegration of old borders. Ms Evans, 'the abortionist' and member of the parents' committee, invades his school and attempts to change policies on uniforms and competitive sport. Her symbolic victory is evident when she succeeds in replacing the annual school tour to Kilmainham Gaol with a trip to Waterworld with the support of Raphael's old friend Father Stokes. 'Terry Krash' (a fictionalised Gay Byrne whose name prophesies Raphael's imminent crash and also contains the echo of 'trash') pollutes his radio with immoral discussions of sex before marriage and women's underwear. Kojak and the Six Million Dollar Man annex the classroom, the playground and the staffroom. The IRA are no longer heroes but are terrorists and murderers. For Raphael this is a war he fights and loses. His intolerance of the seismic shifts in the boundaries of his environment pushes him into a no-man's land of insanity where he attempts to reconstruct the absolutes of his past in his 'Dead School'. When this proves impossible he commits the ultimate transgressive act and kills himself. Ironically it is the spineless Malachy who returns to Ireland, to a form of sanity and to his 'duty' of nursing his invalid mother. Cissie Dudgeon—unfaithful wife, self-pitying widow, rejected mother, petulantly mute and wheelchair bound, a modern Mother Ireland cared for by her pathetic offspring—survives tenaciously, still dominating his life while he wallows in nostalgia for the seventies and a romance kindled by the song 'Chirpy Chipy Cheep Cheep'.

Herron's assertion that the 'interface between modernity and tradition' is imagined by McCabe as 'seriously pathological' seems well worth noting here. As he emphasises '[T]his interface is a zone in which past and present contaminate each other; neither is settled or secure'.[12] This unsettled zone in McCabe's work is not merely temporal but extends continually to the 'boundaries' between apparent fact and apparent fiction. The hermeneutic difficulties which arise from this blurring are least resolvable in *Breakfast on Pluto*. Pussy Braden is, of course, immediately identifiable as liminal in the most obvious sense. To a degree her narrative has integrity in its transgressive performativity; it is always camp or crass or in bad taste. The apparently indiscriminate shifts from the trivial or fantastical to accounts of violent sectarian murder are shocking and gratuitous but it remains impossible to determine if any of the events described in vividly contrasting voices and vocabularies can be understood as outside of Pussy's perpetually attention seeking performance.

Clearly McCabe seems intent upon delving into the troubled subject—selves which are fragile and in doubt. Although

Breakfast on Pluto makes sexual identity an explicit theme, one might remark that the desires of the characters in each of these texts are problematic: Francie Brady is disturbed by a semi-Oedipal longing for Mrs Nugent; Raphael Bell is deeply distrustful of women generally and is predictably deeply repressed; Malachy Dudgeon's desire is blocked by the traumatic memory of his mother's betrayal of his father. Interestingly, McCabe claims not to be attracted to taboo subjects as much as to truths.[13] In particular he refers to the archetypal Oedipal drama which he relates to a primal impulse. His distinction between taboo and primal truths tends to misapprehend the complexity of what Freud has called 'the psychical apparatus' with its labyrinthine mechanisms of repression, substitution and displacement. McCabe baldly states '[a] man wants to murder his father and ride his mother. It doesn't matter whether it's Ireland or Greece', but equally the Oedipal story rises out the depths of social taboos concerning incest and its relation to 'truth' (in whatever sense) is fraught.[14]

In each of the novels families are the crux of tension. While McCabe's female figures never seem more than token—the three novels are essentially 'boys' stories—when women do appear they fare badly indeed. Mothers are killed or kill themselves, they are unfaithful wives, live out their later years in vegetative states or as invalids, smoke endless fags and have whiskers, or abandon their offspring and are never seen again. The Oedipal subtext structures both Francie Brady's fantasy of being suckled by Mrs Nugent and Malachy Dudgeon's peering into the boathouse to watch his mother with Jemmie the cowman. However a more salient element of the narratives which extends from the Oedipal drama is the characters' desire to return to the primal scene, the scene before their own conception or that of their own conception. What is revealed is that this ideal space is in fact a no-place, a utopia.

Obsessive desire to return to the primal scene is perhaps most in evidence in *Breakfast on Pluto* where Pussy compulsively writes and rewrites various versions of the scene of her conception and subsequent abandonment. Pussy cannot forgive her father (whom she believes to be Father Bernard) for impregnating her (virginal) mother, for breaking the hymen Pussy may never possess. Pussy imagines the conception scene variously but a key element in each version is a sense of intrusion into the reproductive space of her mother's body. While this resentment of her conception seems perilously close to a desire for non-existence, it is also entangled with Pussy's jealousy of her own mother's reproductive capacity. Notably, Pussy's other impossible longing is a deathbed fantasy in which she is attended by her numerous loving children. In effect Pussy's utopia is the womb itself, as place of origin and symbol of womanhood.

Pussy's identity is a morass of transgressivity, just as her life and the world around her is seamed with confusion and contradictions. Her escape from Ireland and the growing violence of the North involves crossing to England where, in search of true love, her mammy, and freedom, Pussy becomes a prostitute and is almost murdered by a client. As the Troubles move to England, Pussy's list of fantasy personae expands to include characters like the 'Lurex Avenger'. In spite of the flights of fancy though, the pastiche of femininity produced by Pussy owes much to the stereotypes of 'normal' feminine and masculine sexuality. Just as in *The Crying Game*, Dil is a 'better' woman than Jude, so Pussy surpasses the biological women in the novel in terms of femininity (a keen example is to be found in 'Whiskers Braden'). McCabe has described the book as being 'a fairy story' (*double entendre* perhaps intended):

> [it] is about identity, about borders: gender borders, geographic borders, the borders between mortality and death ... It's a quest for home, which is really a quest for everybody.[...] I see this character as a [...] fictionalisation of Mother Ireland. And she's almost getting there but not quite. She's saying to the reader, 'Why don't you get there? Don't be like this. Reach home.[15]

So where is home, and indeed what is home? McCabe's proclaimed interest in the 'truth' of primal impulse seems closely allied to a quest for authenticity. Indeed since *The Butcher Boy* he has been industriously slaughtering Irish sacred cows. Nevertheless his fiction might also be said to deconstruct notions of authentic identity implied in an attempt to return to primal truths. The three novels discussed here all work in the transgressive spaces of borders and boundaries. What they reveal is that the either/or of madness and sanity, functional and dysfunctional, fact and fantasy, authentic and inauthentic are bleeding categories, texts produced by mutual interaction.

NOTES

1. Patrick McCabe, *Breakfast on Pluto*, London 1999, see cover.
2. Joe Jackson, 'When Love Hurts: an interview with Patrick McCabe', *The Irish Times Weekend*, 10 June 2000, 6.
3. Patrick McCabe, *The Butcher Boy*, London 1992; *The Dead School*, London 1995; *Breakfast on Pluto* London 1999. Further references are to these editions and are given in the text.
4. Jacques Derrida, 'Living On: Border Lines' (Survivre: Journal de bord) in Harold Bloom *et al.*, *Deconstruction and Criticism*, New York 1979, 83.
5. John Hill, 'Crossing the Water: Hybridity and Ethic in *The Crying Game*', *Textual Practice*, 12:1 (1998), 89-100.
6. Hélène Cixous, 'The Laugh of the Medusa' in D. Walder, ed., *Literature in the Modern World*, Milton Keynes 1990, 324.
7. Richard Kerridge, 'Meat is Murder: an interview with Patrick McCabe', *Irish Studies Review*, 3 (1993), 10-12.
8. These terms are not intended in a Lacanian sense here.
9. Kerridge, *op.cit.*, 10-12.
10. Roberta Gefter Wondrich, 'Exilic Returns: Self and History Outside Ireland in Recent Irish Fiction', *Irish University Review*, 30:1 (2000), 1-16.

11. Tom Herron, 'ContamiNation: Patrick McCabe and Colm Tóibín's Pathographies of the Republic' in Liam Harte and Michael Parker, eds, *Contemporary Irish Fiction: Themes, Tropes, Theories*, London 2000, 168-191.
12. *Ibid.*, 168
13. Jackson, *op.cit.*, 6.
14. *Ibid.*
15. Abby Freedman, 'Patrick McCabe's *Breakfast on Pluto*: an interview with Patrick McCabe', 28.1.1999, ww.thedaily.washington.ed...nter/Jan28.99/A6.PatrickMcC.html

Too Soon to Tell: Matthew Sweeney, Stephen Dobyns and the New Narrative Movement in American Poetry

MICHAEL FAHERTY

During one of his many visits to Chile in the 1980s, Stephen Dobyns somehow managed to talk the caretaker of Pablo Neruda's former residence on Isla Negra into letting him wander around inside. He found three photographs on the wall above the desk where Neruda once worked: one was of Walt Whitman, one of Charles Baudelaire and one of Arthur Rimbaud. Dobyns has said, since then, that this was just as it should have been, that this is how all writers should work, that they 'should always be close to the sources of [their] strength', keeping kindred spirits close to them 'like talismans'.[1] If we could get inside Dobyns's house in Boston and wander around his study, the photographs we would most likely find on his wall would be those of Rainer Maria Rilke, Osip Mandelstam, Anton Chekhov and Yannis Ritsos. And if we could get inside Matthew Sweeney's flat in Bloomsbury and take a stroll around it, the photographs we might find there would be those of Franz Kafka, Charles Simic and, possibly, Dobyns himself. Although he is not the sort of writer who decorates his walls with literary icons, Sweeney has said it is only natural for poets to 'piggyback' on other poets to whom they find themselves temperamentally drawn, and that it is almost impossible for beginning writers, especially, to begin any other way.[2] It seems appropriate that, among the three writers Sweeney feels most drawn to, one is Eastern European, one American and one a bit of both, Simic having been born in Serbia but having lived in the States since the age of eleven. It seems just as appropriate that one is best known for his stories, one for his poems and one for both, with Dobyns celebrated as a poet by some readers and as the author of nearly two dozen detective novels by others, including the comic thriller *Cold Dog Soup*. All three writers share Sweeney's obsession with the fantastic, his rather dark sense of humour and his preference for parable and fable, but it is Dobyns alone who shares his interest in bringing narrative back into contemporary verse, and both poets try to tell the sort of story that would welcome readers back to poetry rather than push them away.

Dobyns was only one of many poets in America over the past few decades who began to wonder where all their readers had gone. Although poets and critics like Edmund Wilson, Vivian de Sola Pinto, Delmore Schwartz, John Wain and Leslie Fiedler had been predicting doom and gloom for poetry since the 1930s, it was not until the 1980s that a new generation of poets and critics were willing to admit the end was more than nigh. As far as they could tell, no one in America outside the universities' creative writing programmes could be bothered with poetry at all. Christopher Clausen, Joseph Epstein, Dana Gioia, Dick Allen, Frederick Feirstein and Frederick Turner all noticed that while the general public still read novels, watched films and visited art galleries, almost no one outside the university subculture ever picked up a book of verse. As Gioia said at the time, poets may have begun the century by starving and freezing in bohemia, but they ended it by circling their wagons round the relative security of university life:

> To maintain their activities, subcultures usually require institutions, since the general society does not share their interests. Nudists flock to 'nature camps' to express their unfettered lifestyle. Monks remain in monasteries to protect their austere ideals. As long as poets belonged to a broader class of artists and intellectuals, they centered their lives in urban bohemias, where they maintained a distrustful independence from institutions. Once poets

began moving into universities, they abandoned the working-class heterogeneity of Greenwich Village and North Beach for the professional homogeneity of academia.[3]

Gioia and others believed the worship of poets like Wallace Stevens, Anne Sexton and Robert Bly within the English departments of American universities had resulted in young poets writing nothing but meditative, confessional or deep image poems. For various cultural and political reasons, the free-verse, autobiographical, imagist lyric had become the sole choice for the budding poet, letting the prose writer lay complete claim to such traditional poetic subgenres as narrative, satire and drama. At a gathering in Greenwich Village in 1981 that included Allen, Feirstein and Turner, these contrary poets decided to take the offensive, actively promoting a return to both narrative and metre, and even to traditional forms like the ballad, the sonnet, the sestina and the villanelle. Some managed to recruit a number of influential journals to the cause—*Counter / Measures*, *The Quarterly Review of Literature*, *The Hudson Review*, *The Southern Review*, *The Ontario Review* and *The Kenyon Review* among them—while others, like Mark Jarman and Robert McDowell at *The Reaper*, set up their own journals to publish nothing but narrative verse. They even founded their own press, Story Line Press in Oregon, to issue slim volumes and the occasional anthology. The critics among them launched an almost immediate assault on nearly every twentieth-century American poet admired by the academy and suggested a somewhat quirky, revised canon of Edwin Arlington Robinson, Robert Frost, Robinson Jeffers and Weldon Kees, poets who would never have dreamed of turning their backs on narrative. When it came to contemporary heroes who had spotted the problem with poetry in America early on and attempted to do something about it, Anthony Hecht and Louis Simpson were readily elected to the posts, whether they wanted them or not.

Even to those involved in all this propaganda at the time, it was not clear whether there were two distinct movements afoot or only one. Critics in the 1980s were quick to label anything written in couplets or quatrains examples of the so-called New Formalism, while anything that suggested even a whiff of story was soon classified as New Narrative. In an essay published in a special issue of *Crosscurrents* in 1988 devoted to these new impulses in American verse, Wade Newman was the first to argue that it must be seen as a single movement, inventing the term that has stuck ever since: expansive poetry. Newman argued that it is 'expansive' both in the sense that these poets want to expand the formal possibilities of verse available to them and in the sense that they want to expand the potential audience for their work.[4] Or, as R.S. Gwynn has put it, what unites these two impulses is a common desire to get readers reading poetry once again:

> Perhaps this desire to embrace a larger readership is the essence of what 'expansive' connotes; these poets are giving the elusive common reader the missing ingredients that are most often lamented by those who claim to have given up on modern poetry. Indeed, if we are to think of expansive poetry as a truly populist movement (and I, for one, do, in the most honorable senses of the term), then its poets have simply responded to the audience's call (as opposed to arrogantly disregarding it) for formal elements that can be *heard* and narrative qualities that can be *understood.*[5]

Many of these so-called expansive poets believed the best way to show an interest in this larger readership was to stop talking about themselves and their little worries and start paying some attention to the world around them. As Louis Simpson, the new guru of the expansive movement, had said as early as 1976:

> For some time American poets have been writing almost exclusively about their personal lives. We have become accustomed to poets telling us what they are doing and thinking at the moment. The present moment is everything—there is no sense of the past. Nor is there any sense of community. If poetry is the language of a tribe,

it seems there is no longer a tribe, only a number of individuals who are writing a personal diary or trying to 'expand their consciousness'.[6]

For many American poets in the 1970s and 80s, including Simpson, the obvious alternative to the deadend of solipsistic medita-
tion was narrative. In fact, Simpson suggested at the time that
poets with an interest in narrative might be better off reading
novels and short stories than modern poetry, since most fiction
writers had spent the better part of the last two hundred years
doing their damnedest to 'imitate life' around them, particularly
middle-class life, while most poets had spent those same centuries priding themselves on their 'remoteness from the everyday'.[7] There was a general consensus among expansive poets
that narrative, like the anonymous stories of traditional ballads,
had a natural connection with community, while the lyric could
not care less about anything other than the self. Or, as David
Mason has suggested:

Poets are drawn to dramatic monologues and narratives
when they become bored with the limitations of autobiographical writing, but they end up realizing what all good
fiction writers know, that other peoples' lives are every
bit as important as their own. Empathy, the act of inhabiting a stranger's experience, is a civilizing process. It
implies connection, community, releasing the poet—who
otherwise seems 'Encased in talent like a uniform'—
from isolation. Fiction's advantage has usually been
considered its interest in society as well as the lives of
specific individuals, and poets envy this particularly
when the lyric 'I' has become repetitious, nearly auto-
matic.[8]

Although some expansive poets have gone so far as to pronounce the lyric absolutely, positively dead,[9] Mason argues that
this propaganda on the behalf of narrative verse is probably just
another healthy corrective in the development of modern poetry,
an indication that the preference for the lyric above all other

forms of verse in the nineteenth and twentieth centuries may have finally come to an end, but not that it should be abandoned altogether.

This is not to say narrative has made a comeback only in American poetry. Critics in Britain and Ireland have been noting the gradual disappearance of the lyric and the rather quiet return of monologue, dialogue and story to British and Irish poetry ever since the early 1980s. If readers had not already seen this for themselves, Blake Morrison and Andrew Motion called their attention to it in their introduction to *The Penguin Book of Contemporary Poetry* in 1982, citing the work of James Fenton and Paul Muldoon as particularly obvious examples. However, these early verse narratives did not seem all that reader friendly; they were not the sort of work one would write in order to welcome the average reader of fiction back to the world of poetry. Borrowing the title of Motion's third volume of verse, published in 1983, these poems soon became known as 'secret narratives', bits and bobs of stories whose contexts are never made quite clear. Alan Robinson's response to these secret narratives in the late 1980s is fairly typical of the general critical response to them at the time:

> To explain such experimental works, the associations of the convenient label 'narrative' are misleading. For there is little which corresponds in these elusive poems to the conventional notion of a story. Instead, the reader confronts either the fragmentary traces of a displaced narrative which must be recovered inferentially, or alternatively a palimpsest of apparently discrete, incomplete fictions, the nature of whose interrelationship remains obscure or conjectural.[10]

From that description alone, these secret narratives probably sound off-putting enough to the general reader, but Robinson goes on to talk about the way in which these poems 'seem designed to mock the reader's pursuit of arcane significance, tempting one into comic excesses of overinterpretation'; how they are 'deliberately designed to frustrate any attempt to establish a single context, whether literal or metaphorical, that will adequately explain the poem' and how 'the resolute discontinuity of [Fenton's] poems induces in the reader a disconcerting epistemological confusion'.[11] To be fair to both Robinson and Fenton, Robinson probably has his fellow lecturers and professors of English literature in mind here rather than the nonacademic reader of poetry, but this is a far cry from the sort of narrative verse that the expansive poets were trying to encourage in America. The situation in Britain and Ireland was also different in that their poets had not sought refuge in the universities in the postwar years in the way they had in the States and, consequently, the general loss of readers for poetry that occurred in America did not occur to such an extent on the other side of the Atlantic. In any case, the sort of narrative verse that was being written and published in America in the 1970s and 1980s was not the sort of narrative verse being written and published in Britain and Ireland during those years and the major difference seems to have been their attitudes towards their respective audiences. While American poets like Simpson and Dobyns felt a need at this time to make their poems as accessible to the public as possible in the hope of attracting new readers, British poets like Fenton and Irish poets like Muldoon did not.

Most new movements in poetry over the last two hundred years have begun with a redefinition of the figure of the poet, but this was not so with the expansive movement. According to Gioia, this new movement began with a redefinition of the reader of poetry:

> At odds with the small but established institutional audience for new poetry, these young writers imagined instead readers who loved literature and the arts but had either rejected or never studied contemporary poetry. This was not the mass audience of television or radio, for whom the written word was not a primary means of information. It was an audience of prose readers— intelligent, educated, and sophisticated individuals who, while no longer reading poetry, enjoyed serious novels, film, drama, jazz, dance, classical music, painting, and

other modern arts …. Rather than be bards for the poetry subculture, they aspired to become the poets for an age of prose.[12]

Since it was assumed these prose readers, with their steady diets of fiction and films, had become quite competent at constructing narratives on their own with only a minimum of information, expansive poets decided they could trust their readers more than lyric poets had. While lyric poets were supposed to write best when they pretended no one was listening—that their poems were not meant to be heard but overheard—expansive poets found they wrote best when they knew the reader was definitely there. As Simpson said:

> I know when I am writing well because I start to trust the reader. When you start to have a sense of the reader, a strong sense that you can trust this person, this mind listening to you, then you can move in all directions. I find when I do not have a sense of the listener I try to explain everything and the poem goes dead.[13]

This does not mean, however, that the poet should take advantage of this situation, using the reader of the poem as a mere listener or, even worse, as some kind of confessor. As Dobyns has said, the problem with the confessional poets, despite some rather wonderful poems, is that they still think they are Keats or Shelley, withering away in a Hampstead garden or sheltering from a storm in some Tuscan wood:

> The main reason this sense of self damages the poet is that it violates the poet's relationship with audience. Instead of audience and poet being in the same boat, the attitude of the poet as hero creates a situation where the poet is in a special boat. It keeps the poet from being the reader's representative and lessens the poem's chance to create a sense of community.[14]

Although we may well admire a confessional poem, says Dobyns, we are not invited to participate in it, merely to 'stand in awe' of it as witnesses or onlookers. Such poems only serve to draw attention to the poets and their troubles, not to the world around them:

> The emotional concept that has been deeply experienced by the writer can be exactly reproduced in the reader only if the writer feels that he or she and the reader are more or less in the same boat and, perhaps, that the reader is an extension of the writer. For the grand narcissists, of course, this is no problem.(206)

Like Simpson, Dobyns found the best cure for such narcissistic poetry was a good dose of prose. When he joined the master of fine arts programme at Goddard College in 1978, Dobyns had already published three volumes of verse but felt, like so many other poets then, that he was stuck in a bit of an autobiographical rut. Fortunately, he came to Goddard at a particularly fruitful time, teaching creative writing alongside Joan Aleshire, George Chambers, Louise Glück, Robert Haas, Donald Hall, John Irving, Thomas Lux, Heather McHugh, Lisel Mueller, Craig Nova, Steve Orlen, Greg Orr, Francine Prose, Michael Ryan, Michelle Simmons and Ellen Bryant Voigt. But, more importantly, he quickly became friends with three short story writers there—Raymond Carver, Richard Ford and Tobias Wolff—whose work has been described variously as Minimalism, Dirty Realism, Freeze-Dried Fiction, Low-Rent Tragedies and Post-Vietnam Post-Literary Post-Modernist Blue-Collar Neo-Early-Hemingwayism. They spent many long nights together, telling each other stories and sharing a mutual admiration for Kafka, Beckett and, more than any other writer, Chekhov.

In order to teach himself how to write narrative poetry, Dobyns set himself the task of writing a series of poems based on the paintings of Balthus, inventing a story for each painting that, despite its source, could be understood perfectly well on its own. After that exercise, he began to write poems that clearly showed the influence of the minimalists, particularly the realistic narratives of *Black Dog, Red Dog*, published in 1984. What Dobyns had been learning from this short fiction was the way in which story could function as metaphor and how metaphor could, in turn, involve the reader in the story. By metaphor, Dobyns means something more complicated than the simple use of simile, thinking instead of story working as analogy and allegory, like Carver's 'Popular Mechanics' serving as a metaphor for the effect feuding parents can have on their children.[15] However, this interest in metaphor, like his earlier interest in narrative, comes from a desire to bring the writer and the reader closer together. Like Simpson, Dobyns cannot imagine writing a poem without the reader being present: 'I would find it impossible to write without a conception of the reader, that impossibly ideal figure who holds the other end of the string. He or she is the person I am talking to' (3). What the writer needs to consider, according to Dobyns, is just how much information the reader needs in order to make the metaphor work, to connect the image or the analogue with the object, and just how much information to withhold:

> Every metaphor is based on withheld information that the comparison given by the metaphor tries to uncover. Implied in each metaphor is the question of how the image is like the object. In the act of answering this question the reader becomes a participant by authenticating the comparison from his or her own memory and / or imagination. (17)

Dobyns argues that metaphors, including analogies and allegories, are essentially 'riddles' which the human brain automatically tries to solve, telling itself stories in order to do so. It is crucial, however, that the writer gets the balance right, holding back enough information to make the narrative mysterious, but not so much that the reader gets nowhere at all:

> Many weak poems substitute vagueness for mystery. They withhold information as to the object of the meta-

phor and offer only image or what appears to be image, which gives the poem an aura of mystery and meaning. But image without object is nonfunctional, since its contemplation won't increase our understanding. (15)

Another thing Dobyns learned from his study of narrative is how to use tone in order to make the reader feel more comfortable with the poem, particularly the rather cool tone readers have found so attractive in the short stories of Carver, Ford and Wolff. Here, both Carver and Dobyns acknowledge a debt to Chekhov, the Russian writer who advised one of his friends to show a little less sentiment in her stories about the downtrodden. Writing to Lydia Avilova in 1892, Chekhov suggested, 'When you describe the miserable and unfortunate, and want to make the reader feel pity, try to be somewhat colder—that seems to give a kind of background to another's grief, against which it stands out more clearly. Whereas in your story the characters cry and you sigh. Yes, be more cold' (157). According to Chekhov, such sentiment only draws attention to the narrator and away from the narrative; the teller is trusting neither the story nor the reader of the story. It was important to Chekhov that the teller never judged the tale he or she was telling and that the narrator never considered him or herself above the characters of the story. Readers do not feel comfortable, he argued, when they sense the writer is looking down either at them or at the characters, or that the writer understands the story he or she is telling but cannot be bothered to make the meaning clear to them. What must be clear is that the writer does not understand the story any better than the reader does; that, as Dobyns would put it, they are in the same boat, both scratching their heads trying to figure things out. Or, as two New Narrative poets, Mark Jarman and Robert McDowell, would argue:

The word *story*, when it is traced back through its Indo-European roots, meets the word *veda*: I have seen, I know. We think of storytellers as witnesses, all the more so when they speak in the first person and in a poem. The problem for the poet is to find how what he or she has witnessed can be relived. For as soon as the story is too well understood by the teller or, even worse, distorted to corroborate an ideology, it loses authenticity. To have a story to tell, in the magically flexible form of the narrative, means to react to life as it is lived and not as it is anticipated.[16]

A somewhat older narrative poet who also acknowledges a debt to the short stories of Chekhov and an affinity to the short stories of Carver,[17] Simpson, agrees:

If I can state a problem truly in a poem I feel I've written the poem. I try to state the answer but I never arrive at it. What I really think I'm doing in poems is presenting a situation or a problem as clearly as possible or giving the reader a sense that different things are coming together at this point .... A lot of my poems end with a shrug that says I don't know. On the one hand, yes; on the other hand, yes, and I don't know which way to choose. And damn it, that's how we live. I don't know any people who go through life with a view of life. I know people who go through life with a lot of ideas.[18]

Dobyns thinks he detects a similar shrug, a similar refusal to sum things up for the reader, in the work of the two writers Sweeney admires most, Kafka and Simic. The reticent tone of their stories and poems suggests, once again, that they will not place themselves above the reader, in terms either of compassion or of comprehension. In fact, Dobyns argues that part of the fascination of their texts is in trying to guess what these writers do feel and think about the things they are telling us. In some of their texts, the tone is so cold, so scrupulously objective, that Dobyns says they read as if they simply dropped from the sky: 'What this diminished tone can do in a poem is to give it the appearance of existing without an author, which in turn gives it the appearance of permanence, as if it had always existed, in the way that the Bible exists or that laws exist. It tries to separate itself from a human maker. And isn't that also a tone?' (160-61).

Dobyns also has a weakness for parable, whether it is his story of the working-class residents of a New England resort who suddenly emerge from their mobile homes to conga down the main drag in 'Dancing in Vacationland', his modernisation of Bede's well-known metaphor of the bird passing through the festive meadhall in 'Where We Are' or his tale of the unsuspecting family whose home becomes a slaughterhouse in 'White Pig', huddling in their beds upstairs while the drunk butcher sings hunting and marching songs below. While the tale he retells from Bede probably has the same object today as it had back in the eighth century, the narrative tone in all three poems is as restrained as anything in Kafka or Simic, letting us make the metaphors ourselves, offering us the concrete images but leaving us to provide the objects. In his poem 'What You Have Come to Expect' from *Black Dog, Red Dog*, Dobyns begins by offering us a vaguely familiar film narrative, in which a man bids farewell to his family before jumping on his horse and riding off to war. Since at least some of his readers in the States will have watched these films, as he no doubt did, in the cavern-like atmosphere of postwar cinemas, Dobyns shares the memory by retelling it in the second person and the present tense, hinting that others have sat in this seat before:

> Then, from your seat in the third row, you follow him
> through battles and bloodshed and friends lost
> until finally he returns home: rides up the lane
> as dusk falls to discover all that remains of his house
> is a single chimney rising from ashes and mounds of debris.
> Where is his young wife? He stares out across
> empty fields, the wreckage of stables and barns.
> Where are the children who were the comfort of his life?[19]

Despite the fact that it is highly unlikely Hollywood in the 1950s would have left a movie so open ended—that it would have trusted its audience to fill in the blanks, no doubt assuming we want to know more than our hero does—Dobyns seems to suggest that the film continues to fascinate the boy long afterwards simply because he does not know what happened to the man's family any more than the man himself does. Nor, as readers of the poem, do we. This is neither what cinema audiences have come to expect of films, nor what poetry readers have come to expect of poems. There are a number of other disturbing narratives like this in *Black Dog, Red Dog*, including 'Wind Chimes', which offers us only two disparate moments from an obviously long and complicated life, and 'Night Swimmer', which gives us the isolated thoughts of two political enemies on a night when two children are murdered, trusting us in each case to finish the story.

But the poems in Dobyns's next volume, *Cemetery Nights*, are the ones that most resemble Sweeney's own work. While the two previous volumes had been necessary exercises in narrative, Dobyns finally decided it was time to move away from the sort of realism he had found in the short stories of Carver, Ford and Wolff:

> In *Black Dog, Red Dog*, I had tried writing realistic narratives.... But by early 1982, I had come to an end of it. Furthermore, I had spent six months in Santiago, Chile, and was beginning to believe that realism was an inadequate way to deal with the world's excesses; or rather, a realistic approach came across as fantastic – what people who know nothing about surrealism call surrealistic (307).

This means instead of getting a story about one little boy pointing a gun at another and telling him to pull down his pants, we get a story about a woman who travels to Brazil for plastic surgery, is murdered and shipped back home to a son who no longer recognises her. Unable to pick her out from ten other women at the morgue, the son takes them all, cremates them and sprinkles their ashes over his garden. Then he plants tomatoes because his mother loved tomatoes and, when they are ripe, picks them and takes them into his kitchen, their shape suddenly reminding him of his mother's breasts, their feel reminding him of his mother's hands:

> Mother, mother, he cries, and flings himself
> on the tomatoes. Forget about the knife, the fork,
> the pinch of salt. Try to imagine the filial
> starvation, think of his ravenous kisses.[20]

The humour here is quite typical of the volume, and so are the final instructions to the reader, trusting the reader to return to the poem and see its serious side. Sweeney has always insisted narrative works differently in a poem from the way it works in a short story or a novel, that what is always made explicit in prose narrative is best left implicit in verse narrative:

> When a woman decides to leave her husband in a novel or a play the reader or the audience usually knows exactly why. That reader has been given all the information, realises what's happening, and understands the context of the decision. A poem, on the other hand, must establish its context with very limited means. A situation must be pinned down as simply and surely as an artist captures a likeness with three quick strokes of the charcoal. A poem works, to a great extent, by implication, leaving a lot of the picture for the reader to fill in. (79)

Although he believes the poem must contain just enough information for the reader to construct his or her own context, Sweeney also argues that leaving blanks in the narrative can have the somewhat surprising effect of turning a simple story into allegory: 'When Kafka describes a man on trial, without letting us or his hero ever find out what he's accused of, he creates a mysteriously non-literal parable on the nature of guilt and punishment' (78). For both Dobyns and Sweeney, of course, it is important that this information is withheld from the hero as well as the reader—and one suspects from Kafka himself—so that none of the participants in the story is made to feel uncomfortable in the company of the others.

Sweeney has often said the red pen can be of more use to the budding poet than the black one. In order to make this point, he often tells young writers the story of the fishmonger and his sign:

> It's a bit like the man who puts up a sign saying 'Fresh Fish on Sale Here'. Someone comes up to him and says 'You don't need the "Here". You're not selling them anywhere else.' The man paints out the 'Here', so the sign now reads 'Fresh Fish on Sale'. Someone comes up and says 'You don't need the "on Sale", you're not giving them away.' The man paints out the 'on Sale' so the sign now reads 'Fresh Fish'. Someone comes up and says 'You don't need the "Fresh", you're not selling rotten fish.' The man paints out the 'Fresh', so the sign reads simply 'Fish'. Someone comes up and says 'You don't need "Fish", you can smell them at the bottom of the street'.(49-50)

It was probably just a matter of time, therefore, before Sweeney would call a volume of verse, as he just has, *A Smell of Fish*. Sweeney argues that a poet becomes a good poet by learning what to leave out and that some of the poems he admires most, including a number by Frost, do little more than establish atmosphere, the situation itself suggesting the story, giving the puzzling effect but not its cause. Sample atmospheric poems by Frost might include 'Stopping by Woods' and 'The Draft Horse', while similar examples by Sweeney would be 'Russian' and 'The Blue Taps'. In the first poem, a man wakes up and suddenly finds himself speaking Russian, despite the fact that he has always struggled with foreign languages before. And in the second, another man inexplicably inherits some cacti and blue bathroom fixtures from a recently departed friend, the widow abstractedly reciting the names her husband had given each of his cherished plants. But neither poem tells us why. The wife of the Russian speaker returns home from church only to find the man she thought she knew so well writing Cyrillic in their bed and having an argument in a strange language on their telephone, while the man whose friend has just died will need some time to understand why he was given all these precious cacti and blue taps for his white bath. As with Kafka's stories, these blanks in the narratives tend to make their meanings less literal and considerably more allegorical but, perhaps more importantly, they tell the reader no one has any more information than he or she does. The man in the first poem clearly cannot comprehend why he can suddenly speak Russian, nor can his wife, and the man in the second poem only hopes he will be able to remember the names of all those cacti and that the taps will fit. As Sweeney has said of this second poem:

> I was doing a reading at a writing course tutored by Simon Armitage and Beryl Bainbridge. After I read a poem about someone being left blue taps in a will, Beryl said: 'You poets are all the same. When you tell a story you leave half of it out. For example, that line "I hoped the taps fitted". I want to know whether they fitted or not.' I told her I couldn't care less if they fitted. That was up to the reader to decide. (27)

Although some of the more traditional expansive poets in the States would probably have the same objection to these abbreviated stories that Bainbridge had—including Jarman and McDowell, who argue that a narrative poem must have a beginning, a middle and an end[21]—Dobyns and Sweeney would suggest that such omissions are not intended to exclude readers but to include them more, to put their experiences and their imaginations on a par with those of the poet, not below them.

Apart from Bainbridge, British critics have not complained too much about the bits missing from Sweeney's stories—having become quite comfortable with the secret narratives which poets like Fenton and Muldoon have been publishing since the 1980s—but they have noted his distinct preference for the third person to the first. Ian Gregson, for example, points out that while many British and Irish poets have stopped writing lyrics and started writing monologues instead, Sweeney still seems 'the odd one out', with his tendency towards third person narration giving his poems 'a much less excitable surface than that of the others'.[22] Alongside American poets like Simpson, Simic and Dobyns, of course, he does not seem odd at all, nor does his familiar deadpan tone, but this does not mean Sweeney no longer writes in the first person. Two poems from his most recent volume, *A Smell of Fish*, demonstrate that the first person can be just as clueless as the third when it comes to comprehending the significance of the story being told. In the first poem, 'Long Distance', the narrator returns home, following some minor domestic duties, to hear a voice from his past, from a distant moment in his life that he cannot quite translate into the present:

> At the fifth ring, just as the ansaphone clicks in,
> I drop the groceries, the clanking bottles, and grab the phone.
> Ah, Herr Sweeney, endlich sind Sie da!'
> German! I haven't heard those sounds in some time.[23]

Not unlike the man in the poem 'Russian', with all its Kafkaesque undertones, the narrator here suddenly finds himself speaking a strange language, absorbedly watching himself send signals across his synapses to utter mechanical German sounds and translate them back into English, amazed that he can still do so, that this former self still survives. But because the narrator has no more of a clue who called at the end of the poem than the reader does—this information having been withheld from him, from us and, one suspects, from the poet himself at some point in his past—allegory creeps in once again, the mixture of formal and informal German turning from playful reproach to painful self-accusation. The questioning that occurs in the final lines suggests that, whoever phoned, this incident is going to have greater significance precisely because it is so uncertain, that the simple slip of forgetting to say who called will no doubt cause the narrator to imagine all sorts of potential speakers and possible meanings, including a warning from death itself. A similar story is told in the second poem, 'Incident in Exeter Station', where, this time, an unidentified fellow passenger approaches the narrator and demands a drink:

He came in the door, staring at me,
like he'd known me in another life.
'I've chased everywhere after you', he said.
'... The least you can do is buy me a pint.'[24]

Although this poem seems even more of a dialogue with the self than the other poem does, this story allows for both anecdotal and allegorical meanings simply because, once again, neither the narrator nor the reader really knows just who or what this character is. In fact, the reader gets a definite sense here that the narrator prefers not to know; that the closer he comes to finding out the true identity of this rather scruffy man, and the more he finds they have in common, the less comfortable he becomes. While the incident itself certainly feels real enough and the unkempt character seems vaguely familiar, the uncertain connection between these two figures begins to suggest an allegorical interpretation which the narrator does his best to deny, resisting a reading he is not quite ready to admit even to himself.

A somewhat calmer encounter with death occurs in one of the Dobyns poems selected by Sweeney for the anthology of contemporary poetry he recently edited with Jo Shapcott for Faber and Faber. In that poem, rather innocuously entitled 'Seeing Off a Friend', the narrator is little more than a reporter, asking questions and telling us, as clearly as he can, what his eyes and ears tell him. He only wants to know what his friend has come to know, hoping the story of his life might be worth sharing with others. However, like all good storytellers, the one thing the friend does know is not to place his own experiences, or any conclusions he might have come to as a result of those experiences, above those of his listener, even if he appears to be in a pretty good position to come to some conclusions about them now:

Early April on Broadway, south of Union Square,
a man jumps from a twentieth floor. I
stop him at the tenth. Tell me, I say,
what have you learned in your travels?[25]

The man, however, begs for more time to consider the question and continues his fall to the fifth floor, where he is stopped again and asked the same thing. But he remains reticent: 'These answers / are slow in approaching, he says, / perhaps it is too soon to tell.'[26] No one wants to tell too much here. The suicide is reluctant to tell his story and Dobyns does not want to be any more precise about this incident than telling us it takes place some springtime in Manhattan. As a result, this man's drop to the streets below suddenly becomes ours, its parable as clear as the flight of Bede's bird through that medieval meadhall. Chekhov would argue, of course, that the coolness of tone in a poem like this does not suggest a lack of compassion, but rather an admirable unwillingness to place the poet's emotions above either those witnessing this tragic event or those reading about it. The same goes for comprehension, with the crowd gathered below coming to grips with the significance of that event at the very same moment as its narrator. After the man falls the remaining five floors, strikes a streetlight, bounces off the hood of a blue Chevrolet and finally comes to rest against a parking meter, the people on the street surround him: 'Their hands are open like shopping bags. / Their mouths are open like pits in the earth. / All his answers cover their faces.'[27] His fate may not yet be theirs but, as Dobyns and Sweeney know all too well, it will be.

NOTES

1. Sam Halpert, ed., *Raymond Carver: An Oral Biography*, Iowa City 1995, 116.
2. Matthew Sweeney and John Hartley Williams, *Writing Poetry and Getting Published*, London 1997, 6. Further references are to this edition and are given in the text.
3. Dana Gioia, *Can Poetry Matter?*, St Paul 1992, 12.
4. Wade Newman, 'Crossing the Boundary: The Expansive Movement in Contemporary Poetry', *Crosscurrents*, 8:2 (1988), 142-53.
5. R.S. Gwynn, ed., *New Expansive Poetry*, Ashland, Oregon 1999, 12.
6. Louis Simpson, *A Company of Poets*, Ann Arbor 1981, 310.
7. *Ibid.*, 346.
8. David Mason, 'Other Lives: On Shorter Narrative Poems', in Gwynn, *op. cit.*, 215.
9. Mark Jarman and Robert McDowell, *The Reaper Essays*, Brownsville, Oregon 1996, 160.
10. Alan Robinson, *Instabilities in Contemporary British Poetry*, London 1988, 1.
11. *Ibid.*, 6, 12, 15.
12. Gioia, *op. cit.*, 249.
13. Simpson, *op. cit.*, 277.
14. Stephen Dobyns, *Best Words, Best Order: Essays on Poetry*, New York 1997, 205. Further references are to this edition and are given in the text.
15. Halpert, *op. cit.*, 115.
16. Jarman and McDowell, *op. cit.*, 83.
17. Louis Simpson, *The Character of the Poet*, Ann Arbor 1986, 167.
18. Simpson, *op. cit.*, (1981), 300-01.
19. Stephen Dobyns, *Velocities: New & Selected Poems*, Newcastle upon Tyne 1996, 174.
20. *Ibid.*, 185.
21. Jarman and McDowell, *op. cit.*, 131-42.
22. Ian Gregson, *Contemporary Poetry and Postmodernism: Dialogue and Estrangement*, London 1996, 115.
23. Matthew Sweeney, *Selected Poems*, London 2002, 116.
24. *Ibid.*, 130.
25. Jo Shapcott and Matthew Sweeney, eds, *Emergency Kit: Poems for Strange Times*, London 1996, 279.
26. *Ibid.*, 280.
27. *Ibid.*, 280.

Of Beards and Breasts, Baldheads and Babies:
Muldoon's Mongrel Families

RUI CARVALHO HOMEM

The enumerative and alliterative title of this chapter should not be taken as a dubious attempt to mimic Paul Muldoon's phonetic and semantic games: it is meant, rather, as a reminder of how often this poet's 'whimful' verbal resources (to use one of his favourite self-descriptions[1]) both assist and are enhanced by his treatment of the theme of generation, and by his recurrent and disturbing representations of the family. Further, it signals how such formal and thematic concerns are brought together by the master-theme of hybridity.

The latter theme famously found an anchorage in Muldoon's second book, *Mules* (1977)—in the title poem,[2] and in the poem which will be at the centre of this chapter, 'The Bearded Woman, by Ribera', as well as in such other instances as the woman with 'one brown, and one blue eye' in 'Blemish'. or the freaks and the elusive forms glimpsed in 'Duffy's Circus'. Closely related to this theme is a concern with division and borderline conditions which pervades the following volume, *Why Brownlee Left* (1980), where Muldoon's sly denunciation of the absurdity of arbitrary divisions memorably takes the form, in 'The Boundary Commission', of an image of rain stopping like 'a wall of glass' along a highly artificial border. The continuity of the theme is further confirmed by the representations of liminality in Muldoon's more recent work, which foreground what Ian Gregson has called a 'hybrid of the fictive and the real'.[3] It is significant that the opening poem of *Hay*, 'The Mud Room', should have goats which 'delight to tread upon the brink / of meaning'.[4] Indeed, the emergence of the same concerns in Muldoon's prose writings suggests that 'no fine / blue-green line' should be drawn between his poetry and his other writing: his recently published *To Ireland, I* (*The Clarendon Lectures in English Literature 1998*) is dominated by an interest in 'promiscuous provenance', and an 'essential liminality'; and it focuses on 'a range of strategies devised by a range of Irish writers for dealing with the ideas of liminality and narthecality that are central...to the Irish experience'.[5] These lectures also argue the attraction of the Irish tradition to a 'critically positioned figure, a figure who is neither here nor there, (but) at some notional interface'.[6]

These continuities, and this emergence in later volumes of what Clair Wills has called 'states of suspension or indeterminacy which are the logical extension of the concerns of *Mules*'[7] can also be traced more specifically in Muldoon's representations of the family and its bonds. Three consecutive poems in *The Annals of Chile* (1994) construe the figure of the mother, to whose memory the volume is dedicated, in varying and metamorphic guises: in 'Brazil', as sexually seductive presence, 'one nipple darkening her smock', but also as prudish upbringer and educator, in 'Oscar', as ruthlessly oppressive wife, even posthumously. A capacity to subordinate (or emasculate) the father which in 'Milkweed and Monarch' is confirmed by the son's incapacity to distinguish between father and mother: 'as he knelt by the grave of his mother and father / he could barely tell one from the other' (156).

The representation of the family as weird and dysfunctional had been prominent amongst the delirious 'American' ramblings of 'Immram', featuring a disappeared father, a force-fed mother, and a 'child bride'— all in a poem whose first stanza includes a fictional mongrel genealogy, half direct speech, half inner musing:

My grand-father hailed from New York State.
My grand-mother was part Cree.
This must be some new strain in my pedigree (54).

The theme of mongrel identity in 'Immram' also includes, amidst the fictionalisation of the subject's father as a carrier of drugs, the statement: 'My father had been a mule' (62). This reminds Muldoon's reader of his second book, which I have already referred to as an anchorage for the theme of hybridity, as well as the location of several of Muldoon's more explicitly autobiographical realisations of that theme with regard to family identity. A clear instance of this is 'The Mixed Marriage', an ostensibly autobiographical poem about a 'servant-boy' father and a 'school-mistress' mother which, besides stereotyping the poet's parents respectively as 'genuine' atavistic peasant *vs.* pretentious teacher, defines for himself what will prove to be a poetically recurrent sense of an in-between origin and identity: But 'the volume's most powerful family image',[8] and the most memorable instance of hybridity and in-betweenness, is to be found in 'The Bearded Woman, by Ribera'.

* * *

The poem has an ostensibly visual referent—the famous seventeenth-century painting named in its title. It is thus, from the outset, promised to us as an instance of ekphrasis, a description of a work of art—or rather, in James A.W.Heffernan's simple and apt definition, a 'verbal representation of visual representation'.[9] It is an example of a mode of writing as old as western writing itself, and popular enough for 'at least one poem about a work of visual art [to have] come from almost every major poet of our time'.[10] Indeed, the very first clause of 'The Bearded Woman by Ribera' is a report on '[having] seen': the verbal presents itself as based on an actual, empirical visual experience, but, in the first of many dislocations, what the subject reports seeing is *another* bearded woman, not in Ribera's painting but rather 'in a fairground, /

Swigging a quart of whiskey'. The two opening lines thus define a perspective (and a term of comparison) for the ekphrastic treatment of a museum piece which is that of popular entertainment—the fairground freakshow—in addition to which it brands the woman at the fair as hybrid in all respects, by associating her with disreputable and stereotypically *male* heavy-drinking, as if the facial pilous consequences of a (probably) hormonal imbalance inevitably entailed a social correspondence, inhibiting a more genteel (or 'ladylike') behaviour. The third line, 'But nothing like this lady', prepares the reader for a more surprising view (or rather, for its verbal description) than that which the fairground offers, but the details which support that comparison (with corresponding authorial judgments) will only come with the second of the three seven-line stanzas which, separated by two couplets, make up the poem. The rest of the first stanza appears to be a 'neutral' overall description of the painting, except for the phrasing chosen to describe the peripherality of the husband vis-à-vis the centrality of the woman suckling the baby: 'With what must be her husband / Almost out of the picture'—stressing the insignificance of the male presence.

The two couplets not only occupy a conspicuous position on the page; they are identified by their reflective content—reading almost as afterthoughts to visualisation and description—and by the way they appear to confirm the relevance for Muldoon of Edna Longley's *dictum* that, 'As with Joyce, Catholic Ulster seems to have incubated its own deconstruction'.[11] The first couplet reminds the reader of what must, in a culture with a Catholic matrix, inevitably suggest an analogy for the trio in the painting. The second makes explicit what the very writing of the poem might imply, when the poet avows, despite (or because of?) her 'wrongness': 'I'm taken completely / By this so unlikely Madonna'.

The sense of 'wrongness' and 'unlikelihood' is imparted to the reader from the outset by the information in the title that this is about a *bearded* woman, but the second heptastich makes clear that it is also grounded in other elements found and reported by the poet as viewer. Besides the fact that her luxuriantly black beard gives this mother one of the symbolic features of a father's authority, her physiognomy is actually that of a *grand*father. Ultimately, though, mother and child are surpassed, in their power to draw the viewer's attention, by the inconspicuous third party, 'the figure in the shadows', who is described and judged in the third heptastich, and who gets the last view and the last words of the poem. The authorial voice admits the near unwillingness of this attraction—a confession and a reminder of this poet's persistently complex relationship to father figures. As Ian Gregson points out, 'maleness' is hardly ever treated seriously by Muldoon,[12] and the demotion of this father's maleness comes with his androgyny which is in marked contrast to the woman's robust, central, black-bearded presence. But if the poem began by leaning on an inverted stereotype, it will end by appealing to stereotypes of male intervention in the domestic sphere, both in a *macho* version and in a supposedly effeminate version—since the woman's husband's peripherality in the painting is construed as an accidental appearance.

Such stock domestic chores for husband and wife signal, when the reader gets to these closing lines, that the painting is (inevitably, once the poet refuses the pretence of a non-judgmental attitude of 'mere' description) to be construed in the light of mid-to-late twentieth-century values and mores— social, sexual, familial. And this forcible evidence of the *aggiornamento* to which Muldoon is subjecting the seventeenth-century scene painted by José de Ribera may be, after a preliminary reading of Muldoon's poem, an additional stimulus for the reader to indulge his/her curiosity, to consider the hint contained in the title—which, to the extent that it might be the tag beside the painting on a museum wall or on the page of a catalogue, offers the poem up as a substitute for Ribera's painting—and to judge to what extent and in what ways such a substitution has taken place.

The theoretical demise of a belief in the 'transparency' of representation (in whatever medium it is offered to us), or in the possibility of a 'neutral' appropriation of the real by art, unmediated by a construing and constructing consciousness, demands that a *caveat* be put forward at this point, to emphasise precisely that the ensuing compared reading of Ribera's painting and Muldoon's poem will at no moment aim to gauge the latter's 'fidelity' to its referent as a critical objective *per se*. It will rather be guided by an awareness that ekphrasis always entails a conflict, a 'friction' between the two media involved;[13] and by the wish to investigate the connections between the 'intersexuality' of Muldoon's theme and the intermediality of his ekphrastic gesture.   Indeed it is suggested that both should be read in the context of a basic principle of intertextuality whose inevitability Muldoon's whole *oeuvre* so powerfully demonstrates. What John Carey meant as the most serious of indictments when he stated that, 'If all previous literature vanished, Muldoon's poetry would instantly suffocate'[14] will be perceived by many as the natural condition of all writing, and Muldoon's poetry as a forceful vindication of that perception.

The reader who endeavours to read Muldoon's poem against its stated pictorial referent will probably do so by means of a reproduction, rather than by resorting to the palace in Toledo where the painting hangs. This means of access to visual art (which Muldoon himself foregrounds in another ekphrastic poem, 'Paul Klee: *They're Biting*', by making it clear that he sees the painting as reproduced in a postcard),[15] and the overall range of possibilities afforded by the age of mechanical and electronic reproduction, have in fact provided one of the cultural bases for an increase in the practice of ekphrastic poetry.[16] Additionally, and with much relevance for this reading, they help to query the whole endeavour of a search for an original: departing from a representation of a representation, one searches for the latter only to find it disseminated through the print culture and the cyber-culture, available for multiple possession and for re-viewing (and re-vision?), rather than arcanely preserved in its singleness, or signified (as far as the genesis of the poem is concerned) as a unique object glimpsed on a unique creative occasion.

Alongside the reproduction, the reader will probably access some of those curatorial and catalogue notes which are often so closely involved with the fortunes of ekphrasis, and which in this case will inform one that José de Ribera, Spanish painter at the court of Naples, known to take a particular interest in the grotesque and the out-of-the-way, was commissioned by the viceroy in 1631 to paint a portrait of Magdalena Ventura, aged fifty-two at the time, who fifteen years earlier had suddenly grown a beard and moustache. Indeed, the reader as viewer will not fail to notice that the painting itself includes the equivalent of such a note, in the form of a brief account of the circumstances, inscribed in Latin on a stone surface—a concern with memorialisation, but above all with verification and authenticity, so that those to come would not falsify, misrepresent or construe as fictional what the sponsor and the painter were at pains to guarantee was true.

However, the eye is not primarily caught by the stone inscription, but rather (as made predictable by the outlandishness of the theme, and as enforced by the structure of the painting and by its light) by the woman portrayed. For Muldoon's reader, the visual focus of the painting will first bring confirmation: here are the woman's luxuriantly black beard, her bare right breast 'borrowed by her child', her face like that of an elderly man; and, beside her, a male 'figure in the shadows'. But it will also, promptly, bring surprise, since fundamental aspects of Muldoon's 'description' are not to be found in, or rather are blatantly contradicted by Ribera's painting. Rather than squat[ting] in the foreground, the bearded woman unequivocally *stands* at the centre of the picture. Even if in a peripheral position, her husband's whole frame is within the picture, and he is posing as much as the bearded woman herself. He is not, therefore, in the attitude of an accidental intruder who 'has simply wandered in'; rather, his position in the painting is that conventionally taken by the paterfamilias in family portraits. More surprisingly still, his plain, rather rigid stance, and his features, which are those of an obviously old man, disallow the adjective 'willowy'. His gaunt face, with indrawn cheeks (probably covering a toothless mouth), is covered by an old man's beard, poor in comparison with the 'luxuriance' of his wife's, but in no way describable as 'clean-shaven'.

Within Muldoon's poetics, these 'deviations' from his referent are scarcely surprising: he has spoken of his interest in a disturbing, dislocating vision, that reconfigures one's relationship to the real, and his strategies are often the equivalent of an ironical epistemology, questioning one's capacity to know.[17] His play with elusive family origins comes together in this poem with a dis-respect for the authentic and verified source, with a wilful mis-representation which is indeed an intermedial equivalent of the parodies, distorted allusions, and blatant or discreet misquotations which punctuate his work. One might remember here that 'The Key' to that great subversive summoning of intertexts and of intellectual authority which is *Madoc* and more recently, in *Hay*, Muldoon gave the title 'Errata' to a poem totally made of approximate spellings, near-identities, instances of 'mis-quotation', which include: 'For "mother" read "other"', 'For "ludic" read "lucid"', 'For "anecdote" read "antidote"'.[18]

The friction between Muldoon's poem and Ribera's painting is thus only different in medium from Muldoon's habitual verbal and intertextual play. His ekphrastic gesture lends itself, in fact, to a broad understanding of this mode closer to Claus Clüver's critique of Heffernan's restrictive definition, where Clüver argues for the need to 'change the discourse on ekphrasis from a discourse preoccupied with modes of representation to a discourse of re-presentation, re-writing, and translation'.[19] When Muldoon rewrites (or re-paints) the husband as 'Willowy, and clean-shaven' he is (as pointed out above) accentuating the reversal of the male/female roles and updating them to conform to present-day stereotypes. He is thus re-presenting the painting in a way which confirms the insight of Edna Longley, who, when commenting on two other ekphrastic poems by Muldoon, states that his methods are conspicuous 'not only in calling attention to fictionality and artifice ... , but in weaving narratives rather than dwelling on images ... . Muldoon chooses pictures that potentially tell a story or whose morally emblematic quality he can translate into verbal parables. Text usurps image.'[20] But this is, in fact, actualising to the full the workings of ekphrasis, according to Heffernan: 'ekphrasis is dynamic and obstetric; it typically delivers *from* the pregnant moment of visual art its embryonically narrative impulse, and thus makes explicit the story that visual art tells only by implication'.[21] From another angle, it is also as if Muldoon were describing not an actual but rather an imaginary painting, offering us then an instance of what John Hollander has called 'notional ckphrasis'.[22]

In a concomitant rather than alternative way, though, the painting Muldoon ultimately describes will not have to be imaginary; rather, the referent he makes up may result from an imaginary collage of Ribera's and other, actual paintings which will be so many other intertexts for his poem. Those intertexts may be strictly locatable or not: Michael Riffaterre's argument that a 'presupposition of intertext' will often be enough for the intertextual web to be activated (and thus for a perceptive reading to take place) may, in this case, prove productive. As Riffaterre puts it, 'When we speak of knowing an intertext ... we must distinguish between the actual knowledge of the form and content of that intertext, and a mere awareness that such an intertext exists and can eventually be found somewhere'.[23] The intertextual web is thus based on the application of a simile one might phrase as *an intertext like...* For this to be made possible, though, in Riffaterre's model, the reader has to identify in the text a trace of the intertext, 'the connective for an interpretant intertext',[24] often an ungrammaticality. It is my contention that the mismatches between Muldoon's poem and his pictorial referent may provide those indices.

In broader terms, the two couplets begin by aligning Ribera's painting with the full range, or rather the whole tradition, of representations of the Holy Family—a connection whose necessity might otherwise not be perceived. The very breadth of the tradition ensures that the reader who departs on a quest for possible intertexts may find him/herself on a wild-goose chase: bearded Madonnas, after all, may prove difficult to find, and those preliminary hints apparently dropped by the very titles of paintings (to be found in catalogues and directories of different kinds) may also prove misleading. That would be the case, for instance, of Raphael's famous 'Madonna with Beardless St Joseph' (1506, presently at The Hermitage, St. Petersburg): the title (and the facial particularity it describes) might make it relevant to our purposes, but not its treatment of the theme; St Joseph is indeed (to retrieve Muldoon's phrase) 'clean-shaven', but the structure of Raphael's painting is not homologous to Ribera's. As for the characterisation of the child as 'ninety, ... if he's a day', the reader familiar with medieval painting may recognise in it not the summoning of a specific intertext, but rather of a whole stage in the history of the representation of children: of 'Holy Families' in which the child looks like a grown-up, and often elderly, there will indeed be plenty—an example amongst many others being the late thirteenth-century 'Gualino Madonna', by Duccio di Buoninsegna, where the proportions of the body, the facial features and the receding hairline of the child can give it the appearance (from a present-day perspective) of an elderly gentleman sitting on the Madonna's lap.

* * *

One may look closer to home, though, in what might otherwise prove a somewhat aleatory quest for possible intertexts; and the means for narrowing the search can be found in Muldoon's text. His quip, (an *interrogatio*) on 'the Holy Family / Gone wrong' can be read as directed, at both the dysfunction of his familial referent, and (sardonically) at a possible failure of the artist when trying his hand at the pictorial genre of the 'Holy Family'—a genre the artist may elsewhere have attempted with other results. This will remind the reader/viewer that Ribera himself is credited with at least two paintings of 'The Holy Family'. In one of them, 'The Holy Family with St Catherine' (a 1648 painting, presently at the Metropolitan Museum of Art, New York), a bearded St Joseph is indeed (as in Muldoon's poem) 'in the shadows', 'Almost out of the picture', and (even if he faces the viewer in exactly the same way as Mary) in a bodily attitude more easily construable as that of someone who has 'simply wandered in'. If we were to mind the incongruity between the standing position of the bearded woman in Ribera's painting and her description as 'squat[ting]' in Muldoon's poem, we would notice that in 'The Holy Family with St Catherine' the Madonna *sits* at the front of the picture. But in the other 'Holy Family' by Ribera (1639, Museo de Santa Cruz, Toledo) we indeed have a lady who squats in the foreground' to tend to the baby. The figure of St Joseph, busy with his carpentry and delineated against an area of shadow, is here that of a much younger man, whose light-coloured beard does not cover all of his face. He stands and works by Mary's side, his body in a dynamic attitude; his leg flexed; his head bent, looking down at the child; his hands wide apart, holding a long and slightly curved piece of wood (almost a visual metonymy for his body): 'willowy' would not misapply.

This is a quest potentially as unending and as indeterminate as the process verbalised at the close of Muldoon's 'Something Else': 'which made me think // of something else, then something else again'.(125) Looking at an image, and realising that we only invest it with meaning by summoning other images, is a way of considering his poetics in which Muldoon has long been educating his readers, as when he declared, in an interview almost twenty years ago, 'we mustn't take anything at face value, not even the man who is presenting things at face value';[25] or when he coins the word 'imarrhage' for that 'slippage or ... bleeding of the image',[26] that 'tendency towards the amalgam, the tendency for one event or character to blur and bleed into another'[27] which he identifies in Joyce and to which he claims an allegiance; or even when, still with Joyce in mind, he produces yet another coinage to describe how the 'range of reference' can be extended by heaping quotations 'in a technique I think of as "conglomewriting"'[28]—a word, itself a hybrid, which aptly describes the accretionary, intersectional and palimpsestic production of meaning which this article has tried to investigate.

NOTES

1. See Clair Wills, *Reading Paul Muldoon*, Newcastle 1998, 11.
2. Paul Muldoon, 'Mules', *New Selected Poems 1968-1994*, London 1996, 35. Unless otherwise indicated, Paul Muldoon's poems will be quoted from this edition; page references will be given in the text.
3. Ian Gregson, *Contemporary Poetry and Postmodernism: Dialogue and Estrangement*, Basingstoke 1996, 54.
4. Paul Muldoon, *Hay*, London 1998, 3.
5. Paul Muldoon, *To Ireland, I: The Clarendon Lectures in English Literature 1998*, Oxford 2000, 5.
6. Muldoon, *ibid.*, 8.
7. Wills, *op. cit.*, 136.
8. Tim Kendall, *Paul Muldoon*, Bridgend 1996, 57.
9. James A.W. Heffernan, *Museum of Words: the Poetics of Ekphrasis from Homer to Ashbery*, Chicago, Ill. 1993, 3.
10. Heffernan, *op. cit.*, 135 and *passim*; see also Edna Longley, *The Living Stream: Literature and Revisionism in Ireland*, Newcastle 1994, 227ff.
11. Longley, *op. cit.*, 52.
12. Gregson, *op. cit.*, 42.
13. Heffernan, *op. cit.*, 6-7, 136.
14. Quoted by Kendall, *op. cit.*, 123.
15. Paul Muldoon, *Meeting the British*, London 1987, 32.
16. Heffernan, *op. cit.*, 139.
17. See Longley, *op. cit.*, 55, 169.
18. Muldoon, *Hay*, *op. cit.*, 88-9.
19. Claus Clüver, 'Ekphrasis Reconsidered: Jorge de Sena's transformations of art and music', in Margarida L.Losa *et al.* (eds.), *Literatura Comparada: os novos paradigmas*, Porto 1996, (39-48) 45.
20. Longley, *op. cit.*, 240, 242 .
21. Heffernan, *op. cit.*, 5.
22. Cited by Heffernan, *op. cit.*, 7.
23. Michael Riffaterre, 'Compulsory reader response: the intertextual drive', in Judith Still and Michael Worton (eds), *Intertextuality: theories and practices*, Manchester 1990, (56-78) 56.
24. Riffaterre, *op. cit.*, 71.
25. Quoted by Kendall, *op. cit.*, 209.
26. Wills, *op. cit.*, 201.

27. Muldoon, *op. cit.*, 2000,74.
28. Muldoon, *ibid.*, 56.

Travesties, Transvestisms, and Transgressions: Cross-dressings and Re-dressings in Nuala Ní Dhomhnaill's Poetry

MARYNA ROMANETS

Among specific usages of female bodies as territories in the symbolic production of Western culture, gendering an uncharted landscape as feminine and equating woman with untrodden desiring-zones have undiminishable surplus value. While focussing on the forms of encoding of male desire in European literature within various historical and geographical frameworks, Klaus Theweleit emphasises that as long as 'the body of woman continues to serve as a territory of desire in place of the body of the earth, which is withheld, there is no need for historical images to die away'.[1] In the case of Ireland, where the collective psychological matrix has been determined to a considerable extent by a traumatic sense of history, the land traditionally allegorised as woman is 'laden with a history and mythology of invasion, dispossession, plantation, famine, eviction, land wars, emigration, and rural depopulation'.[2] By emblematising the earth's body as the body of infinite womanhood, woman is confined to a representational function, her world reduced to the cyclical time of nature. The female body traversed by relentless mapmakers, converting its curved spaces into flat charts, is allotted to the place both of a body outside discourse and of the site for the production and operation of power. Structuring, channelling, manipulating, and restricting desire by personalising it in woman and thus territorialising it into sexuality, dominant cultural formations provide a guiding metaphor for males as avatars of desire and conquerors of 'virgin territories' instrumental in affirming an ideology of control.

Through a discussion of the representation of the female body/land as the locus and articulation of desire in Nuala Ní Dhomhnaill's work, and in that of a number of male writers, I intend to examine here the ways in which she calls into question the procedures of representation implemented by canonical traditions, and the mechanisms of her reshaping of an entire territory on which signs and images circulate.

While surveying the desiring-territories of texts authored by men, Ní Dhomhnaill conducts her study into products of what might be called an unconscious intertextuality in the flows of male desire. By exercising the power to redefine the borders and expand the limits of existing cultural maps, she undertakes the project of conceptual reterritorialisation. Her poetic territory becomes her spatial and cognitive matrix for redrawing the map of male supremacist culture in which a man transgresses marked borders, violating laws and boundaries, making the territory his possession, and claiming exclusive rights to charter and define.

In 'Amhrán An Fhir Óig / Young Man's Song', Ní Dhomhnaill explores a strict conceptual gridiron according to which man and woman inhabit differently defined spaces. Her pastiche, where woman is metaphorically a stationary landform and man is a dynamic agent who moves freely on and across feminine terrain, is comprised of the recurrent images in the male poetic repertoire, lexical clichés and commonly used, stereotypical imagery, combining the poetic fetishisation of woman's body which runs through the canon with a Gaelic resonance based on the author's knowledge of folkloric conventions. Ni Dhomhnaill's description of the lover's skin, for example, is structured as pragmatic repetition based on the associational row of colour and texture progressing from a neutral, seasonal snow, to a more practical, prosaic lime and, further on, to a vivid rural image of flax[3.]

The strategy of employing this trite figurative language, fixed in the oral tradition, clearly brings out the conventionality of male questing and the banality of an unpretentious rural courting in patterns that have been replicated for centuries. But this inanity of rural routine contains the dormant seeds of a pervasive will to conquest. They flourish in the climax of the poem and are associated with a masculine emblematic self-image of a ploughman accompanied by rural, intrusive phallic symbols, and with subjective female images of furrows that relate woman's body to an object of sexual tillage in yet another act in a precarious monodrama of vulnerable femininity assaulted by aggressive masculinity:

Osclaíonn trínse	A trench is opened up
faoi shoc mo chéachta.(80)	by the sock of my plough.(80)

Such male charting of the female body, read as an open space, an uncultivated virgin land that has to be courted and deflowered, equivocally celebrates the act of penetration when a horizontal movement changes its vector and becomes vertical, ingressive, claiming male dominion. By deliberately restricting the poem to a rural background, which in such poets as Patrick Kavanagh signifies a departure from the authority of Yeatsian mythographies, Ní Dhomhnaill constructs a new myth of virility *rusticana*, unsentimentally disabling recognisable tendencies in Irish poetry to romanticise and idealise pastoral pleasures.

The same system of imagery occurs in Michael Longley's 'Furrows' from the Lares' series, a poem with explicit erotic implications, where the images of a woman and the earth are interchangeable.

The title, evoking the Roman deities of cultivated fields, entwines the piece with the unavoidable sexual nature of the body-land connection established in classical times. While metaphorically matching female corporeal parts with landscape features, Longley shapes a wasteland, with scattered 'knuckles' and 'small bones', as if implying that its bareness can be transformed into fertility if properly propitiated, in this case, by the vigorous ploughman whose 'horses stumble' at the end of the furrow. [4]

The semantic structure of 'Furrows' operates within the same lexico-semantic field as in Ní Dhomhnaill's poem. The speaker of

'Amhrán An Fhir Óig / Young Man's Song' reaches the furrow's end with escalating intensity: 'raidim' (80) / 'I buck' (81). Likewise, Longley introduces his stumbling horses in the climactic penultimate line. The appearance of the equine image in male/female relations in both poems is not just a conventional accessory to create a 'rustic' atmosphere. Generally, it is a masculine and 'heroic' symbol *par excellence*. Another source of this image is the ritualistic representation of a king as a stallion with great sexual power in ancient Irish inaugural ceremonies that involved a symbolic act of mating between the king and the land of Ireland. [5] This allusion turns Ní Dhomhnaill's young man into a degenerate descendant of the royalty of ancient lore by providing him with an archetypal counterpart.

Irony is also latent in the young man's monologue when he compares himself to a powerful *púca*, a mighty legendary spirit greatly feared in Ireland, appearing after nightfall to create harm and mischief in the guise of a dark horse with sulphurous yellow eyes, terrifying and destructive. But *púca* can also take the shape of a horse or a bull, a goat or an ass. Though horns of antlered animals represent force and virility and are associated with aggression and lasciviousness, attributing them to a goat diminishes their noble status. In addition, Angela Bourke writes that in some parts of the country *púca*, completely deprived of any sinister connotations, 'is a sort of horse that fouls blackberries every year at Halloween, making them unfit to eat'. [6] In 'Amhrán An Fhir Óig / Young Man's Song', desire for possession completely eradicates any possibility of enjoyment. The young man, like a number of his doppelgängers from other poems by Ní Dhomhnaill, lays claim to the female territory, his claim containing an allusion to the bog, one of Seamus Heaney's complex and ambivalent feminine key-symbols that has 'bottomless' connotation. The tendency to employ generic plot and imagery in an exploration of the morphology of body/land is explicit in both Ní Dhomhnaill's 'Oileán / Island' and Longley's 'Galapagos'. Both poets use a corporeal island as a ready-made framework by projecting open body spaces onto a natural landscape; both invent their body landscapes to undertake metaphoric mappings of the regions of desire; both present a map-like body view. The image of the island itself is underlaid with multiple connotations, for it reflects the Irish insular psychology, it is one of the key symbols of Celtic mythology where it embodies paradise, and has been replicated in the Irish literary heritage since ancient times.

Ní Dhomhnaill's 'Oileán / Island' begins with a panoramic view of the body in the great ocean as seen by the author's cartographic eye. This part of the poem is traditionally romantic in its visual mode. The opening lines of the three initial stanzas form the following structural pattern:

Oileán is ea do chorp / Your body an island (I)
Toibreacha fíoruisce iad t'uisí / Your forehead a spring well (II)
Tá do dhá shúil / mar locha sléibhe / Your eyes / are mountain lakes (III)

Much of its poetical arsenal—trite epithets and metaphors in the manner of established clichéd images—is appropriated from male-authored poetry. Ní Dhomhnaill's subversive analytic mimicry, which allows her to 'quote' freely from different sources, imparts parody to the text. Simultaneously, accumulated water imagery works to dissolve the solidities of conventional imagistic constructions.

If for Longley the traveller is a scientist, even on his way to the islands of enchantment—a sophisticated stranger who celebrates his intellect as he pays tribute to a body/island that is his to explore and discover in terms of masculinist epistemology—for Ní Dhomhnaill, the poetic persona is a romantic sailor. The 'travelling' part of her poem is distinguished by its colour tonality defined. White sails allude to a victorious journey as in the folktale of Céatach, Son of King Cor from Ireland, wherein white sails hoisted on his return from Greece would signal to his wife that he was alive, while black sails would signify his death. Ní Dhomhnaill's speaker is going to navigate under the billowing sails of Irish folkloric imagery, for her description of the boat reproduces the recurrent passage from the legend, 'Art, King of Leister', almost verbatim,[7] thus making the poem a collage of assorted images and textual blocks from oral tradition. Besides, a compressed repetition of the island image at the end, which completes the frame initiated by the opening line of the verse, brings to the surface the associations both with *aisling* and with *immram*, the voyage to the Paradise of the Pagan Irish consistently reappearing on old maps.

In Longley's 'Galapagos', the woman/island correlation may be considered as a double allusion in which both elements are interpreted by each other as in the surrealist game of *l'une dans l'autre*. The poem adds yet another example to an impressive corpus of male poetic production cited and analysed by Theweleit, supporting the scholar's statement that 'in all European literature (and literature influenced by it), desire, if it flows at all, flows in a certain sense *through women*. In some way or other, it always flows in relation to the image of woman.(It is far rarer for it to flow *aimlessly...*)'.[8]

The spatial definition of both poets is based on a cinematic representation of the island; but whereas Ní Dhomhnaill's is a panoramic shot permeated with images of fluidity, Longley's is a tracking one that narrates the body in a fragmentary fashion: 'Breasts, belly, knees, the mouth of Venus'.[9] Longley accentuates conventional symbols of female sexuality, which Ciaran Carson regards as archetypal, claiming them to be immanent to Celtic sensibility. 'The Insular Celts' is a poem about the colonisation of Ireland that also reflects Carson's fascination with maps. His first 'mapmakers' establish their patterns of iconography of the Irish landscape by constructing a 'sexual space' superimposed on the land, which becomes a double-valanced site for acquisition, subordination, and settlement:

> They will come back to the warm earth
> and call it by possessive names...
> to hard hills of stone they will give
> the words for breast ...
> ... to firm plains, flesh ....[10]

These 'topographers' exercise their power of naming, a crucial aspect of both geographical discovery and rituals of conquest, and thus establish their proprietorial claim over the territory, for, as Geoff King suggests, fixing names onto the map is 'an act of conceptual appropriation inseparable from the seizure of the land itself '.[11] By leaving their topographic tracks, they verbalise the uncharted space, converting a land into a coherent corporeal text for generations to read and utilise.

Opposing such surveying techniques in representing the female body, Ní Dhomhnaill romanticises her personal geography, being concerned with forehead, eyes, and eyelashes. As if complying with the convention of patriarchal explications of sexuality that promote body-charting techniques restricted to genitals, Longley seems to apply mapping that is determined in advance. He observes fragmented, disunited/united (by their function in the sexual act) parts of the female body: erotogenic zones, available for male penetration and knowledge. His selectively designed corporeal cartogram in a way resembles medieval portolan charts, used to map small areas for navigation purposes. Although magnetised by an exotic world of Galapagos, Longley's speaker remains a scientist, classifying and categorising as part of his rationalising project. Under his taxonomic eye, a kind of prehistoric life of the instincts emerges: the tortoise, which tends to live almost for ever; the iguana, with stable, unshifting eyes; the night-dwelling lemur. Natural, organic species inhabiting this feminised landscape emphasise its instinctiveness, unconsciousness, and sensuality completely excluding the mental or spiritual. This oscillated, insular world is invaded by its antagonist, a traditionally male protagonist, a scientist whose mind is ready to explore the/a female realm, explicitly emphasising the binary mapping of the masculine, progress-oriented civilisation and the feminised natural unhistorical world. The idea of a triumphant male intellect is intensified by the reference to Darwin's *Beagle*. Longley's scientist is very much like an inquisitive nineteenth-century English gentleman, a focal point in the evolution of the species: under the mythic sails of evolutionary theory, he embarks on an exploratory quest voyage constrained by the limits of a phallogocentric horizon. The poem also resorts to generally accepted use of gender in the discourse of discovery.

While Longley's visual surveillance of island/woman, with desire as surveying instrument, implies latent violence suggested by metaphoric dismemberment, Seamus Heaney's 'Act of Union' shifts into the domain of blatantly inclement politics where the Anglo-Irish relations are represented in terms both of a gendered landscape and of a sexual act:

> ....I caress
> The heaving province where our past has grown.
> I am the tall kingdom over your shoulder
> That you would neither cajole nor ignore.[12]

Female bogland is helplessly prostrated, with no role other than enforced submission, under the gaze and in the possession of the aggressive, warrior-like masculinity of an imperial male speaker. speaker with his assertively active lexicon and syntax. He inflicts pain that is like pulsating explosions within a mined territory, rending, battering, burst[ing]. Besides the pain of childbirth, the description contains a more sexually violent variant of interpretation; that of rape, penetration, ejaculation. The connections among conquest, colonisation, and rape and the employment of the traditional Irish poetic trope of 'the rape of the (female) land by the (male) invader'[13] are made even more explicit in Heaney's poem, 'Ocean's Love to Ireland' with its repetitive pattern of 'possessed and repossessed ... ruined maid'.[14]

Both Heaney's discourse of the perpetrator of violence and Longley's discourse of discovery and desire differ from Ní Dhomhnaill's anthropomorphic island which is not specifically gendered. Her deterritorialisation of sexuality erodes an established grid and nullifies the binarism of masculine and feminine. Her island somehow becomes an island of a manly woman and of a womanly man, to paraphrase James Joyce.[15] Although it is very tempting to read the poem in terms of gender role reversal, in which an autonomous female subject of erotic desire directs and focuses her gaze on a male object, I disagree with Patricia Boyle Haberstroh who insists that 'Oileán / Island' 'describes a man's body', and interprets it as Ní Dhomhnaill's tribute to the 'male muse'.[16] I consider the description to be essentially androgynous if it is compared to other Ní Dhomhnaill poems—those addressed to a man, where she is very frank in emphasising male virility. In a number of poems she delights in assuming different voices and gender roles, teasing her reader with the question, 'Who is speaking to whom?' She thus ensures herself the freedom to trespass assumed gender norms. The poet casts a seductive spell of metaphoric cross-dressing, re-dressing, and transvestism that ultimately leave in suspense the definiteness of such constructs as sex and gender and any fixed character of subject-object relations. But if one wishes to position Ní Dhomhnaill's ambiguous corporeal island gender-wise, a close, monocular reading will provide a number of indications that the body in the ocean is female: first, because the author employs the poetic form of aisling that is already culturally gendered; and second, Ní Dhomhnaill's serene, almost puritanically chaste depiction is disturbed by the metaphor of ploughing, which is recurrent in her poetry and is correlated with the male perspective. Additionally, the image of the spread limbs is associated with the erotic spreading of a woman's legs, and third, the piece contains an abundance of images traditionally associated in male poetry, as Theweleit suggests, with woman as a territory for desire: woman-in-the-water, woman as a cooling stream, woman as a fountain from which man drinks, vagina as wave, love as a sea voyage.[17] Reading from this particular, intertextual perspective calls into question the validity of Haberstroh's view of island/body as Ní Dhomhnaill's tribute to her male muse.

In 'Oileán / Island', Ní Dhomhnaill sails along, to use Cheryl Herr's expression, 'the channels of Irish psychohistory'[18] to Ireland-as-body, utilising a traditional symbolic representation of Ireland as female, which derives from the sovereign goddess figure of Irish native tradition and from its modifications in medieval literature. In seventeenth-century poetry, Ireland was allegorised as woman as a consequence of the suppression of the indigenous Irish culture. Irish poets used this trope to establish a poetic convention where an emblematised female became a sky woman, *spéir bhean*, and the beloved was often substituted for Ireland in love lyrics.

This allegory further evolved into the eighteenth-century classical poetic genre, *aisling*, which evasively allowed for the subversive expression of political dissent through the erotic coding. Moreover, in the interview with Rebecca E. Wilson, Ní Dhomhnaill refers to the female muse. While speaking of this muse's multiple appearances and shapes, she concludes:

> The greatest muse in Ireland is the country—Eire, again seen as a woman, and the whole sovereignty of Ireland. That's what lies deepest in our hearts here in Ireland. There has been an ongoing love affair between the people and the land and the land and the people here for millennia. And we have lavished our imaginations on it until we have projected on to it the depths of our own psyches.[19]

By employing various systems of associated commonplaces that have been operative for centuries, Ní Dhomhnaill slices up and reorders the continuum of tradition. Her positioning of rhetorico-ideological conventions outside of their historical context blurs margins that appeared sharp and inviolable. By putting inherited imagistic and linguistic configurations, conventional poetic genres, archetypes, and folklore back onto her poetic map, she merges the border between oral and written traditions and, correspondingly, between male and female spheres of literary influence.

While re-textualising male models of imagery, Ní Dhomhnaill brings them to an extreme and thus creates implications of collaged travesty. She undertakes a voyage, challenging prefabricated female identities. Her quest narratives are opposed to conquest voyages like Longley's traditional discourse of the explorer who charts the land in a quasi-sexual way; Heaney's enactment of political and colonial suppression both in terms of a gendered landscape and the sexual act; and the map-making practices of Carson's Celtic discoverers who superimposed sexual spaces on the natural landscape and exercised their power of naming while colonising Ireland. Ní Dhomhnaill operates within the framework of a 'minoritarian' map determined by the 'Irishness' of her poetry; the male authors tend to accept majoritarian codes by adopting what Edward Said calls 'a great *topoi* of colonial culture'.[20]

For both Ní Dhomhnaill and the male authors discussed here, there is the final destination of their journeys, the other's territory. For the male writers this territory is the essentialised female body, the body of the other, who becomes a rationale through which male identity (be it sexual, cultural, or national) is defined. This body has become an object of a double aggression to exterior malefactors and interior benefactors. The anthropomorphic, feminised, and sexualised territory/landscape either becomes exposed to a male gaze or is subjected to intrusion. Opposed to this politics of representation, Ní Dhomhnaill's anthropomorphic and geomorphic configurations challenge the gender-bound power dynamic. Her poetry, with its pluridimensional spaces and richly allusive lexico-semantic textures, charts a whole new territory of desire. Ní Dhomhnaill crosses patrolled borders of male poetic domains to engage in the conversion of her assemblages, her citations, imitations, and reworkings of a wide range of literary conventions, themes, images, and tropes, into a new discursive form.

NOTES

[1] Klaus Theweleit, *Male Fantasies. Volume 1: Women, Floods, Bodies, History*, trans. Stephen Conway in collaboration with Erica Carter and Chris Turner, Minneapolis 1987, 359.

[2] Catherine Nash, 'Remapping the Body/Land: New Cartographies of Identity, Gender, and Landscape in Ireland', in Alison Blunt and Gillian Rose, eds, *Writing Women and Space: Colonial and Postcolonial Geographies*, New York and London 1994, 244.

[3] Nuala Ní Dhomhnaill, *Selected Poems / Rogha Dánta*, trans. Michael Hartnet, Dublin 1988, 80. Further references are to this edition and are given in the text in parentheses.

[4] Michael Longley, *Poems 1963 - 1983*, Edinburgh and Dublin 1985, 62.

[5] Miranda Green, *Animals in Celtic Life and Myth*, London and New York 1992, 187.

[6] Angela Bourke, 'Language, Stories, Healing', in Anthony Breadley and Maryann Gialanella Valiulis, eds, *Gender and Sexuality in Modern Ireland*, Amherst, Massachusetts 1997, 301.

7. Sean O'Sullivan, ed. and trans., *Folktales of Ireland*, Chicago and London 1966. The description is replicated three times in the text of the legend (99, 101, 107).

8. Theweleit, *op. cit.*, 272.

9. Longley, *op. cit.*, 69.

10. Ciaran Carson, 'The Insular Celts', in John Montague, ed., *The Faber Book of Irish Verse*, London 1974, 379.

11. Geoff King, *Mapping Reality: An Exploration of Cultural Cartographies*, New York 1996, 28.

12. Seamus Heaney, *North*, London and Boston 1975, 49.

13. Steven Matthews, *Irish Poetry: Politics, History, Negotiation. The Evolving Debate, 1969 to the Present*, London 1997, 119.

14. Heaney; *op. cit.*, 47.

15. Declan Kiberd, *Inventing Ireland*, Cambridge, Massachusetts 1995, 344.

16. Patricia Boyle Haberstroh, *Women Creating Women: Contemporary Irish Women Poets*, Syracuse 1996, 186.

17. Theweleit, *op. cit.*, 283

18. Cheryl Herr, 'The Erotics of Irishness', *Critical Inquiry*, 17 (1990), 7.

19. Rebecca E. Wilson, 'Nuala Ní Dhomhnaill', in Gillean Somerville-Arjat and Rebecca Wilson, eds, *Sleeping with Monsters: Conversations with Scottish and Irish Women Poets,* Edinburgh 1990, 153.

20. Edward Said, *Culture and Imperialism*, New York 1994, 30.

'Shifting Ground': The Object and Post-Colonialism in Eavan Boland's Poetry

ERIN V. OBERMUELLER

In her book *Object Lessons*, Eavan Boland writes that 'the way to the past is never smooth. ... Every step towards an origin is also an advance towards a silence'.[1] Pursuing a personal past or a national past for the post-colonial Irish subject is the work of reconstructing and restoring. But, as Boland poignantly remarks, silences and absences mystify the path. Her solution is to 'make free with the past' by piecing together fragments and silences into a history.

David Lloyd suggests that the role of the national poet is wrought with the dangerous assumption that he or she ought to create a 'sense of Irish identity that would transcend historically determined cultural and political differences and form the reconciliatory centre of national unity'.[2] Lloyd importantly illustrates that 'fetishization' of the lost culture accompanies this unified image and transforms the Gaelic past into a primitive, regressive culture. Furthermore, this narrative of national unity legitimises the imperial project by glossing over the ruptures and discontinuities in Irish history as caused by the alien British influence. Anyone who participates in the discourse of Irish nationalism, then, inevitably bears the responsibility of revealing the fractured experience. In her poem 'The Harbour', Boland acknowledges this challenge of representing the complexity of a personal and national past. She writes:

I am your citizen: composed of

your fictions, your compromise, I am
a part of your story and its outcome.
And ready to record its contradictions.[3]

How does Boland record the contradictions? One significant
way is through her use of the cultural object. Boland employs
engravings, jewelry, paintings, statues, maps, and souvenirs to
structure an overt confrontation with history. Furthermore, she
takes potentially abstract concepts such as 'colony' and
'language' and renders them tangible by translating them into
objects and highlighting their external structures. Her poetry has
the quality of an art installation that enacts what Luke Gibbons
describes as 'different registers of memory'.[4] Here, the official
versions of history sealed in museums and monuments are
countered by examples of a heterogeneous collective memory. In
his work on post-colonial Irish identity, Gibbons cites two
exhibits, one by Philip Napier and the other by Alice Maher,
which combine media that signify various strains of Irish history
such as Irish music, hunger strikers, and pre-famine women's
labour. The exhibits unlock codified representations of Irish
history and foreground the disjunctions within the art object. So
too does Boland use objects because of their ability to house
'different registers of memory'. She says in an interview:

> I'm interested in how [objects] really are fractured pieces
> of a dialogue about power. An object has no power but
> often is a part of power —whether it's a status symbol or a
> doll or an ornament or a piece of gold. ... When you look
> at objects you're really looking at failed witnesses: they
> can't speak but they were there.[5]

The objects offer a perfect site for negotiating identity; they are
fragments produced by particular cultural conditions and are now
imported to another set of circumstances.

Boland investigates the way that knowledge arises out of
exchange between the present and the past. She uses the object to

go 'beyond' the present, not in the sense of a linear step to the future, but to travel within the past and return to a present which has been displaced by the act of travel. In a visit to an installation that explored such 'in-between' moments, Homi Bhabha explains:

> such art does not merely recall the past as social cause or aesthetic precedent; it renews the past, refiguring it as a contingent 'in-between' space, that innovates and interrupts the performance of the present. The 'past-present' becomes part of the necessity, not the nostalgia, of living.[6]

When applied to Boland's work, we see that she gives us a version of 'now' that is unstable and purposefully transformable.

Her emphasis on the transformation of the present is an indication of 'the ability to shift the ground of knowledges', or to engage in the 'war of the position,' to mark 'the establishment of new forms of meaning, and strategies of identification' (Bhabha 162). I would like to focus on the 'shifting ground' in Boland's poetry, particularly in the ways she uses objects to embody the fractures of post-colonial experience. Other critics have explored a 'dual postcolonialism' or the feminisation of masculine forms in Boland's poetry, both of which attend to the development of an Irish female identity inside the realm of Irish literature.[7] Whereas I do not discount the idea that Boland offers a version of the Irish woman that is perhaps more representative than the myth-making female iconicity of the male Irish canon, I believe that Boland is less concerned with illustrating marginality than she is with the 'the "middle passage" of contemporary culture' which 'is a process of displacement and disjunction that does not totalize experience'(Bhabha 5). We see this disjunction framed in the space of an object where the past-present dwells. By utilising these localised images of culture, Boland resists the temptation of the national poet to give us a unified national identity and instead specifies the contemporary transitional subjectivity. She places us 'in the middle of things' through a rupture which is read as both a physical split and a shift in knowledge. Her poetry embodies the shifting process that creates post-colonial identity by narrating a space of the past that transforms the present.

The poem 'Object Lessons' most directly dramatises the act of fracturing the mythical past to interrupt the present. Boland uses an everyday object, a coffee mug inscribed with a pastoral hunting scene, as an avenue towards a better understanding of the disjunctions of Irish history and contemporary existence. The scene on the mug is unified and seamless: a huntsman kissing a maiden in a fertile meadow ornamented by wine jugs and a singing thrush. The innocence of the image is replicated in the locale of the poem, a new house where a young couple unpacks and anxiously anticipates the future. However, the maiden signifies 'land ... before disaster/ strikes,' a vulnerable terrain that can be violated.[8] When the mug breaks, the land (figured in the woman) suffers a metaphorical rape. The fractured mug resembles the fracturing of the Irish culture by British colonial rule, dismembering the Irish past. Boland's poem comments both on the mythical quality of the 'original' past as well as its fragmentation by intrusion. It also captures the 'the shiver / of presentiment' of the present scene, displacing the young couples' knowledge about their life (23). The broken pieces lie on the floorboards that were never sanded or varnished and thus stand unprotected from this intrusive 'disaster'. Boland uses the mode of colonisation—fracturing a culture—as a mode of knowing the past. The object lesson then is a personal example for the young couple (that idyllic love eventually breaks open) as well as a history lesson that articulates how a land can be violated by a huntsman and break apart. The object comes to occupy what Gayatri Spivak describes as the 'most negotiated position ... because you must intervene even as you inhabit those structures'.[9] It holds captive the scene of the hunt and ruptures itself so as to re-inscribe the story of its making.

Other post-colonial theorists recognise this duality of inhabiting and intervening in dominant structures. In the introduction to their book, *The Nature and Context of Minority*

Discourse, Abdul R. JanMohamed and David Lloyd discuss ways in which minority discourses resist the practices and values of hegemonic culture. They claim that:

> one aspect of the struggle... is the recovery and mediation of cultural practices that continue to be subjected to 'institutional forgetting', which, as a form of control of one's memory and history, is one of the gravest forms of damage done to minority cultures. Archival work, as a form of counter-memory, therefore is essential to the critical articulation of minority discourse.[10]

Such a recovery mission or 'archival work' allows the interpellated individual, namely the post-colonial subject, to redefine the terms of his or her existence. The project of remembering is intrinsic to Boland's understanding of the post-colonial condition and appears in many of her poems. Boland emphasises in 'The Emigrant Irish' the assimilative habit of erasure, the forgetting of the past: 'Like oil lamps, we put them out the back—// of our houses, of our minds' (*OH* 108). After this sobering reminder, Boland writes:

> that their possessions may become our power:
>
> Cardboard. Iron. Their hardships parcelled in them.
> Patience. Fortitude. Long-suffering
> in the bruise-colored dusk of the New World.
>
> And all the old songs. And nothing to lose.(*OH* 108)

She insists that reclaiming the objects of old transforms one's present condition. Boland articulates the very process that JanMohamed and Lloyd describe: the loss of history, both conscious and sublimated, and the retrieval of that history. The subtext suggests that there are master narratives at work, such as the celebrated 'progress' of modernity and the unified national

Irish identity that seeks to submerge incongruities and render the Irish past as 'backward' and unnecessary. Boland attempts to establish a counter memory by highlighting the freeplay between the past and the present within the space of the artifacts. She invokes parcels of 'hardships' as a way of objectifying experience, packaging it for recovery. In the poem, the object of the 'oil lamp' elides with our 'lights' and thus formulates a space for the past-present.

Boland also captures the method of remembering in her poem 'That the Science of Cartography is Limited'. The poem embodies a series of confrontations with cultural objects. First, the speaker and her companion travel to the 'borders of Connacht' and enter a wood. [11] This position on the 'edge' suggests an aptitude for rewriting the past as one is nearest the conditions for shifting knowledge. As a cultural symbol, the famine road conjures up many signifieds. It is a heteroglot object that allows us to encounter the Irish past more directly. Cultural theorist Iain Chambers asserts that in contemporary experience we 'migrate across a system that is too vast to be our own, but in which we are fully involved'—a condition he describes as a hybrid state.[12] He explains, 'the tension, the gap, between *different symbolic regimes and their shared occupation of the same signs* simultaneously draws us into historical specificity and potential communalities'.[13] The famine road leads us to the historical specifics, that in '1847, when the crop had failed twice,/ Relief Committees gave/ the starving Irish such roads to build.// Where they died the road ended'(*TV* 7). The road embodies contrarieties: that of British imperial power and their warped version of 'relief'; and the starved Irish subjects building roads, a labour which would help to kill them. The sharing of the same sign by different regimes creates a gap, the 'border' that the post-colonial Irish stand upon. It brings a 'communality' in the sense that the present of the poem, in the internal plot and the external reading of it, is now transformed by confronting the past. The present subject can re-member the map as a result of the encounter.

A fine example of how Boland shifts the meaning of an object to confront the past occurs in her poem 'Imago'. Here, Boland begins with a catalogue of objects:

> Head of a Woman. Half-Life of a nation.
> Coarsely-cut blackthorn walking stick.
> Old Tara brooch.
> And bog oak.
> A harp and a wolfhound on an ashtray. *(LL 21)*

We bluntly confront the objects as recognisable images of Irishness, the commodified national identity. Boland then rewrites their meanings. In a counter-hegemonic act, she displays the ideology of this 'anti-art: a foul skill/ traded by history/ to show a colony// how to make pain a souvenir' *(LL 21)*. Here, the signifier takes on a new signified as Boland exposes the apparatus of nationalism. David Lloyd, in his article 'Nationalisms against the State', investigates the ideology of '[mobilizing] the populace through appeal to cultural or ethnic identity posed against modernity'.[14] He later describes how this attempt at creating traditional images to unify a nation achieves a 'vertical integration' based on 'political solidarity against a common enemy rather than a horizontal integration based on class antagonisms'.[15] The objects in Boland's poem represent this production of national identity; they are the conduit for Lloyd's vertical integration. Yet, the objects now represent a very different history from that originally intended because they reveal the irony of building a national identity by making 'pain a souvenir'. The resignification of the objects marks Boland's method as post-colonial, as Gayatri Spivak suggests that the 'general mode for the post-colonial is citation, re-inscription, re-routing the historical'.[16] Boland re-routes an object's historical significance, which inevitably transforms the present way of knowing Irish national identity.

The shifts in Boland's poetry—the breaking out of the interpellated subject position—is a mode of resistance against a

containment of identity by the British centre. Homi Bhabha aptly
warns of marginalised cultures: 'it is ... the demand that, in
analytic terms, it be always the good object of knowledge, the
docile body of difference, that reproduces a relation of
domination' (Bhabha 31). Boland recognises the docility of the
Irish Other as a chief enabler of replicating the power structure;
she therefore writes against the 'docile body' and makes the body
speak. In her poem 'Lava Cameo', Boland imagines real bodies,
those of her grandparents, and makes those bodies the poet's
place to carve an identity from the Irish past. Her method is
comparable to creating an image, a beautiful face, out of a
substance that has covered the ground and even damaged or
destroyed the past. The process of making a cameo carries
through to making a story of our ancestors:

> except that it is not a story,
> more a rumor or a folk memory,
> something thrown out once in a random conversation;
> a hint merely. (*TV* 46)

Boland begins with very little then, a hint of a story like a slab of
volcanic rock. But this open field empowers the speaker and
allows a reworking of history in which the docile body breaks
free. The cultural object is a terrain of possibility for Boland as
she explains the methodology of shifting ground:

> there is a way of making free with the past
> a pastiche of what is
> real and what is
> not, which only can be
> justified if you think of it
> not as sculpture but as syntax:
> a structure extrinsic to meaning which uncovers
> the inner secret of it. (*TV* 46)

The pastiche is an object of freedom that narrates a past that may or may not have happened. Boland's method of encounter relies upon syntax, a system of representation more malleable and transformable than a sculpture of volcanic rock. The text of the cameo—extrinsic to meaning—allows for the inscription of meaning that history imbues. Boland imagines that the past directs the present as the speaker of the poem asks the woman to 'show' her 'the obduracy of an art which can/ arrest a profile in the flux of hell.// Inscribe catastrophe' (*TV* 47). It is the obduracy or the unyielding quality of art that will allow Boland to read the contradictions of the past and form a threatening body of knowledge. For post-colonial history, this means taking the damaged terrain (the volcanic rock) and re-constructing a present based on an encounter with a past.

Boland further pushes the obduracy of art by actually placing the present inside a cultural artifact representing the past. 'An Old Steel Engraving' literally embodies the transformable now. In it, Boland gives us two images: the first is that of a wounded patriot who is helped by a passerby; the second is a revision of the first, which includes contemporary participants. She writes of the first image: 'this hand which can barely raise/ the patriot/ above the ground which is/ the origin and reason for it all' (*OH* 45). The ground figures in the scene as an impetus for action, as the 'Helen of Troy' for the patriot and the passerby.[17] Later, the ground is replaced by 'spaces on the page. They widen/ to include us' (*OH* 45). Now, the present 'us' is implicated in the scene of the battle for land. The spaces also become the realm of history where

nothing can move until we find the word,
nothing can stir until we say this is
what happened and is happening and history
is one of us who turns away
while the other is
turning the page. (*OH* 45)

The agency of the land is quelled until the *present* subject narrates the nation. Importantly, this story will be about 'what happened and is happening' in an ongoing dialectic between the past and present circumstances. Like the famine road, Boland attempts to describe the historical incongruities mapped into a post-colonial space and tell the double story of one turning away and the other 'turning the page.' Thus, we become figures in the object of history—a steel engraving—and engage in the process of negotiating an identity within the new position.

It is this shifting of the ground of knowledge within the space of the past-present that leads Iain Chambers to write:

> Our previous sense of knowledge, language and identity, our peculiar inheritance, cannot be simply rubbed out of the story, cancelled. What we have inherited—as culture, as history, as language, as tradition, as a sense of identity—is not destroyed but taken apart, opened up to questioning, rewriting and re-routing.[18]

Chambers outlines the terms of the post-colonial project: the past cannot be erased or severed from the present but it can be opened and reworked. That we find ourselves 'making free with the past' in Boland's poetry is not surprising; she has inscribed the 'catastrophe' and turned the page of history. Chambers further argues that 'identity is formed on the move'.[19] As part of this identity formation we see what Homi Bhabha calls dissemination, where 'the performative introduces a temporality of the "in-between"' and 'the nation split[s] within itself' (Bhabha 148). Here, a most profound intervention takes place, in that post-colonial subjects work against homogeneous self-representation of their nation. This is an internal fracturing which carves the 'middle ground' for the emergence of new forms of knowledge. The splitting is a fundamental activity in the post-colonial epistemology, for to negotiate one's past and to intervene in current structures require a dislocation and the creation of a new space. The ways in which Boland's work registers this split are mapped onto localised cultural artifacts and are also apparent in her objectification of concepts such as 'colony' and 'language'. She emphasises their external structures and the gaps within them.

In her many poems about the colonial space, Boland clearly marks borders and edges, imagining an actual 'split'. For example, in her poem 'The Mother Tongue' she discusses the idea of dividing land. The poem begins with the image of 'the old pale ditch' which is also 'a line drawn in rain/ and clay and the roots of wild broom' *(LL* 21). Boland illustrates the physical separation of land, which in essence forms a colony's boundaries. However, she also shows us how the boundary has changed: what was 'the ancient barrier of mud and brambles/...is now a mere rise of coarse grass' *(LL* 21). The doubleness in the boundary is a representation of other splits in the nation. Boland highlights these by listing Irish patriots whose names can be said 'two ways' and who are the representatives of those 'who came to the limits of this boundary' *(LL* 21). Both the colonial and post-colonial subjects arrive at the edge that allows for the shifting of knowledges between the alien influence and the colonised Irish and also between the colonial and post-colonial. As Bhabha explains:

> the space of a modern nation-people is never simply horizontal. Their metaphoric movement requires a kind of 'doubleness' in writing; a temporality of representation that moves between cultural formations and social processes without a central causal logic (Bhabha 141).

Boland's poem shows this multi-dimensional space in the sense that a present scene of a mother and child is drawn atop the scene of the battle for land. The speaker's 'forked tongue of a colony' signifies the linguistic splitting of a nation, further complicated by the dream of an 'undivided speech' *(LL* 21). The transfer and transformation of knowledge along the dividing ditch illustrates the way in which the 'split' reveals itself in the objects of the post-colonial context and encounters history.

The images of a wound and scar appear repeatedly in Boland's poetry and are perhaps the best examples of how she literalises the splitting of the national subject. 'The Scar', for example, first describes a young child whose 'skin felt different' after being cut by glass and healing *(LL* 22). Boland suggests that the nation's identity, like the child's skin, feels different after the cut. However, she also posits that the colony is still a 'wound' that hasn't healed. The colony is an opening, vulnerable and tender, that has yet to find a restorative. It knows no answers to the question: 'After such injuries,/ what difference do we feel?' *(LL* 22) One way to read the 'wound' in Boland's poetry is to see it as what Bhabha calls the 'supplementary question' (Bhabha 155). The supplement gathers and accumulates meanings, while simultaneously adding to the original; in Derridaen terms it differs and 'defers'. Bhabha explains that 'coming "after" the original, or in "addition to" it, gives the supplementary question the advantage of introducing a sense of "secondariness" or belatedness into the structure of the original demand...it may disturb the calculation' (Bhabha 155). For Boland's colony, one may see that the wound holds those qualities of coming after the original, or disturbing modes of order. The wound weakens the body (the colony) but also threatens its unified sense. The Gaelic past and the fabricated notion of homogeneous national experience are *supplemented* (and thus displaced) by the wound. Boland also offers the granite statue of Anna Liffey as the supplementary question to the river which 'hides// the long ships, the muskets and the burning domes.// Everything but this momentary place' *(LL* 21). The river covers history only to be recovered in the 'flawed head' of Anna Liffey that stares at the head of the speaker *(LL* 21). The cultural object—the 'emblem of this old// torn and traded city'—breaks the seamless flow of the river *(LL* 21). The supplementary questions posed by the wound and statue make the entry of new meaning possible. They seek to locate identity not in a transcendental signified but in the negotiation of the historic past and present. The questions disrupt causal logic and call attention to the 'differences' in the skin that are present in the wound and will be present in the scar.

The 'colony' is disruptive in the sense that it itself slips in meanings. We see it as a wound, but also find that it is an argument or a place of making meaning. In 'Witness', Boland asserts that the contemporary voice of the colony embodies 'The men and women/ they dispossessed'*(LL* 18). This is a clear example of the past-present inside a contemporary national subject. Boland further develops the idea of historical figures speaking through present figures in her closing rhetorical question:

> What is a colony
> if not the brutal truth
> that when we speak
> the graves open
> And the dead walk? *(LL* 21)

Boland foregrounds the conjunction between the present and past here, and directly challenges the notion that a colony is somehow free from its history. As we have seen in Chambers's and Bhabha's works, the idea that the past is not *in* the present is a misrepresentation of post-colonial experience. Boland shows that we cannot exist in the middle ground of post-colonial Ireland without reaching for the objects of the past to inform a present identity. In this way, the docile body of knowledge is used as that potent supplement for the order which submerges the past. Boland suggests that the very nature of the colony is to hear and see the dead simultaneously with the living. It is that scene that reveals the splitting of the nation within itself.

Boland insists on hybridity within poetic structures in the same way that she insists on splitting an object so that the past-present can dwell within it. I am careful here not to suggest that post-colonialism 'is more of an abstraction available for figurative deployment in any strategic redefinition of marginality'[20] as applied, for example, to the marginalised role of a female poet. Boland's post-colonialism does intersect with her feminist methodology but not as 'a free-floating metaphor for cultural embattlement'.[21] Gender participates in the 'cultural embattlement' that Boland articulates in the shifts and displacements within the space of language. Language is the object that Boland has reclaimed for the female post-colonial subject, in her poem 'Mise Eire' (*OH* 78-79). The title, Gaelic for 'I am Ireland', followed by the line 'I won't go back to it' in English, sets up a confrontation between language forms which explores the role of language in national identity (*OH* 78). David Lloyd's work on the history of the language split is pertinent:

> Irish nationalism thus emerges at the moment of virtual eclipse of what would have been its 'natural' language, and mainly among a [middle] class which was already, necessarily, estranged from that language. The peculiar forms taken by Irish nationalism develop from this vividly apprehended dislocation and from the consequent absence of the political legitimation available to other European nationalisms through the putatively a priori transcendent unity of a national language.[22]

Lloyd explains how the fall of a 'natural language' results in a nationalism that is built on a dislocation. Ireland's colonial national identity is from the beginning 'split' because of the linguistic divide between English and Irish within its own populace. Boland points out the 'peculiar forms' of Irish nationalism: 'old dactyls,' 'oaths,' 'songs,' and 'words' that 'bandage up the history' and 'make a rhythm of the crime// where time is time past' (*OH* 78). These forms of language are the objects she ruptures. In addition she rejects their representations of Ireland as a (masculine) atavistic 'land of the Gulf Stream' and 'small farm' (*OH* 78). She shifts this history by introducing two images of women who don't figure into the given national picture; she also intervenes in the current structure of the poem to make it a space for the past-present. Boland writes, 'I am the woman—/the sloven's mix/ of silk at the wrists' (*OH* 78). The fact that woman is a 'mix' signifies the hybridity of national identity that is inherent in the colonial and post-colonial subject. She highlights the 'beyondness' of contemporary existence by using the present tense 'I am' for the female historic person. Then, 'the quick frictions/ the rictus of delight' (*OH* 78), for which the woman gets paid emphasises Gibbons's collective 'register of memory'[23] in the sense that it re-members a historical act which is not present in the former object (the dactyl and songs).   Boland returns to the issue of language loss and formation in her second image of an Irish woman. Placed on a ship, this woman is an immigrant who holds a 'half-dead baby' to her:

  She is a person,
mingling the immigrant
guttural with the vowels
of homesickness who neither
knows nor cares that

a new language
is a kind of scar
and heals after a while
into a passable imitation
of what went before. (*OH* 79)

The hybridity of speech here, its 'mingling' qualities, suggest the rupture and displacement of the old language by the new. A shift takes place in the process of breaking and healing as English is seen as a 'passable imitation' of the Gaelic language which preceded it.[24] Boland makes a meta-text on her own craft (her object) in the sense that we read her language as a scar. The properties of that scar recall the 'wound' of the colony and literally figure a split in an object (the poem) and its meaning. Boland looks at both national languages and poetic forms and how they house versions of history. She breaks these open and reinscribes them through a female figure of the past-present.

Boland further meditates on language itself in her poem 'Habitable Grief' *(LL* 32). She now turns her focus to the absence and loss that is inherent in language rather than focusing on the 'bandaged' meaning. The absence appears on many levels. First, the speaker is physically removed from Ireland: 'Long ago/ I was a child in a strange country:// I was Irish in England' *(LL* 32). There, the speaker learns the 'lingua franca of a lost land' *(LL* 32). The idea of a common language for the Irish is a vexed issue, especially since this *lingua franca* is learned in and imported from another country. Ireland becomes 'lost' in this acquisition of language that ironically subverts the idea of unity which a *lingua franca* promotes. Boland comments on this fragmentation when she says that this dialect holds 'that contrary passion/ to be whole'*(LL* 32). Language reflects the desire for a unified national identity, but for Boland that unity is unachievable. Instead, the losses which language represents become its chief quality. Boland describes language as a 'habitable grief,' suggesting that it is the absence (the thing we grieve for) which is where we dwell in language. The space of absence is physically objectified in the poem. The line 'of losses such as this'*(LL* 32) is followed by exactly that: loss. There is nothing listed but empty space on the page to illustrate what we have lost in acquiring a new language. Importantly, Boland uses the image of the 'scar' again to show how we adapt to such gaps, covering and healing so as to make a new self. She ends the poem by saying that the loss/grief/scar 'heals just enough to be a nation' *(LL* 32). Boland posits that the object of absence is a necessary part of post-colonial identity and that when we break open language we find not only meanings inscribed but also gaps where meanings might have been.

Boland's shifting of the ground of knowledges is heightened by her use of absence. She is able to present the many dimensions of post-colonial experience by focusing on gaps and spaces within a structure. As her poem 'Fruit on a Straight-Sided

Tray' suggests of the fruit, 'the true subject is the space between them' (*OH* 148). This is Boland's most literal embodiment of absence as object as she focuses her poem on the meaning of the 'in-between'. The poem also offers an interesting parallel to the art installations described at the beginning of this essay as Boland discusses the process of creating an object (the painting) through representing other objects (fruit and space). She calls the situating of fruit on a tray the 'assembly of possibilities;/ a deliberate collection of cross purposes' (*OH* 148). The possible meanings are heterogeneous but still held in a 'collection', much as a colony embodies a hybrid existence. Boland works against a traditional reading of a painting as she shifts the meaning from what it literally represents to that which exists on the edges and in between. Furthermore, she talks about a painting that is still in the stage of 'becoming,' which helps to emphasise the process of negotiation in a liminal space.

The poem eventually comes to the conclusion that the 'study of absences' is a 'geometry of the visible, physical tryst/ between substances, disguising for a while the equation/ that kills' (*OH* 148). Boland pushes us past the 'tryst' and asks us to consider its consequences, that 'you are my child and between us are// spaces, distances. Growing to infinities' (*OH* 148). The spaces do not stay static or small but rather multiply. Boland's use of the parent and child relationship helps to dramatise what is lost in the growing gap as the child moves towards defining an individual identity apart from the parent. Relationships change in this liminal space. The study of absence can kill but it also can bring a realisation of one's identity in relation to another. Gayatri Spivak articulates the difficulty of describing that identity and its space of origin: 'No one can quite articulate the space she herself inhabits. My attempt has been to describe this relatively ungraspable space in terms of what might be its history.'[25] So too has Boland attempted to historicise the space of the present, the gap between the many polarities of post-colonial existence. She articulates it by objectifying absence and reading its splits and trysts.

The emphasis on the space between objects, a liminality that produces a post-colonial identity, resides within the cultural object. These objects are physical and conceptual signs of the ways in which post-colonial identity rises out of a split. They directly reflect the contradictory substance of the middle space that supplements and defers meaning. Boland's role as a national poet is to explore national identity through the realm of the 'in-between'. She claims:

> The Irish nation, materializing in the songs and ballads of these centuries, is a sequence of improvised images. These songs, these images, wonderful and terrible and memorable as they are, propose for a nation an impossible task: to be at once an archive of defeat and a diagram of victory.[26]

Here, Boland suggests that the reified forms of national identity hold within them an (impossible) exchange between defeat and victory. As a self-proclaimed 'fictional interventionist,'[27] she suggests that to know the present one must excavate the past, and shift the present through this excavation. This is an act of improvisation. The objects in her poetry bear witness to the multifarious experience of the post-colonial Irish. Boland interrogates these artifacts and objectifies abstract concepts in order to re-member a past and transform a present. Thus, the 'sequence of improvised images'—these signs of culture—shift the ground of knowledge and invite intervention via the splits, the trysts, and the 'assembly of possibilities' (*OH* 148).

NOTES

[1.]   Eavan Boland, *Object Lessons: The Life of the Woman and the Poet in Our Time*, New York 1995, 23-24.

2. David Lloyd, *Anomalous States: Irish Writing and the Post-Colonial Moment*, Durham 1993, 35.

3. Eavan Boland, *The Lost Land*, New York 1998, 16-17. Further references are to this edition and are given in the text as '*LL*' followed by the page number.

4. Luke Gibbons, *Transformations in Irish Culture*, South Bend 1996, 172.

5. Eavan Boland, Interview with Margaret Mills Harper, *Five Points*, Winter 1997, 87-105.

6. Homi Bhabha, *The Location of Culture*, New York 1994, 7. Further references are to this edition and are given in the text as 'Bhabha' followed by the page number.

7. See Rose Atfield's article 'Postcolonialism in the Poetry and Essays of Eavan Boland', *Women:A Cultural Review*, 8.2 (1997), 168-182, for her exploration of a dual postcolonialism. See also Kerry Robertson's article 'Anxiety, Influence, Tradition and Subversion in the Poetry of Eavan Boland', *Colby Quarterly*, 30.4 (1994), for an examination of Boland's revision and subversion of (male) poetic conventions.

8. Eavan Boland, *Outside History: Selected Poems 1980-1990*, New York 1990, 22-23. Further references are to this edition and are given in the text as '*OH*' followed by the page number.

9. Gayatri Spivak, 'The Post-colonial Critic', in Sarah Harasym, ed., *The Post-colonial Critic: Interviews, Strategies, Dialogues. Gayatri Chakravorty Spivak*, New York 1990, 72.

10. Abdul R. JanMohamed and David Lloyd, 'Introduction: Toward a Theory of Minority Discourse: What Is To Be Done?' in Abdul R. JanMohamed and David Lloyd, eds., *The Nature and Context of Minority Discourse*, Oxford 1990, 6.

11. Evan Boland, *In a Time of Violence*, New York 1994, 7-8. Further references are to this edition and are given in the text as '*TV*' followed by the page number.

12. Iain Chambers, *Migrancy, Culture, Identity*, London 1994, 14.

13. *Ibid.*, 14, italics mine.

14. David Lloyd, 'Nationalisms against the State' in Lisa Lowe and David Lloyd, eds., *The Politics of Culture in the Shadow of Capitalism*, Durham 1997, 175.

15. *Ibid.*, 176.

16. Quoted in Chambers, *op.cit.*, 23.

17. It is worth noting that the conflicts in Irish history have been cast as a battle for 'Mother Ireland' and land is described as a mythical female not unlike Helen.

18. Chambers, *op. cit.*, 24.

19. *Ibid.*, 25.
20. Sara Suleri, 'Woman Skin Deep: Feminism and the Postcolonial Condition', *Critical Inquiry*, 18:3 (1992), 759.
21. *Ibid.*, 759.
22. Lloyd, *Anomalous States, op. cit.*, 44.
23. Gibbons, *op.cit.*, 172.
24. I do not mean to suggest that the Irish language is lost today (nor does Boland, I believe), as poets like Nuala Ní. Dhomhnaill eloquently illustrate its vitality.
25. Spivak, *op.cit.*, 68.
26. Boland, *Object Lessons, op. cit.*, 129.
27. *Ibid.*, 10.

'To Cry with Terror':

Crossing the Ultimate Border in Chris Lee's

The Map Maker's Sorrow

DONALD E. MORSE

'I began to cry with terror at the blankness of me, and
the blankness of the world.'
Alan Garner, *The Voice that Thunders: Essays and
Lectures*[1]

Albert Camus famously asserted in *The Myth of Sisyphus and Other
Essays* that 'Judging whether life is or is not worth living amounts to
answering the fundamental question of philosophy'.[2]   But this
question of staying within or crossing over that ultimate boundary
between life and death remains coldly abstract if raised and considered without regard for individual case histories. Examining individual examples of suicide leads to the disquieting realisation that
chemical or pharmacological imbalance, emotional or psychological
disturbance, delusional or fantastic threats usually play a far greater
role in the person's decision to end life than any philosophical con-
siderations. 'The world I am living in now,' wrote the Japanese
writer Ryuunosulke Akutagawa who was paranoid and highly delusional, 'is the icily transparent universe of sickly nerves. ... Of
course, I do not want to die, but it is suffering to live'.[3] Akutagawa's
suicide, prompted in part by his delusion of having maggots in his
food, does answer the 'fundamental question in philosophy' for him.

For life under such agonising circumstances proved insupportable. Yet his example may at best suggest the unfathomable nature and variety of humans rather than answer questions about the worth or lack of it in life. Martin Amis offers an alternative approach in suggesting that 'Suicide is a mind-body problem that ends violently and without any winner'.[4]

It is this 'problem,' this raw wound, this unanswered and unanswerable question that the Irish playwright Chris Lee explores in *The Map Maker's Sorrow* (1999)[5] through having an older child wilfully and knowingly take his own life. Jason, son of Morag and Henry, decides coldly and quite deliberately to kill himself. 'At the moment I'm attempting to decide on the best method ... Hanging is most likely the best way' (42), he tells an acquaintance the week before his death. His is no random accidental death, nor is it one caused by some inexplicable 'act of God,' but by his inability to believe he is 'worth saving' (44).

Although Lee deals with this important, often unacknowledged social problem of young adult suicide, he uses this occasion—somewhat in the manner of Thornton Wilder in *Our Town* (1938) and Jean-Paul Sartre in *Huis Clos* (1947)—to discuss larger issues of the place of death in contemporary society and the ultimate relation of death to life. There is an observable paradox in contemporary society of people living longer yet with a great increase in numbers and rates of suicides.[6] At the end of act one, Death updates the traditional image of life as an arrow coming from the past and going into the future, moving from birth through life to death.

> It might be said that a life is fixed like a line on a map of space-time. Science says there is fate. Quantum mechanics, on the other hand, celebrates the chaos of unpredictability, ... a life is like a sub-atomic particle. You can never know where it will be if you also want to know how fast it's moving (54).

Through the figure of Death and her soliloquies, the play exfoliates out to include 'Death the nightmare' of contemporary society and 'Death the mystery' (6)—the ultimate mystery of life and death in the cosmos of space-time.

'We live in an old chaos of the sun'[7]—that is, we live life with unpredictability. Only with hindsight do the pieces fall into place in the puzzle of Jason's suicide and even then those left behind have mostly unanswered questions. According to Death, for Jason 'All sorrow lies in the past. There is no future. And the present is closing its eyes' (88). For his parents, Morag and Henry, there is a life to grieve and 'No one tells you how to grieve' (88). When Morag says to Henry 'Let's cry. Let's start from there' (90)—the last line heard in the Peacock production—she is suggesting that their tears will slowly wash grief away, leaving memory and love (90). Her admonition becomes strengthened through the last scene in the published text of *The Map Maker's Sorrow* where Death urges humans to accept their and others' death as the natural end of all life, including that of the suicide. Unfortunately the Peacock production sacrificed not only the symmetry of Death ending each act but also, and perhaps more importantly, Lee's insistent look at contemporary society's inability to face death. By bringing down the curtain on the emotional impact of the parents' grief, the production effectively shifted the play's focus away from the cost of contemporary western society's current practice of hiding death. For at the beginning of the twenty-first century, most people will face death in isolation and with terror—two of the characteristics of the suicide's death. 'You are more terrified of death now than at any time in history. ... Death and dying have become strange events that take place in strange surroundings watched over by strangers' (91). Lee's valid point—clear in the published text but obscured in this production—is that suicide becomes an unavoidable means of revealing death to the living.

Having put humanity in its rightful place, somewhat lower than the bacteria in *The Electrocution of Children*,[8] Lee in *The Map Maker's Sorrow* (his Dublin Theatre Festival debut) negotiates human relationships at the very edge of unrefined experience. *The Electrocution of Children* had a macrocosmic focus, presenting a disquieting and often unnerving portrait of an atomised humanity in a catastrophe-prone universe. *The Mapmaker's Sorrow* by contrast has a microcosmic focus portraying an estranged couple who despite their talents, intellect, energy, and good will are, like any parents, fundamentally unequipped to deal with a teenager who wants

nothing to do with them and appears hell-bent on killing himself.
Whatever their limitations, the death of their son forces them to deal
with one another and the reality of loss. 'Being a parent means
watching a beautiful energy slowly spiral out of your control. You
can't mark the boundary where your failure meets his pain,' says
Morag to Henry at the end of the play. '... our boy is dead. ... Let's
cry. Let's start from there' (90). Mourning their loss becomes yet
another beginning as they attempt to accept the death of their son
along with their own mortality.

As God was the guiding, highly ironic presence in *The Electrocution of Children*, so death, 'lovely and soothing death',[9] governs
all life in *The Map Maker's Sorrow*. Against all expectations of the
stock figure of bones, hourglass, and scythe, Lee's death appears as a
beautiful, purposeful, and composed woman offering the last kiss of
forgetfulness to those who embrace her, 'the best kisser in the universe' (23). Within this human as well as cosmic context, Morag and
Henry confront the inexplicable to wrestle with Camus's question of
life's purpose or lack of it. Lee's play is poignant, playful, comic,
and desperate by turns as once again he demonstrates an impressive
mastery of his craft.

Morag, the map maker of the play's title, experiences a mid-life
crisis involving fundamental questions about her profession and
marriage. Her professional life appears to be stagnating. She and her
husband, Henry, have split up, leaving behind the economic debris
of his horrendous gambling debts. Her son often assumes the guise
of an unfathomable alien who refuses to share her cherished assumptions—ones that she has based her life upon. She is a worka-
holic who does take time for her son, but most of their encounters
end in temper, frustration, departure. An expert on cartography, she
now faces his ultimate act which lies beyond any rational or public
map-making.

For the essential nature of suicide remains non-rational and in-
tensely private, unknowable and terrible. No traveller has returned
from this bourne and the very route itself is appallingly mysterious,
often even to the person committing suicide. Several of Sylvia
Plath's poems, for instance, appear to verge on the hysterical in her
attempt to bring coherence to what has no coherence—her embrace
of self-destruction. To maintain the verbal coherence necessary to

communicate thought and emotion, the poet used poetic form as the control rather than logical reasoning, sequencing of events, or symmetry in details; all of which are absent in suicide. 'Dying / Is an art, like everything else. / I do it exceptionally well,' but this is Plath the poet speaking and not Plath, the silent suicide.[10] Suicide rarely if ever becomes 'an art.' Instead, it usually produces a chaotic unformed mess that others are left to clean up. Lee makes this point in *The Map Maker's Sorrow* by placing Jason's death by hanging at the very beginning of the play rather than elsewhere. (The end of the first act was surely another possibility, if he wanted to emphasise logical or progressive development.) In so doing, Lee announces his subject while at the same time he negates or at least forgoes logical development, clear sequencing of events, and symmetry of scenes. The Peacock production created confusion by inserting a scene before the action of the play began in which all the characters walked somewhat somnambulistically around the stage. This intrusive scene was followed by a blackout, followed by the first scene, 'Hanging' (compare with the published text, 5). That unnecessary intrusion of the characters before the first scene muddied the issue of the incomprehensibility of suicide for those left behind by violating the play's structure.

The play's structure reflects Lee's use of a map's 'simultaneous spatial logic'(40) rather than his heeding the mapmaker's imperative to 'reduce complexity in order to be useful' (6). While the division into scenes in *The Map Maker's Sorrow* superficially resembles that of *The Electrocution of Children*, here it serves a quite different dramatic purpose. *The Electrocution of Children* progressed serially from a clear ironic beginning through a development of action and character to a bleak but still ironic conclusion. *The Map Maker's Sorrow* begins abruptly and confusingly with the suicide of a character the audience does not know and has not met and then proceeds through no clear development to a harmonious end. At the very beginning of the play, the audience finds itself in a position similar to that of the bereaved family in the play or that of any survivors who find a member of their family dead by his or her own hand. Suicide, like Lee's opening scene, declares the strangeness of the other. In contrast, *The Electrocution of Children* moves sequentially through a series of scenes drawn from the debris of lives and the isolation of relationships to the seemingly more remote but perfectly plausible and all too probable collision of the earth with an asteroid. 'A slight error' as God admits. Regrettable, but still 'for humans at least it's goodnight'.[11] In *The Map Maker's Sorrow*'s non-linear spatial form, rather than one scene logically following another, scenes are grouped by contiguity. 'Maps are not mirrors of reality', warns Morag (5). But maps still do relate to reality, however approximately, as the scenes in this play relate to, but do not attempt to reproduce, bereavement or to elucidate what remains inexplicable. Lee's subject by definition resists conventional knowledge—there are no forms, no shapes that fit this act. 'Suicide will have seemed to its perpetrator the last and best of bad possibilities, and any attempt by the living to chart this final terrain of a life can be only a sketch, maddeningly incomplete'.[12] Key Redfield Jamison, in her authoritative study of suicide, *Night Falls Fast*, contends:

> Suicide is a particularly awful way to die: the mental suffering leading up to it is usually prolonged, intense, and unpalliated. There is no morphine equivalent to ease the acute pain, and death not uncommonly is violent and grisly. The suffering of the suicidal is private and inexpressible, leaving family members, friends, and colleagues to deal with an almost unfathomable kind of loss, as well as guilt. Suicide carries in its aftermath a level of confusion and devastation that is, for the most part, beyond description.[13]

It is this level of confusion that *The Map Maker's Sorrow* dramatises.

One reviewer, ignoring Lee's mapping of this harsh, confused reality, erroneously described as a negative dramatic effect what proves to be a positive one. 'Although every scene has its point, like a sound-bite, few last long enough to develop into something probing or revealing, and many end with punch lines that effectively abort what might otherwise have moved into more complicated terrain'.[14] But this objection confuses dramatisation with characterisation. To take the reviewer's own example of Jason and Jess's conversation about his approaching suicide in the scene 'Fuck' (41-45), their dialogue ends with two hard-hitting 'punch lines' but both emanate from deep within the character's experience and personality:

> JASON: I'll fix us something to eat.
> JESS: You know I don't have any money.
> JASON: It's not a problem.
> JESS: Are you asking me to fuck for my rent?
> *Pause.*
> JASON: Look, I'll be dead before you learn to hate me (45).

Given Jess's profession as a young prostitute, her suspicion of a sexual trade-off for food is well grounded and it might appear strange if she did not confront the issue. Jason, on the other hand, has worked hard at disengaging feelings and avoiding confrontation as well as nursing his low self-esteem. His line is doubly in character in reiterating his preoccupation with suicide and in devaluing himself. Moreover, within the context of his suicide, Jason's 'I'll be dead' appears neither boastful nor pretentious but purposely consistent. In a landmark study of one hundred and thirty-four suicides, Eli Robbins and his colleagues at the Washington University School of Medicine in St. Louis conclude that 'The high rate of communication of suicidal ideas indicates that in the majority of instances it is a premeditated act of which the person gives ample warning'.[15] Jamison agrees: 'Most who commit suicide explicitly and *often repeatedly* communicate their intentions to kill themselves to others ... before doing so'[italics added]. Such communication 'is fortunate (... in that) it allows at least the possibility of treatment and prevention'.[16] True it does—unless that suicidal person communicates to someone, such as Jess in the play, who remains aloof, uninvolved, and indifferent (42, 45). The result here, as throughout the play, is one in a series of short scenes—those last bits of 'confusion and devastation'—that form *The Map Maker's Sorrow*.

Since suicide produces fragmentation, a work of art focusing on it may well be fragmented itself. Further, Lee's series of vignettes, fragmented scenes that are themselves fragments—post-modern fragments shored against our ruin—prevent an audience from a too easy sympathy with any of the characters. As Morag says, 'Fragmentation defeats empathy' (89). Those relatively short scenes of

varying length continually interrupt any emotional engagement by
the audience thus avoiding even a semblance of sentimentality. 'We
ache for more of the relationship between parents and son', percep-
tively wrote Dorothy Louise; 'hints at first tantalise, then irritate, as
we realise that we will never get closer to any insights on why these
relationships have developed as they have'.[17] For Louise, this irri-
tation over the course of the play proves negative. But surely Lee's
point that there is no real insight to be had remains valid—these
relationships simply happened. There is no why. In this particular
mind-body problem there can be no answers to questions about
human motivation and relationships. (The key informant cannot be
interviewed or testify to being dead.) Clearly, we are meant to face
the insoluble nature of this ultimate act.

Lee does give voice to the suicide, however, through retrospective
exposition where all the seemingly innocuous remarks, frustrations
and inexplicable temper tantrums acquire significance through
hindsight. As we follow Jason's scenes sporadically inserted in the
action, we can see 'the slippage into futility is first gradual, then
utter'.[18] This progress into futility mirrored in the play is far truer to
the experience of suicides than if Jason had 'report[ed] the causes of
his feelings' as one reviewer naively wished. This same reviewer
apparently would have liked to see another play—one that tidied up
all the emotions to show logically and clearly exactly why Jason felt
the way he did and how that led him inevitably to his hanging himself.[19] But such wishes, understandable as they are and frequent as
they are, cannot be granted.

> When Morag asks Jess [Jason's recent acquaintance] if Jason
> hated her, Jess replies: 'He didn't hate you. He was hurt by
> you. He couldn't bear the weight of expectation. That's why
> he cut himself off'. But this is feeble because we never see
> Morag pressuring Jason, so we have to wonder about Jason's
> accuracy in reporting the causes of his feelings. And why
> could he not just as well have been spurred to accomplishment
> by his mother's ambition for him, assuming she harboured
> such a prospect?[20]

But an audience might equally wonder about Jess's accuracy in reporting what she did or did not hear Jason say. She certainly wants to wound Morag and lower her self-esteem since she sees the older woman as behaving as if she were her superior. As for why Jason 'could ... not just as well have been spurred to accomplishment by his mother's ambition for him', there can be no answer. Morag is a good mother—ambitious for herself and, one could presume, for her son as well. We see her and Jason together in scenes where neither one understands the other. For instance, at his mother's request Jason has mastered various statistics about the solar system but sees no point in them. Finally, as the scene builds he rattles off a complicated recipe in all its detail then runs off in frustration shouting, 'Who cares? Who cares about anything?'(17). Each of the living Jason's scenes ends abruptly either with his physically leaving or his clearly ending the conversation (17, 45, 63, 78)[21]. The visual image of Jason fleeing not just his parents but any true confrontation with them or with his own feelings typifies not only his actions in the play (compare 48) but that of virtually all suicides. Suicide is an escape from what has become intolerable. Why it should become intolerable is rarely known. What this reviewer noted as negative—'we remain in the dark about what his [Jason's] parents have done'(22)—is dramatically positive and psychologically true. Not only do 'we [in the audience] remain in the dark', but so do Henry and Morag and everyone else Jason has left behind to clean up his mess.[22]

'Death is the mother of beauty' declared Wallace Stevens.[23] The psychiatrist, Rollo May, went further suggesting that:

> This awareness of death is the source of zest for life and of our impulse to create not only works of art, but civilisations as well. ... awareness of death also brings benefits. One of these is the freedom to speak the truth: the more aware we are of death, the more vividly we experience the fact that it is not only beneath our dignity to tell a lie but useless as well.[24]

Jason, all too aware of death, still has no zest for life; nor does he wish to help create a civilisation, but he does tell the truth as he knows it—often shockingly so.

Nietzsche suggested that 'The possibility of suicide has saved many lives'.[25] But Nietzsche must have been describing a person intellectually engaged with the question of suicide rather than one prone psychologically or emotionally to commit suicide. One of the great strengths of Lee's play remains his focus on the pathology of suicide framed by other non-suicidal lives rather than either the intellectualisation or rationalisation of suicide. The mind-set and emotional state of the suicide is fundamentally at variance with those of others. Jamison wisely cautions:

> Although it is tempting to imagine suicide as obituary writers often do—as an 'understandable' response to a problem of life, such as economic reversal, romantic failure, or shame—it is clear that these or similar setbacks hit everyone at some point in their lives. ... For every grief or strain that appears to trigger a suicide, thousands of other people have experienced situations as bad or worse and do *not* kill themselves. The normal mind, although strongly affected by a loss or damaging event, is well cloaked against the possibility of suicide.[26]

In *The Map Maker's Sorrow*, for instance, Jason's parents find themselves, both together and individually, in almost impossible positions economically, emotionally, and professionally, yet neither contemplates suicide. Henry has gambled himself into huge debt to underworld figures that threaten to maim and/or kill him if he fails to repay the loan within a very short time. He has also wrecked his marriage, alienated his son, and lost his job. Still he perseveres, creating a freelance consulting business based on his profession as a polysomnographic technician and meeting adversity and danger armed with an ironic sense of humour, verbal agility, and a baseball bat. Morag has had the very foundations of her research and lifework destroyed. What she took for a bright new wave of the future in the building of the Rajasthan Canal in India (45-50) turns out to be a tsunami that drowns and destroys people, their lives, work, and culture (88-89)—a 'savage waste of progress,' as Henry calls it (89). Her only son, in whom she believed and for whom she had such high hopes, killed himself, yet she, like Henry, never thinks of killing herself. Like Henry and millions of others she may drown her sorrows in alcohol to the point of endangering her health but this is a short-term non-remedy that she appears capable of jettisoning. Both parents feel understandably that their lives individually and together are shattered by Jason's suicide and their own failures, yet unlike Jason and those who are genuinely suicidal they do not feel total paralysis of 'all the otherwise vital forces that make us human'.[27] They are not confined to the suicide's world that A. Alvarez described so fittingly as 'airless and without exits'.[28] They appear baffled but not buffaloed. There is no 'slippage into futility' so typical of suicides.[29] By contrast, Jason continually experienced the utter futility of his life.

Unlike Willy Loman, one of the most famous suicides in modern drama, Jason's death is not motivated by a desire to 'solve' any problem, either of his own or his family. In *Death of a Salesman* (1949), Willy decided to kill himself because he believed his death would actually solve all of his and his family's problems through the proceeds from his life insurance. In his mind, the insurance becomes 'a guaranteed twenty-thousand-dollar proposition ... like a diamond shining in the dark, hard and rough, that I can pick up and touch in my hand'.[30] But there are no prospective diamonds for Jason. The existential psychoanalyst Ludwig Binswanger, discussing a suicidal patient he calls Lola, also describes Jason's mood and reasoning: 'In Lola's case [...] despair is not only, as in other cases, despair at having to be in the world in a particular way and no other; it is despair at being-in-the-world at all!' For Lola, all life consisted of 'conflict between the ideal and the resistance from the dull world ("reality")'.[31] Keith Hawton concludes from his research that '... it is now recognised that a sense of hopelessness, rather than general depression, is a major factor in determining suicidal behaviour'.[32]

In *The Map Maker's Sorrow* Lee presents suicide as a direct challenge to a belief in life as the progression from birth through maturity to death, for Jason's death attempts to deny not just the zest for life in the face of mortality but also the very premise of lived life itself. By denying the future, suicides like Jason attempt to negate the past carried in memory. The Greeks envisioned Mnemosyne as the mother of all the muses since memory is the basis of all the arts. The suicide denies this premise in emphasising that memories are too much to live with; bring not consolation but pain; provide no enjoyment through recall; and are to be destroyed rather than built upon. The twin goals of the suicide become to lessen the hold of both the living and the compulsion of memory. Thornton Wilder put the promise of death well for such people: '... the dead don't stay interested in us living people for very long'.[33] One hypothesis for the high suicide rate among holocaust survivors, for example, contends that such people cannot face living when so many others perished. One by one they commit suicide. Whether true or not, far too many people of genius who are both compassionate and articulate and who survived the death camps have killed themselves. Primo Levi the chemist, holocaust survivor, and witness to the terror unleashed in the twentieth century wrote compellingly of his and others' unimaginable ordeals. Yet years—decades—later after considerable fame and success as a writer, he killed himself.[34] Jason has no such memories of or guilt feelings about being a survivor. His life has barely begun. Rather he forms part of the acute, painful mystery of young adult suicide that in many countries has reached almost epidemic proportions. 'One percent of all suicides occur in the first fifteen years of life, but 25 percent occur in the second'.[35] 'Suicide in the young, which has tripled over the past forty-five years, is, without argument, one of our most serious public health problems. Suicide is the third leading cause of death in young people in the United States and the second for college students.'[36]

W. H. Auden once distinguished between two kinds of necessary art: 'There must always be two kinds of art, escape-art, for man needs escape as he needs food and deep sleep, and parable-art, that art which shall teach man to unlearn hatred and learn love'.[37] *The Map Maker's Sorrow* belongs in Auden's second category of parable-art—art that teaches people 'to unlearn hatred and learn love.' Confronting one of the most difficult of all human situations in the loss of their child compounded by that child's suicide, Morag and Henry struggle to accept their loss and to accept their son's choice of death over life as the means of ending his torment.(89) Jason 'finding no comfort, no remedy in this wretched life, ... [is] eased of all by death ...'.[38] As a young adult suicide, Jason also exemplifies the values of a contemporary society that weighs the worth of the young more than the old, and hence views the suicide of a young person as almost the ultimate tragic loss. Lee then constructs his contemporary parable of life lived in the knowledge of and with the acceptance of death on this incident. In his parable—as in life—Death has the last but one word about crossing the ultimate border. 'I want you to live and to live beautifully', concludes Death. 'Live, but remember also to die'.(91) But the last word in the play is given not to Death but to Nature that rains 'upon all the living and the dead'.[39] 'It rains on Henry and Morag. It rains on Jason and Jess . . . .' during Death's speech. Then 'it is still raining' on the five characters as the curtain falls.

NOTES

I wish once again to thank Ms Judy Friel and the Peacock Theatre, Dublin for graciously supplying me with the unpublished script of *The Electrocution of Children* and to thank Chris Lee for permission to reproduce its text.

1.   Alan Garner, *The Voice that Thunders: Essays and Lectures*, London 1997, 209.
2.   Albert Camus, *The Myth of Sisyphus and Other Essays*, New York 1995, 3.
3.   Quoted in M. Iga, *The Thorn in the Chrysanthemum: Suicide and Economic Success in Modern Japan*, Berkeley 1986, 82-83.
4.   Martin Amis, *Night Train*, London 1998, 67.
5.   Chris Lee, *The Map Maker's Sorrow*, London 1999. All further references are to this edition and are given in the text in brackets. Chris Lee, the Abbey Writer in Association for the 1999-2000 season, had an auspicious Abbey Theatre debut with his brilliant *The Electrocution of Children* that shared the annual Stewart Parker Trust New Playwright Bursary for 1998. *The Electrocution of Children* was an intellectually ambitious play superbly directed by Brian Brady with an outstanding cast. *The Electrocution of Children* depicts a world in which people have forgotten how precious the gift of life is and how fragile human beings are. 'Humans ... here by the luck of the draw' (Stephen Jay Gould, *Full House*, New York 1996, 175) and as 'glorious accidents of an unpredictable process' (Gould, *op.cit.*, 216), squander their opportunities to be creative, turn their backs on relationships, fail in their attempts to communicate, and prey upon one another. For a detailed analysis of the play and this production, see Donald E. Morse, '"The Simple Magnificence of Bacteria": Chris Lee's *The Electrocution of Children*', *Irish Studies Review*, 8:1 (2000), 91-98.
     The 1999 Peacock entry in the Dublin Theatre Festival, *The Mapmaker's Sorrow* reunited Lee, Brady, and the imaginative designer, Paul McCauley

with several key actors from *The Execution of Children*, including Chris McHallem (as Henry the freelance polysomnographic technician, feckless husband, and father) and Catherine Mack (as an alluring and very self-assured Death). Ingrid Craigie played the title role of Morag the map-maker, reluctant teacher, and mother.

6. Lee, *The Mapmaker's Sorrow*, 22. Suicide does remain an option for many elderly, however. Although Jamison's 'focus is on suicide in those younger than forty,' she emphasises that 'this in no way means to downplay the terrible problem of suicide in those who are older. Study after study has shown that the elderly are inadequately treated for depression—the major cause of suicide in all age groups—and that suicide rates in the elderly are alarmingly high'.(Key Redfield Jamison, *Night Falls Fast: Understanding Suicide*, New York 1999, 21.) All the more surprising that Tom Kirkwood in his otherwise thoroughly researched book on the science of human aging fails to mention suicide. (Tom Kirkwood, *Time of our Lives: The Science of Human Aging*, London 1999.)

7. Wallace Stevens, 'Sunday Morning' in Holly Stevens, ed., *The Palm at the End of the Mind: Selected Poems and a Play*, New York 1972, 5-8 (line 7).

8. Chris Lee, *The Electrocution of Children*, 1998, unpublished, np.

9. Walt Whitman, 'When Lilacs Last in the Dooryard Bloom'd', in Sculley Bradley and Harold W. Bodgett, eds, *Leaves of Grass* (1965), New York 1973, 328-337, 1.135.

10. Sylvia Plath, 'Lady Lazarus', in Ted Hughes, ed., *The Collected Poems*, New York 1983, 245.

11. For a description of this disastrous eventuality of an asteroid striking the earth, see Paul Davies, *The Last Three Minutes: Conjectures about the Ultimate Fate of the Universe*, New York 1994, 1-7 and especially 1-2.

12. Jamison, *op.cit.*, 73.

13. *Ibid.*, 24.

14. Dorothy Louise, 'Observe the Irish Playwrights Marching Towards the Screen', *Irish Theatre Magazine*, 1:4 (1999), 23.

15. Quoted in Jamison, *op.cit.*, 237.

16. *Ibid.*, 236.

17. Louise, *op.cit.*, 22.

18. Jamison, *op.cit.*, 104.

19. Louise, *op.cit.*, 21, 21-22.

20. *Ibid.*, 21.

21. 'Look, I'll be dead before you learn to hate me' is, of course, verbally abrupt. It is not, however, a solid ending for a 'sound-bite' (Louise, *op.cit.*, 21) but a viciously effective, narcissistic termnation of a discussion.

22. Jason's bleak closed-in view of his diminished life does not include or permit his lending anyone a hand. Louise, however, objects to Jason's inactivity. '... Jason describes watching an old woman pulling a shopping trolley against the wind for an hour to prove his point (that 'life is shit'). 'Then I had to look away. That's how hard life is.' Can we help wondering why it apparently never occurs to him, over the course of that hour, to offer the woman a

hand?' asks Louise.(22) But surely the point of his story is that as with all of Beckett's characters there is 'Nothing to be done'. Jason identifies with the old woman only in her helplessness for it reflects his own. 'I understood that that woman was the future. The future for all of us', he concludes.(43) By which he means that in his experience it is impossible to 'achieve ... something in the course of ...time'.(43) So there would be no point in going to her aid. Instead, her plight reinforces his determination to commit suicide.

23. Wallace Stevens, *op.cit.*, 1.63.
24. Rollo May, *Freedom and Destiny*, New York 1981, 103.
25. Quoted in May, *op.cit.*, 103.
26. Jamison, *op.cit.*, 199.
27. *Ibid.*, 104.
28. A. Alvarez, *The Savage God*, Harmondsworth 1971, 293.
29. Jamison, *op.cit.*, 104.
30. Arthur Miller, *Death of a Salesman: Certain Private Conversations in Two Acts and a Requiem* (1949), London 1969, 442-443.
31. Ludwig Binswanger, *Being-in-the World: Selected Papers of Ludwig Binswanger*, trans. Jacob Needleman, New York 1963, 286, 287. Ellen West, an adult caught between a manic desire to be slender and the need for food to sustain life, 'escaped ... by way of suicide'. (Binswanger, 'Lola Voss', 287; see also Binswanger, 'The Case of Ellen West' for a more complete analysis of this person's tragic life.)
32. Keith Hawton, *Suicide and Attempted Suicide Among Children and Adolescents*, London 1986, 90.
33. Thornton Wilder, *Our Town* (1938), in *Three Plays by Thornton Wilder*, New York 1965, 52.
34. In his introduction to *The Drowned and the Saved*, Paul Bailey warns against reading the third chapter, 'Shame' (52-67) as many have as providing clear reasons for Levi's own suicide.(*xii-xv*) 'Améry's suicide, Levi observes, "like other suicides, allows for a nebula of explanations." The same has to be said of his own', Bailey cautions.(*xiv*) (Paul Bailey, 'Introduction', in Primo Levi, *The Drowned and the Saved* (1986), trans. Raymond Rosenthal, London 1992.)
35. Jamison, *op.cit.*, 202.
36. *Ibid.*, 21, and see also 22-24. In England and Wales suicide rates per 100,000 among 20-24 year old males more than doubled between 1960 and 1981 (National Centre for Health Statistics 1984, quoted in Hawton, *op.cit.*, 22). 'In 1975 [...] suicide was the second or third leading cause of death in 15-24 year olds in several European countries, with the rates for males generally higher than those for females'.(*Ibid.*, 25) '... in the United States during the 1960s and 1970s, there was a very serious increase in deaths by suicide among older teenagers and those in their early twenties, this being more marked among males than females, and among whites as compared with nonwhites.'(*Ibid.*, 21) 'Between 1960 and 1975, rates among 20-24 year olds rose by 130%. Since 1975, the rates in this age group have remained relatively stable'(*Ibid.*, 19).

37.   W.H. Auden, *The English Auden*, Edward Mendelson, ed., New York 1977, 341-342.

38.   Suicide was vividly described by Robert Burton in his monumental *An Anatomy of Melancholy* close to four hundred years ago. 'There is ... in this humour the very seeds of fire. ... In the midst of these squalid, ugly, and such irksome days, they seek at last, finding no comfort, no remedy in this wretched life, to be eased of all by death ... to be their own butchers, and execute themselves.' (Robert Burton, *The Anatomy of Melancholy*, 3 vols., London 1832, 1.431-432.)

39.   James Joyce, 'The Dead' (1914), in *The Essential James Joyce*, Harry Levin, ed., Frogmore 1977, 173.

'Who is the father of any son?':
Sebastian Barry's *The Steward of Christendom*

VIVIAN VALVANO LYNCH

In the 'Scylla and Charybdis' section of *Ulysses*, Stephen Dedalus, a son who has attempted to dismiss his father, asks: 'Who is the father of any son that any son should love him or he any son?' even as he undergoes his singular search for self-identity.[1] His question underscores the recurrent theme of father-son relationships in Irish literature; a theme that reaches one of its most potent acts of creativity in Synge's Christy Mahon. Christy, a symbolic rather than an actual parricide, succeeds, to the unabashed delight of his father, in achieving autonomy. To such action, Declan Kiberd, in *Inventing Ireland*, attributes no less than effective revolution: the son, representing the colonised country, overthrows but does not destroy the parent, or coloniser; no longer having need of any parent, he also dismisses any surrogate.[2] Christy, the son, invents a self and can then lead his parent into the future. Metaphorically speaking, the son crosses the border into adulthood, wins the father's approval and assumes his due place as the dominant person of the future. Kiberd credits Synge above all other writers for his dramatisation of this moment of self actualisation. It is the moment articulated by Fanon in *A Dying Colonialism*: it is the moment 'when the person is born, assumes his autonomy, and becomes the creator of his own values.'[3] Fanon elucidates: 'The father stood back before the new world and followed in his son's footsteps.'[4]

Sebastian Barry's *The Steward of Christendom* presents a catastrophic antithesis to this meaningful border crossing. At one point in the play, Thomas Dunne, the hero of Barry's play, cries out:'Damn history'.[5] If we keep in mind Kiberd's assertion that, 'insurgency makes history possible' and that '(t)he ensuing search for a father-surrogate may be rooted in a desire to erase the memory of the necessary patricide, but no surrogate and no actual father can suffice for the child who must invent a self'[6] then, as evidenced by the case of Christy Mahon, Dunne's cry is indeed heartfelt and to the point. The loss of Thomas Dunne's docile son, Willie (ironically in battle) constitutes a loss of potential for dynamism, and leaves Thomas in a world that, no matter how dramatically its trappings have changed, is ultimately stagnant and hopeless. Barry positions Willie's primal lack of rebelliousness and consequent failure to attain maturity and self-identity against numerous large scale revolutionary and/or militarist activities that serve as historical backdrops: the Great War, the Rising, the Anglo-Irish War, the Civil War. For all that, neither meaningful revolution nor effective evolution occurs for the son of this play's protagonist-father.

In 1932, when the play is set, Thomas Dunne is an anachronism; an Irish Catholic loyal to the crown of Britain but willing to live under any rule so long as there is peace; a man who often recalls his past and his service in the Dublin Metropolitan Police (DMP) as a utopian time. In 1932, Willie is already a memory and a ghost, who returns to haunt his father. He appears paradoxically clothed as the young soldier who met his death at the Front in the Great War, but embodied as the boy-child who was, in fact, completely subservient to his father To understand Thomas, whose tortured mind cannot face the full reality of his present day world, and to comprehend why he cried like an owl in a tree all night long when he received the news of his son's death, we need to examine some of Thomas's memories, and the relationship between the father and the son, as well as the quasi-father and quasi-son, and their resonances in the play.

Thomas Dunne, who is seventy-five in 1932, was born in the middle of the nineteenth century, and has seen extraordinary changes in the development of his country. His memories are focused on his family and his employment. On his paternal side, Thomas hails from generations of the stewards of the great estate, Humewood. He marries his young love, fathers three daughters and a son, and survives the death of his much loved wife. His children's lives are a source of troubled anxiety to him: a physically afflicted spinster daughter lives a life of frustration; another daughter has married but lives far from contentedly and is apparently on the edge of hysteria; the youngest daughter has emigrated to America, and his only son dies at the Front. Thomas's professional life in the Dublin Metropolitan Police locates him at the centre of Ireland's political and governmental maelstrom—a position that increasingly bewilders him.

Thomas's reveries about his career are somewhat suspect. Repeatedly, he reminds us of his attainment of the rank of Chief Superintendent—the highest rank a Catholic could attain in the DMP—but at one point he admits that his final promotion, after forty-five years of service, was really a matter of form. Repeatedly, he articulates his pride in his position, but eventually admits that he only became a policeman because he had failed at school; his disappointed father sent him into a job that he considered appropriate for fools. And repeatedly, he voices memories of a utopian Ireland, memories infused with orderliness, security, peace, loyalty, and service. By way of example, Thomas recalls Victoria's reign:

The great world that she owned was shipshape as a ship. All the harbours of the earth were trim with their granite piers, the ships were shining and strong. The trains went sleekly through the fields, and her mark was everywhere, Ireland, Africa, the Canadas, every blessed place. And men like me were there to make everything peaceable, to keep order in her kingdoms. ... We were secure, as if for eternity, the orderly milk-drays would come up the streets in the morning, and her influence would reach everywhere, like the salt sea pouring up into the fresh waters of the Liffey. Ireland was hers for eternity, order was everywhere, if we could but honour her example. She loved her Prince. I loved my wife. The world was a

wedding of loyalty, of steward to Queen, she was the very
flower and perfecter of Christendom. (14)

Of the DMP, Thomas recalls years of efficiently maintaining
order in the city 'with nothing but our batons and our pride' (10).
Perhaps a few heads got broken at an illegal gathering, as during
the 1913 Lockout, but the meticulous DMP, according to
Thomas, was a far cry from the armed Royal Irish Constabulary.
He recalls his colleagues as simple country men for the most
part, lovers of crown and country and keepers of order on the
urban streets and grids, not armed routers of the Easter Rising,
not armed opponents of the Black and Tans.

But Thomas's memories are at best woefully incomplete and
frequently inaccurate. Listening to him, one would have no idea
that the centre of Dublin in the late nineteenth century was, as
Roy Foster has succinctly stated, 'a byword for spectacularly
destitute living conditions'.[7] To hear Thomas reminisce, one
would assume that there had been no discomfort or disquietude
in the DMP until the coming of the new Irish government after
the Treaty and the consequent decisions that had to be made by
the men as to whether to join the new *Garda Siochána*. In
reality, by 1914 at the latest, the poor pay and long working
hours common to the force had engendered serious discontent.
Mary Scanlon's excellent work on the DMP[8] is a useful
counterbalance to Thomas's rosy memories. According to
Scanlon, the clearing of the streets during the 1913 Lockout that
Thomas recalls with such pride actually necessitated frequent,
arduous overtime. Jim Larkin himself argued for a pay rise for
the DMP, and further argued that the two shillings per week rise
given in 1914 was paltry; in fact, it was the first rise granted to
the force since 1882. In 1916, a DMP constable made between
25 and 33 shillings per week, a sergeant between 37 and 39
shillings, the lowest rates for police service throughout the
United Kingdom. After the Easter Rising, during which there
were some DMP men on the streets (three of whom were killed),
members demanded a weekly rise of 12 shillings and one penny,
plus a weekly four shillings war bonus. Extra policing duties
followed the Rising, and wartime inflation seriously affected the
men. For the first time, the DMP was trained in fire-arm use, but

they had to bear transportation costs to the courses and laundry bills for the increasingly dirty uniforms themselves. Perhaps part of Thomas's fixation on his clean, crisp uniform of old harks back to the days when the uniform must have been muddied and stained by fire-arm practice and he was obliged to take pains to return it to its pristine condition. The British government decided to pay only the war bonus, angering the men. A subsequent offer of a three shillings and six pence rise was rejected; volatile meetings followed despite orders from the DMP Commissioner prohibiting same, and, in contravention of the DMP oath of allegiance that Thomas Dunne holds so dear, a DMP branch of the forbidden Ancient Order of Hibernians was formed. Many members of B Division, the 300-man division under the command of our man of repressed memories, Thomas Dunne, attended AOH meetings. By late 1916, the DMP was granted a war bonus of three shillings and six pence weekly, and basic pay was increased by three shillings after 20 years of service; an extra five pounds was awarded for Christmas 1916. The cases of five men labeled as insubordinate for fomenting the propagandistic use of the AOH were heard; one was dismissed, four fined and transferred. However, the transferees staged a demonstration in the form of a mock funeral; they were quickly dismissed.[9] So much for Thomas's utopian golden age.

> Thomas Dunne, who plaintively entreats his God,
> put the recruits back in their barracks in Fitzgibbon Street,
> put the stout hearts back into Christendom's Castle, and
> troop the colours once more for Princess and Prince, for
> Queen and for King, for Chief Secretary and Lord
> Lieutenant, for Viceroy and Commander-in-Chief. (37)

swiftly recognises the impossibility of his prayer being answered. He ends his prayer for a return to Ireland's colonial past with the simple acknowledgement, 'But you cannot' (37). Difficult as it is for Thomas to live in the new Ireland, he *is* able to do so, and perhaps it is his selective perception of the glories of the past that comforts and enables him to do so. Replaying the fabled day in 1922 when he turned the Castle over to Michael Collins, Thomas recalls the bittersweet situation. With the promise of peace in the land, he will accept the new scheme of things:

> I hope I guarded his [the King's] possession well, and helped people through a terrible time. And now that story is over and I am over with it, and content. I don't grieve. (42)

Thomas does not, in fact, grieve for the loss of his old, idiosyncratically remembered, utopian Ireland. He regrets its loss, surely, but that is not the same as grieving. He grieves for the loss of his son. It is the loss of Willie that drives Thomas into bouts of madness, not the loss of designations of the British Empire on Dublin highways and byways.

Recalling the birth of his last child, Dolly, the birth that killed Cissy, Thomas articulates an important component of his personal philosophy:

> [I]t was a moment in our life when daily things pass away from you, when all your concerns seem to vanish, and you are allowed by God a little space of clarity and grace. When you see that God himself is in your wife and in your children, and they hold in trust for you your own measure of goodness. And in the manner of your treatment of them lies your own salvation. (38)

Tending the family, the relationship with one's wife and lover, the nurturing of one's child—these, for Thomas, are the fulcrums of a man's existence. He laments his failure with his son, the failure that caused him to hold on to the boy for too long. 'What big loud talking fools are fathers sometimes. Why do we not love our sons simply and be done with it?'(47), Thomas asks the singing boy-soldier Willie on one of his ghostly appearances. As more than one sage has suggested, to love completely is neither to hold, nor to possess, but to allow freedom. Willie never had the chance to make his own choice. His mother encouraged his youthful singing, to Thomas's dismay; and his father apparently expected him to follow in his own footsteps. But Willie enlisted in the army because he was not tall enough to be a policeman, and Thomas suffers recriminations, knowing that, with no conscription, there was no actual need for Willie to go. Willie, however, was his father's loyal son. What better way to imitate his father than to serve the Crown that his father had served for so many years? If an accident of physical stature meant that a career in the police force was out of the question, the British Army beckoned.

The motif of Thomas's fixation on children and parent-child relationships underlines his feelings of guilt at Willie's death. Many of his memories revolve around his childhood at rural Humewood and his dealings with his parents, particularly those with his somewhat fearsome father; and many involve the raising of his own children. Some even involve the father-daughter relationship of his wife, Cissy, and her father. Cissy's father, it seems, did not understand his girl; he always believed that she would prefer to dance than to keep house, but Thomas gently chides that his father-in-law was wrong: 'What does a father know?'(25). Thomas loves the very smell of children; he reads Tom Sawyer and children's adventure stories, and he sorely misses contact with his grandchildren, whom he has unfortunately frightened and alienated. Most significantly, when he recalls Michael Collins on the day of the Castle turnover, he praises Collins's rough and ready American-style glamour and good looks, and says: 'I would have been proud to have him as my son' (49). Moreover, noting that he 'felt rough near him', he goes on to say: 'I thought too as I looked at him of my father, as if Collins could have been my son and could have been my father' (50). Thomas Dunne, loyal servant of the British crown, soon 'closed his heart' against the 'shadow of loyalty' (50) that he felt for the charismatic leader, Collins, but he cannot revoke his musings on Collins's attraction to him as both son- and father-figure. Collins serves here as a meaningful symbol of a successful son because he has reached maturity and become his own man; he has made his own decisions, and has taken up his adult place in the world. In relation to Collins, Thomas feels as Old Mahon feels in relation to the exuberant, mature playboy Christy: he feels inferior rather than superior, ready to be led. It is the revolutionary moment, in which the son has grown beyond the father and can therefore effectively assume the father's role of leadership; and so, by way of this moment, the progress of life (and history) can continue. But of course, Michael Collins is not Thomas Dunne's son; Thomas is desperately searching for a pseudo-son to replace the one lost through his decision to serve in the British army; the one who never had the chance to become his father's leader.

Thomas Dunne believes he has been 'stupid and silent'(38) in the matter of raising Willie, and I daresay many fathers have similarly berated themselves.[10] On a level more complex than stupidity or silence, he failed to grasp that mysterious facet of the human comedy: at some point, a boy must leave the father's path and make his own choices, whether correct or mistaken. Even Thomas's father, who was such a stern disciplinarian and so cruel when his son failed in school, recognised such a moment in Thomas's own development. When the young Thomas disobeyed his father's directive to lead their old dog, Shep, to slaughter for killing a ewe but instead hid out with the dog overnight in the cold, he expected a violent parental response. Instead, he felt a fond embrace and heard a prayer of thanks for his safety. Thomas concludes: 'And I would call that the mercy of fathers, when the love that lies in them deeply like the glittering face of a well is betrayed by an emergency, and the child sees at last that he is loved, loved and needed and not to be lived without, and greatly' (65). Thomas's father may not have been perfect, but here he recognised, perhaps subliminally, that in the child lies the future, and the effectively maturing child will not blindly follow the father.

Consider Willie's last letter from the Front. Barry's knowledge of trench warfare is superb, and the absurdity and haphazardness of the scene is palpable. Willie, entrenched with fellow soldiers and abundant rats, and never having even seen the enemy writes to Thomas:

> It gives me great comfort to write to my father. ... God keep you all safe, because we have been told of the ruckus at home, and some of the country men are as much upset by that as they would be by the present emergency. I know you are in the front line there, Papa, so keep yourself safe for my return, when Maud will cook the

fatted calf! The plain truth is, Papa, this is a strange war and a strange time, and my whole wish is to be home with you all in Dublin, and to abide by your wishes, whatever they be. I wish to be a more dutiful son because, Papa, in the mire of this wasteland, you stand before my eyes as the finest man I know, and in my dreams you comfort me, and keep my spirits lifted. (57)

Poor Willie sounds like a chastened prodigal son trying to make amends for profligacy and dissipation. But paradoxocally, in his complete subservience to his father, he is poignantly wrong rather than prodigal. He will die a soldier, but not a man—a child in an adult's body.

Stephen Dedalus suggests, in 'Circe', that he must symbolically commit patricide in order to reach an independent identity; he taps his brow and says, 'in here it is I must kill the priest and the king'.[11] It is the very thing that Willie Dunne never matured sufficiently to do. Kiberd calls the shedding of the father of such creditable revolutionaries as Stephen and Christy Mahon versions of the 'Anti-Oedipus, which saw the ancient tale not as awful tragedy but as happy comedy'.[12] Barry allows us to see the tragedy of the undeveloped, immature son peripherally in The Steward of Christendom, as he focuses most of his attention on that son's anguished father. Without his son, the child who is 'needed and not to be lived without', hope for a meaningful future has disappeared. 'I would kill, or I would do a great thing, just to see you once more, in the flesh' (47), says Thomas to Willie. That being impossible, he finally sleeps, apparently understanding, at last, the enormity of his loss.

NOTES

1. James Joyce, *Ulysses*, Gabler Edition, Hans Walter Gabler, ed., New York 1986, 9.845-6.
2. Declan Kiberd, *Inventing Ireland:The Literature of the Modern Nation*, London 1996, 176.

3.   Franz Fanon, *A Dying Colonialism*, tr. Haakon Chevalier, London 1970, 86.

4.   *Ibid.*, 86.

5.   Sebastian Barry, *The Steward of Christendom*, London 1995, 78. Further references are to this edition and are given in the text in parentheses.

6.   Kiberd, *op. cit.*, 388.

7.   R. F. Foster, *Modern Ireland: 1600-1972*, London 1988, 436.

8.   Mary Scanlon, 'Trouble in the Force', *History Ireland*, 5:2 (Summer 1997), 5-6.

9.   *Ibid.*, 5-6.

10.   I would caution here against labeling Thomas as a 'bad' father. It is all too tempting to castigate a parental mistake. Even the bull headed Creon of *Antigone* elicits cathartic compassion when one realises that he missed Haemon's direct statement that the stubborn father would never again see the son alive.

11.   Joyce, *op. cit.*, 15.4436-7.

12.   Kiberd, *op. cit.*, 388.

Beyond *Bailegangaire:* Authority And

Transgression in Martin McDonagh's

'The Beauty Queen Of Leenane'

MONICA RANDACCIO

Shaun Richards has maintained that Thomas Murphy's *Bailegangaire* is the strongest expression of a sense that the dominant tropes can be deconstructed without the collapse of meaning.[1] My purpose is to see whether such an interpretation can be applied to Martin McDonagh's *The Beauty Queen of Leenane*, which, since both works address such notions as 'national identity' and 'history', invites comparison with *Bailegangaire*.

National identity and history were the major issues debated in the 'eighties by those intellectuals, engaged in a re-evaluation of the Irish cultural identity in the wake of the country's modernisation in the nineteen-sixties and 'seventies, when the Northern Ireland question had become one of the main issues on the political agenda. Careful consideration was given to Seamus Deane's exhortation that 'everything including our politics and our literature has to be re-written, i.e. re-read'.[2] Brian Friel was well aware that this necessitated a revision of the relationship between Ireland

and its English legacy. In his words, the Irish 'have been pig-
mented by an English home... and the rejection of all that, and
the rejection into what, is the big problem'.[3] A solution to Friel's
dilemma was suggested by Mark Patrick Hederman and Richard
Kearney in the 'fifth province'. This province, defined by them as
'not a political or geographical position, (but) more like a disposi-
tion',[4] was acknowledged by Friel as 'the place for dissenters,
traitors to the prevailing mythologies in the other four prov-
inces'.[5] The laborious process then underway was what Declan
Kiberd has called 'inventing Ireland', where the term 'invention'
is to be interpreted as 'both the discovery of extant thought and
the proposal of a future thought'.[6] This necessitated a re-
examination of received ideologies and tradition, and of the central notion cherished by early nationalist ideology that Ireland,
once free and Gaelic, 'would return to the childhood innocence of
its once and future Arcadia'.[7]

According to Edward Said, what is inevitably emphasised in
the first moment of anti-imperialist resistance is the primacy of
the geographical element. One of the main tasks of the culture of
resistance is 'to reclaim, rename and reinhabit the land'.[8] If the
land is recoverable at first only through the imagination, it comes
as no surprise that charting the imaginative geography of the West
of Ireland became an indispensable part of the process of liberation. The search for authenticity in the West, however, was not
only an exercise of pre-eminently geographical imagination, but
also a hypothetical reappropriation of time. To look to the past for
authenticating images meant acknowledging a pre-colonial presence on the landscape, and establishing a continuity with the denied 'glorious' history of Ireland.

Luke Gibbons has identified three characteristics defining the
image of the West of Ireland elaborated by the Anglo-Irish contributors to the Literary Revival.[9] In choosing Synge's *The Playboy of the Western World* as the most exemplary actualisation of
what the Irish western imaginary stood for, he states, first, that the
West has represented an escape from individualism and the fragmentation of community which Synge believed to be an inevitable consequence of the process of modernisation. Second, he
notes that the appeal of the West lies in the fact that it offered a

refuge from the puritan ethos and suffocating morality of the emergent Catholic bourgeoisie. Third, he concludes that the central preoccupation with violence derived mainly from a rejection of law and order imposed by a centralised state power. However, these peculiarities of the West of Ireland automatically subsume their oppositional terms: the community is inextricably linked to the individual, aristocratic nationalism, to the puritanism of orthodox Catholic nationalism, and the violence of the rural West to the order of law and progress. Thus, fragmentation and discontinuity appear as the peculiar hallmarks of the Irish national tradition. The controversial relationship between the individual and the community has been the most revealing facet of this discontinuity and has proved most productive in Irish literature and drama.[10]

The general uncertainty of the 'eighties demonstrated that the equation of urbanisation and industrial development with enlightenment values of progress was no longer viable. This failure has been variously attributed to the lingering malaise of rural ideology[11] or to the attempt to restore a view of rural nostalgia to the countryside.[12] However, as Gibbons points out, these arguments have revolved around the false assumption that the rural myths cultivated during the revival conformed to the lived experience in the countryside—an assumption easily demolished by an analysis of Irish emigration. Therefore, Gibbons continues, 'the backward look towards a peasant arcadia does not represent a form of *continuity* with the rural past, but a *break* with it' .[13] The invocation of the past was not an assertion of vestigial ideology but of an invented tradition.

Irish society was, in fact, 'labouring under two separate and inconsistent value systems': 'the cultural residue of a traditional peasant society' and 'the massive growth in the international flow of information [which had] resulted in a situation in which every Irish household each evening [played] host to a cast of characters whose motives and actions [were] conditioned by a culture different from their own'.[14] As the country entered the postmodern age, it became clear that such concepts as 'culture', 'tradition' and 'national character' were being subjected to a rigorous interrogation. Jean François Lyotard maintains that in postmodernism we wit-

ness a massive delegitimation of the mastercodes, the 'disman-
tling of Grand Narratives… in favour of little narratives (*les petits
récits)'.*[15] The ultimate referent of postmodern narrative is not
some totalising centre of meaning but other narratives, which are
multiple, diverse, not subsumable into some final solution. Thus,
history is constructed not as a continuity leading inexorably back
to a lost paradise or forward to a bright future, but as collage.
However, postmodernism's dangerous tendencies are readily
apparent: the loss of totalising models of identity in the name of
'dissensus' may give way to mere relativism or lazy pluralism.
An attempt to recapture the density of historical circumstance has
been made by leftist critics, but Ihab Hassan has argued that their
need to grant politics priority in the justification of human existence is constricting, as is their readiness to confuse their beliefs
with universal values.[16] However, it is one among these critics,
Edward Said, who suggests, first, that in order to achieve identity,
post-colonial countries must achieve 'a new integrative or contrapuntal orientation in history that sees Western and non-Western
experiences as belonging together because connected by imperialism'; and, second, that they have to develop 'an imaginative, even
Utopian vision which reconceives emancipatory (as opposed to
confining) theory and performance'. Finally, they have to '[in-
vest] neither in new authorities, doctrines, and encoded orthodoxies, nor in established institutions and causes, but in a particular
sort of nomadic, migratory, and anti-narrative energy'.[17]

I would argue that Murphy's *Bailegangaire* is a 'contrapuntal
reading' of the Ireland of the past with its legacy of imperialism,
and the Ireland of the present, endangered by postmodern erasure
of difference. Murphy tries to achieve a reconciling vision of a
cultural-social identity which is both modern and Irish and, at the
same time, he releases an 'anti-narrative energy' which allows
him to cross over from local history into the general dimension of
Irish history.

Bailegangaire is set in 'the kitchen of a thatched house' in the
West of Ireland and is contained within two time scales: 1984 and
the rural Ireland of the 'fifties. There are two narratives at work in
the play: Mommo's narrative of the laughing-contest, and the present lives of her two granddaughters, Mary and Dolly, who, as

their stories unfold, are waiting for their past to be fully revealed to them. In this play, the West of Ireland serves to 'explode the myths of revivalist drama'[18] and Murphy, like Synge, exposes the pieties, pretences and contradictions of rural life. Having already reversed the revivalist transposition of urban to rural in *The Morning After Optimism* and *The Gigli Concert*, Murphy testifies to that *break* with the rural past, and reveals how the backward look towards a peasant arcadia was the result of the sense of dislocation consequent on modernisation. In starkly juxtaposing Mommo's tale of the 'fifties, and the uncertain progress of the 'eighties, he warns against the dangers of neo-traditionalism and denounces its false notion of continuity.

However, Murphy's purpose in *Bailegangaire* is to restore a link with history, with a past which forms a *continuum* with the present and may allow the possibility of a future. The play, which has been termed 'a search for home'[19] and 'a search for meaning'[20], brings on stage three women, whose lives nobody was watching because 'they were an unfashionable subject .... in an Ireland bent on proving itself a fully modern member of the European Community/Union'.[21]

Feminist criticism has been suspicious of *Bailegangaire* as Murphy's answer to the male dominated world of his earlier works. As Murphy has admitted, he wanted to write the play because he still recalled the first night of *A Whistle in the Dark* in 1962, when a woman approached him after the play and said: 'If you don't mind, Tom, you know nothing about women'.[22] Does *Bailegangaire* then allow women space by the simple expedient of keeping men off stage altogether?[23] It is true that the recognition of women's position may lead to the 'oppositional mode', to alternative readings and to a celebration of the periphery; the danger is that women may first welcome but then become entrapped by the possibly marginal positions ascribed to them. As Gillian Beer points out, 'the list of the inhabitants of the periphery becomes a carnivalesque group—the mad, the poor, women and workers—who are idealized as outside the power centre'.[24] However, the risk of such an idealisation perpetuating exclusion is avoided in *Bailegangaire*. Murphy's characters live in a suspended vacuum, still in search of their position in the world they inhabit. They have to negotiate their being in terms of male established rules, and are deeply aware of the struggle this search for definition involves.

According to Gayatri Spivak, naming, which is the central metaphor of the play,[25] is never a neutral activity.[26] As in Brian Friel's *Translations*, 'words ... are matters having to do with ownership, authority, power, and the imposition of force'.[27] *Bailegangaire* opens on the senile, bed-ridden Mommo, who is trying to articulate the story of how the town of Bochtán 'came by its new appellation, Bailegangaire, the place without laughter'.[28] Mommo's mock-epic accounts for an uneasy interaction between the sociosymbolic order and the semiotic. The image of Mommo 'as a female King Lear ... scorning the "good" granddaughter, [Mary], and playing up to the "bad" one, [Dolly]' [29], actually reinforces the patriarchal order.[30] On the other hand, her fragmented narrative, interspersed with Gaelic expressions and sometimes acquiring a child-like inflection, pertains to the domain of the semiotic. Mommo's narration resembles the rhythmic babble which characterises the semiotic and introduces difference: her silences, her gaps, her difficulties at 'naming' experiences from the past indicate resistance to a male-dominated world. Thus Mommo simultaneously takes her place and challenges the symbolic order, the 'order of the father'. Through her storytelling, Mommo asks for 'insertion into history and [for] the radical refusal of the subjective limitations imposed by this history's time'.[31] Her narration is a continuous attempt to overcome these limitations; her project is to enter women's monumental and cyclical time. Mommo's story is therefore a 'myth of origin', but also 'an expiatory myth'[32] because in the end when she can purge her guilt, she will reappropriate her time.

The basic structure of Mommo's story is the 'nativity of Christ':[33] the Strangers, Seamus and Brigit, arriving at the town of Bochtán shortly before Christmas. The action is set on the day of the Tuam fair where the inhabitants in their poverty and desperation are forced to sell everything they have to provide for the coming Christmas. This situation of helpless deprivation has placed them ever more firmly under the control of John Mahony, 'groggy-patriot-publican-general-shop-man',[34] and representative of the venal, gombeen mentality of the small proprietor so detested by Synge. His pub will become in fact the arena for the contest. As Mahony starts to take bets on it, the laughing-contest between the native Costello and the Stranger, Seamus, acquires an economic connotation in which Mahony's interests are pitted against those of his community. Mahony supports the Stranger, the others support Costello. When Seamus and Brigit enter the pub, she is sobbing and worrying over the three children waiting for them at home. The couple is immersed in fear and death, and premonitions of more deaths to come cause Brigit to challenge Costello, a challenge which comes out of grief, and defies the force that has robbed her of her nine sons. As the contest progresses to see, in Brigit's words, 'He who laughs last',[35] Costello collapses, apparently dead. While the crowd drives the Strangers out of the pub, and Mahony insists that he has been victorious, Costello rises for one last laugh, symbolically signifying the people's victory over their economic enemy.

The agrarian community portrayed by Mommo carries within it an inturned competitive aggression, which easily spills over into violence. For those who have only their destitution, 'intense energy is invested in identification with their own community … which spurs the Bochtans on in support of Costello'.[36] The West of Ireland is once again the place where violence is celebrated and where the outsider, like Christie Mahon, is finally rejected by the community, confirming the discontinuity which lies at the heart of Irish tradition. However, the West is also the repository of patriarchal order, to which Mommo has regretfully yielded. The story Mommo cannot bring to its conclusion needs Mary's intervention. Mary helps Mommo to recognise herself as the Brigit of the story, and to admit her responsibility in having endorsed the socioeconomic order behind the laughing-contest. When she can finally tell of the deaths of her youngest grandchild, Tom, and of her husband, Seamus, Mommo achieves her liberation. The rhythmic babble of her narration gives way to a liberating laughter which discloses new hopes for the future. Mommo's final revelation illuminates Mary's and Dolly's contemporary lives and enhances a more comprehensive apprehension of their past. Like Mommo, they are products of a patriarchal order, but they have not fully accepted their imposed roles. Mary has given up her job as a nurse, contravening the patriarchal principle that her social function is to cure and comfort mankind, while Dolly, married to a husband who brutalises her and the mother of numerous children, has turned into a 'whore'. She has casual sex in ditches as a revenge against men, and threatens abortion or infanticide as a desperate response to her unwanted pregnancy. So Mary's despairing response to Dolly, 'I failed. It all failed. I'm as big a failure as you, and that's some failure',[37] laments a 'failure' in patriarchal terms, and testifies to two women's position at the far limit of the symbolic order. As Toril Moi has remarked, 'It is this position which has enabled male culture sometimes to vilify women as representing darkness and chaos, ... as Lilith or the Whore of Babylon' or 'as the representatives of a higher and purer nature, ... as Virgins and Mothers of God'.[38] Nonetheless, in joining Mommo's laughter, Mary and Dolly successfully conclude their struggle against an oppressive patriarchy. But they achieve even more, and *Bailegangaire* thus becomes 'Murphy's Ireland'.[39] In fact, 'the end of [the three women's] excursions is to make *a time* and *a place* comprehensible',[40] that place and that time which, according to Said, must be reappropriated to make way for national liberation. The theatrical space of *Bailegangaire*, therefore, widens not only to embrace Mommo's, Mary's, and Dolly's liberation, but also to represent a national space, in which discontinuity is abolished when 'the sense of [its] brutal reality is ... linked, crucially, to the past of Mommo's story'.[41]

The thematic rejection of the sociosymbolic and the emergence of a renewed national space is skilfully reinforced at a dramatic level. I shall focus on three salient moments in the play's development. When *Bailegangaire* opens, Mary is serving food to Mommo. The reverse image—of the child nourishing her mother, rather than the mother feeding her children—underlines Mommo's refusal of the patriarchal order. She is no longer the traditional personification of Ireland as *Sean Bhean Bhocht* or Cathleen ní Houlihan. The idealisation of womanhood had coincided with the colonisation of Ireland, and had provided a compensatory elevation in the order of the mystique. Ireland was equated with a virginal motherhood, whose native purity of faith and morals was to be safeguarded against the threat of an alien culture.[42] In this process of sublimation real women were not given any socio-economic power, but only a 'representational' role. They became, in psychoanalytic terms, a powerful unconscious symbol for forfeited or forbidden origins, and represented the idealised mothers feeding their faithful sons who would redeem Ireland from colonial violation. As Margaret Kelleher has noted in *The Feminization of Famine*, famine is conveyed in images of women unable to feed their children, so that 'again, and again, images of women are used to figure moments of breakdown or crisis',[43] ascribed to the natural order. The resulting implication is that famine is a natural rather than a political or economic event, and that women are associated with this natural order, being denied access to men's political discourse. Unlike Mother in *Famine*, who is the 'pragmatic provider for her family' and 'eloquent opponent of the men's actions',[44] Mommo in *Bailegangaire* refuses the role of the nourishing mother and partakes in the order of a male-dominated world. Her liberation, however, will begin with the admission of her complicity.

The end of Act I marks the turning point of the play, when Mommo's senility, which gave rise to the tale of Brigit and Seamus, seems to hinder its completion. Senility in *Bailegangaire* plays the role that female madness has played in Western culture. For centuries a privileged relation has been established between women and madness, in which female psychology is shown to have been conditioned by an oppressive, patriarchal culture. The social role assigned to a woman was that of daughter, wife or mother, serving an image, authoritative and central, of man. Madness is therefore 'either the acting out of the devalued female role or the total or partial rejection of [woman's] sex-role stereotype'.[45] But madness is also the opposite of rebellion: it is 'the impasse confronting those whom cultural conditioning has deprived of the very means of protest or self-affirmation'. 'Mental illness' becomes a '*request for help*',[46] the request that Mommo is indirectly making for help in finishing her story.

Mary's character, the homecomer in search of reconciliation, is central to the play's development; and when she urges Mommo to conclude the story, the play achieves its technical and emotional resolution, while the narratives of the past and the present unite. However, the reconciliation taking place after her intervention in the story is manifold, and results in the three women's decision to keep Dolly's baby. In metaphorically bringing home the two 'outsiders', she not only reconciles Mommo with her past, and Dolly and herself with their lives, but also the sociosymbolic with the semiotic, and the '*petit recit*' of *Bailegangaire* with the Official History of Ireland.[47]

It is indeed this image of reconciliation which is difficult to find in *The Beauty Queen of Leenane*. The situation is reminiscent of *Bailegangaire*. Maureen, a forty-year-old spinster is trapped with her old mother, Meg, in 'the living-room/kitchen of a rural cottage in the West of Ireland'.[48] The West of Ireland portrayed by McDonagh has become a powerful expression of that dangerous neo-traditionalism which does not look to history for continuity, but rather selects and manipulates 'traditions' from the past and reduces them to mere commonplaces. In the set of *The Beauty Queen of Leenane* pre-modern and post-modern Ireland are brought on stage side by side. The 'fifties is superimposed on the 'nineties: the mores of rural Ireland with its tyrannical mothers and returned Yanks co-exist with the contemporary chaos of Australian soap operas and sexual liberation. Although the set is redolent with traditional pieties—Our Lady, the Sacred Heart, John and Bobby Kennedy—the focus of the family life is the television hosting 'a cast of characters whose motives and actions are conditioned by a culture different from the Irish'.[49] McDonagh's West of Ireland, located at the margins of a globalised culture, is even more remote and lonely than Synge's. It is true that for Martin McDonagh, a Londoner of Irish parents, 'there was none of the exile's longing, none of the proper nostalgic clutch of the ould sod'.[50] Nationalism is an empty word for this 'citizen of an indefinite land that is neither Ireland nor England but that shares borders with both'.[51] He finds any definition restrictive: 'I'm not into any kind of definition ... I've come to a place where the ambiguities are more interesting than choosing a strict path and following it'.[52]

McDonagh's *Leenane Trilogy* revolves around such ambiguities. In *A Skull in Connemara* and *The Lonesome West*, it is almost impossible to establish whether the protagonists, Mick Dowd and Coleman Connor, have committed murder or are only believed to have done so. In *The Beauty Queen of Leenane* the whole notion of 'truth' has become completely evanescent. In the concentrated, rural community of Leenane, whose credo is gossip, Meg and Maureen Folan lead idle lives, incessantly bickering and hurting each other's feelings. Their claustrophobic, near desperate domestic situation is occasionally interrupted by the arrival of Ray Dooley bringing messages for the two women. Maureen is portrayed as a compelling and unlikely blend of dejection and bloody-mindedness, a psychological picture whose complexity is revealed only when she attempts to seize what she regards as her last chance for love and freedom, represented by Ray Dooley's loquacious and diffident, older brother, Pato, momentarily returned from England. Meg, in a fit of fright and anger burns the letter which Pato has sent to Maureen asking her to go to Boston and marry him. When Maureen discovers what Meg has done, she tortures the old lady by pouring hot oil over her, and rushes off to meet Pato at the railway station. Once returned home, Maureen finds her mother has died, but she does not seem to be concerned as her thoughts are all on the promise she has exchanged with Pato who will wait for her in Boston. Later, however, after Meg's funeral, Ray Dooley says that his brother left 'be taxicab' and not by train, and that he got engaged with a girl he will marry in a year. Whilst there is no doubt of Maureen's distress, the audience is incapable of establishing the 'truth' about what really happened.

The play, characterised by McDonagh's flamboyant, stage-Irish theatricality, fails to avoid the pitfalls of a misinterpreted postmodernism. McDonagh does not make it clear whether he is in favour of an *a priori* relativist refusal of any truth, or whether he surrenders to a postmodern hermeneutic of indeterminate truth, according to which any truth is as good, or as bad, as any other. In analysing how mere relativism does not lead to a final reconciliation, I shall deal with three moments in *The Beauty Queen of Leenane* which invite comparison with those highlighted in *Baile-gangaire*.

At the beginning of the play, Maureen, like Mary in *Bailegangaire,* is serving food to Meg. Maureen's life revolves almost entirely around the acquisition and preparation of a bland diet of porridge, Complan and Kimberly biscuits for her mother, her only power over her adversary being the withholding of food or the making of 'lumpy' Complan. Food, which is 'both metaphor, running joke, bargaining chip and the *radix malorum* of the piece',[53] does not have the wider implications of Murphy's play. It is not the means by which the sociosymbolic is rejected but rather provides the context of Meg's supine acceptance of whatever happened in Irish history, the story Mommo is painfully struggling to articulate. In rejecting the old tongue and advocating the benefits of English in the job market, Meg is denying the loss of national identity perpetrated by the coloniser, one of the main issues on the post-colonial agenda.

If senility, which in *Bailegangaire* has the same function as madness, gives rise to Mommo's tale and represents her request for help, madness in *The Beauty Queen of Leenane* becomes itself storytelling. Meg forces Maureen to tell Pato how she was put into a mental hospital. Maureen, who had worked in England as a cleaner, collapsed under the hostility she found there and suffered a nervous breakdown. Maureen's narration, far from being a rejection of 'woman's sex-role stereotype'[54] heading towards liberation, reproposes in all its urgency the figure of woman as victim. In Maureen's case, this victimisation takes on a more sinister connotation, being perpetrated by her own mother. Maureen's violent reactions, which will lead her to murder Meg in the hope of achieving a belated womanhood, have to be interpreted as the response to what Kristeva has termed the 'difficult connivance of the young girl with her mother'. The girl's great difficulty in detaching herself from the mother, and in thus refusing the patriarchal eternal equation, woman-mother, 'makes [her] more vulnerable within the symbolic order, more fragile when she suffers within it, more virulent when she protects herself from it'.[55]

Finally, the homecomer, who has such a relevant role in *Bailegangaire*, is the ineffectual Pato, who is completely unable to offer Maureen a longed-for release. Although 'his sensitivity is a welcome relief from the mix of coarseness and duplicity in most

stock male roles in Irish drama',[56] he does not represent the agent
of change, and does not help Maureen in 'her search for meaning'
and liberation. This is confirmed at the end of the play when Ray
shouts angrily at her: 'The exact fecking image of your mother
you are'[57] making it clear that there are no new possibilities in
store for her future, only reiterations of the past's old models.
What prevails in Martin McDonagh's play is a sense of loss and
displacement for those people who live on the margins of a globalised culture. For Maureen and Meg there is no family or Irish
community available at the end of their journey.

However, if it is interpreted as a parody of *Bailegangaire,* then
The Beauty Queen of Leenane reveals its potential for resistance
both to the postmodern erasure of difference and to the immobi-
lising presence of the past. Parody is one mode of coming to
terms with the texts of a rich and intimidating legacy of the past,
and signals less an acknowledgement of the inadequacy of the definable forms of the past than a desire to refashion those forms to
present needs. Parody is thus 'a form of imitation ... character-
ized by ironic inversion', 'repetition with critical distance'.[58]
Against the Foucaldian reading of the role of parody as a mode of
discontinuity, Linda Hutcheon sees 'parody as operating as a
method of inscribing continuity while permitting critical distance'(29).

The Beauty Queen of Leenane, therefore, can be seen as following a structural modelling process of revising, replaying, invert-
ing, and 'trans-contextualizing' (7), that is, 'giving a new context'
to *Bailegangaire.* In this process the nature of parody is revealed
as simultaneously implying 'authority' and 'transgression'. According to Mikhail Bakhatin, in parody 'languages and styles actively and mutually illuminate one another'.[59] Bakhtin, however,
identifies another underlying principle of all parodic discourse,
'the paradox of parody' (74), which is its authorised transgression
of norms. The motivation and the form of the carnivalesque are
both derived from authority. The carnivalesque, however, can
also be seen as a threatening force, which puts into question the
legitimacy of the norms. In Bakhtin's terminology, it can be cen-
tripetal or centrifugal. At the roots of this apparent contradiction
lies the paradox of parody's authorised transgression: 'parody is

normative in its identification with the Other, but it is contesting in its Oedipal need to distinguish itself from the prior Other' (77).

How, therefore, are we to read the three moments in *The Beauty Queen of Leenane* which parody *Bailegangaire*'s central and 'serious' notions, such as food, madness, and homecoming, and their wider implications? The postmodern period has witnessed a proliferation of parody as one of the modes of positive aesthetic self-reference because we live in a technological world in which culture has replaced nature as a subject of art. The sense of a challenging of norms which permeates our contemporary culture has thus become the privileged subject of artistic creation, and parody establishes that art's connection with the world. The world, in fact, does not disappear in parody, but the parodic appropriation of the past, as Linda Hutcheon concludes, 'reaches out beyond textual introversion and aesthetic narcissism to address the text's situation in the world' (116).

NOTES

1. David Cairns and Shaun Richards, *Writing Ireland: Colonialism, Nationalism and Culture*, Manchester 1988, 150.
2. Seamus Deane, 'Remembering the Irish Future', *The Crane Bag*, 8 (1984), 84.
3. Fintan O'Toole, 'The Man from God Knows Where: An Interview with Brian Friel', *In Dublin*, 28 October 1982, 22.
4. Richard Kearney and Mark Patrick Herderman, *The Crane Bag Book of Irish Studies (1977-81)*, Dublin 1982, 10-11.
5. Patrick Quilligan, 'Field Day's Double Bill', *Irish Times*, 18 September 1984, 10.
6. Richard Pine, *The Diviner: the Art of Brian Friel*, Dublin 1999, 19.
7. Fintan O'Toole, *Tom Murphy: The Politics of Magic*, Dublin 1994, 94.
8. Edward Said, *Culture and Imperialism*, London 1994, 273.
9. Luke Gibbons, *Transformations in Irish Culture*, Cork 1996, 23.

10.   In *Philadephia, Here I Come!* Friel chooses two characters to represent the 'public' and 'private' selves of his protagonist Gar O'Donnell; in *A Crucial Week in the Life of A Grocer's Assistant* Murphy uses his favourite theatrical device, that of the outside/inside. The downstage area stands for the 'outside' world with which John Joe Moran is in conflict, and serves the purpose of juxtaposing public exchanges and his innermost feelings. Similarly, in *The Death and Resurrection of Mr Roche* the arrival of Mr Roche makes evident the unease of the protagonist in coming to terms with his public and private dimensions.

11.   Declan Kiberd, 'The Moral Superiority of Rural Villages', *Irish Times*, 9 December 1986.

12.   Fintan O'Toole,. 'Going West: The Country versus the City in Irish Writing', *The Crane Bag*, 9 (1985), 112-113.

13.   Gibbons, *op. cit.*, 85.

14.   Frank Barry, 'Between Tradition and Modernity: Cultural Values and the Problems of Irish Society', *The Irish Review*, 8 (1986), 24-26.

15.   Richard Kearney, *Postnationalist Ireland: Politics, Culture, Philosophy*, London and New York 1997, 63.

16.   Ihab Hassan, *The Postmodern Turn: Essays in Postmodern Theory and Culture*, Columbus, Ohio, 1987, 203. Hassan refers in particular to Frederic Jameson's 'dialectical criticism', Edward Said's 'secular criticism', Gerald Graff's 'literature of assertion', and Frank Lentricchia's 'criticism for social changes'.

17.   Said, *op.cit.*, 337.

18.   Richard Kearney, *Transitions: Narratives in Modern Irish Culture*, Dublin 1987, 163.

19.   O'Toole, *op. cit.*, 242.

20.   Shaun Richards, 'Refiguring Lost Narratives—Prefiguring New Ones: The Theatre of Tom Murphy', *The Canadian Journal of Irish Studies*, 15 (1989), 80-100.

21.   Nicholas Grene, 'Murphy's Ireland' in *The Politics of Irish Drama: Plays in Context from Boucicault to Friel*, Cambridge 1999, 240.

22.   Anthony Roche, *Contemporary Irish Drama: from Beckett to McGuinness*, Dublin 1994, 147.

23.   Grene, 'Murphy's Ireland', *op. cit.*, 239.

24.   Gillian Beer, 'Representing Women: Re-presenting the Past' in Catherine Belsey and Jane Moore (eds.), *The Feminist Reader: Essays in Gender and the Politics of Literary Criticism*, Houndmills and London 1997 (1989), 83.

25.   O'Toole, *op. cit.*, 241.

26.   Catherine Belsey and Jane Moore, 'Introduction: The Story so Far' in Belsey and Moore (eds), *op. cit.*, 13.

27.   Edward Said, *The World, the Text, and the Critic*, London 1991, 48.

28.   Tom Murphy, *Bailegangaire in After Tragedy: Three Irish Plays by Tom Murphy*, London 1988, 43.

29.   Roche, *op. cit.*, 147.

30.   Anne Kelly, 'A Feminist Reading of the Plays of Tom Murphy (Part Two)', *Irish Theatre Forum*, 2.3 (1999) http://www.ucd.ie/~rthfrm/issue4.h tm. See also Anne Kelly, 'Bodies and Spirits in Tom Murphy's Theatre', In Eamonn Jordan (ed.), *Theatre Stuff: Critical Essays in Contemporary Irish Drama*, Dublin 2000.

31.   Julia Kristeva, 'Women's Time', in Belsey and Moore (eds.), *op. cit.*, 202.

32.   Joseph Swann, 'Language and Act: Thomas Murphy's Non-Interpretative Drama' in Jacquelin Genet and Richard Allen Cave (eds.), *Perspectives of Irish Drama and Theatre,* Gerrards Cross 1991, 145.

33.   O'Toole, *op. cit.*, 240.

34.   J. M.Synge, *The Playboy of the Western World* in Anne Saddlemyer (ed.), *Collected Works*, London 1968.

35.   Tom Murphy, *Bailegangaire* in *After Tragedy: op.cit*

36.   Grene, 'Murphy's Ireland', *op. cit.*, 238.

37.   Murphy, *Bailegangaire*, *op. cit.*, 68.

38.   Toril Moi, 'Feminist, Female, Feminine' in Belsey and Moore (eds.), *op. cit.*, 112.

39.   Grene, *op. cit.*, 219.

40.   Desmond Maxwell, 'New Lamps for Old: The Theatre of Tom Murphy', *Theatre Research International*, 15 (1990), 65.

41.   Mark Lane, 'Theatrical Space and National Place in Four Plays by Thomas Murphy', *Irish University Review*, 21 (1991), 219-228.

42.   Kearney, 1997, *op. cit.*, 117-120.

43.   M Kelleher, *The Feminization of Famine: Expressions of the Inexpressible,* Cork 1997, 6.

44.   Anne Kelly, *A Feminist Reading of the Plays of Tom Murphy (Part One)*, 1998, http://www.ucd.ie/~rthfrm/index3.htm.

45.   Shoshana Felman, 'Women and Madness: the Critical Phallacy' in Belsey and Moore (eds), *op. cit.*, 118.

46.   *Ibid.*, 118

47.   According to Lynda Henderson, however, this possibility of achieving a reconciliation is denied as the play does not offer its female characters access to the level of the spiritual, mystical or metaphorical. Lynda Henderson, 'Men, Women and the Life of the Spirit in Tom Murphy's Plays' in Jacqueline Genet and Wynne Hellegouarc'h (eds.), *Irish Writers and Their Creative Process*, Gerrards Cross 1996, 92.

48.   Martin McDonagh, *The Beauty Queen of Leenane,* in *Plays: One,* London 1999, 1.

49.   Barry, *op. cit.*, 24-26.

50. Fintan O'Toole, 'Nowhere Man', *Irish Times (Weekend Supplement)* , 26 April, 1997, 1.

51. *Ibid.*, 1.

52. *Ibid.*, 1.

53. C. L. Dallat, 'A Last Chance for Love', *Times Literary Supplement,* 15 March 1996, 10.

54. Felman, *op. cit.*, 118.

55. Kristeva, *op. cit.*, 211.

56. Dallat, *op. cit.*, 20.

57. McDonagh, *The Beauty Queen of Leenane, op. cit.*, 60.

58. Linda Hutcheon, *A Theory of Parody: The Teachings of Twentieth-Century Art Forms*, London 1985, 6. Subsequent references to this work are given in parenthesis in the text.

59. Michael Bakhtin, *The Dialogic Imagination,* Austin, Texas and London 1981, 76.

Index

274

Notes on Contributors

Louis Armand has lived in Prague since 1994, where he directs the InterCultural Studies programme at Charles University. His work has appeared in various publications, including *Poetry Review, Sulfur, Stand, TriQuarterly, Genetic Joyce Studies,* and the *James Joyce Quarterly*. He has authored, edited or co-edited a large number of texts, including *Techne: James Joyce, Hypertext & Technology* (Karolinum: 2003); *Giocomo Joyce: Envoys of the Other* (ed. with Clare Wallace; Academica: 2002); *Night Joyce of a Thousand Tiers. Petr Skrabanek: Studies in Finnegans Wake* (ed. with Ondrej Pilny; Litteraria: 2002). He is editor of the PLR (*Prague Literary Review*), an advisory editor to *Rhizomes* (Washington State University), and an editor of *Litteraria Pragensia*. www.louis-armand.com

Michael Faherty is Senior Lecturer in English Studies at De Montfort University Bedford. He has published a number of essays on Irish and American poets, including two previous pieces on Matthew Sweeney. His book The Poetry of W.B. Yeats: A Reader's Guide to Essential Criticism will be published by Palgrave in 2004.

Rui Carvalho Homem is an Associate Professor of English at the Faculty of Letters, University of Oporto (Portugal). He has published on a variety of themes in Irish Studies and in Early Modern English drama. As a member of a team currently preparing a new *Complete Shakespeare* in Portuguese, he has published a translation of *Antony and Cleopatra* and is currently working on *Love's Labour's Lost*. Other translations include collections by Seamus Heaney (1997, 2003) and Philip Larkin (forthcoming). He is also a founding member of a research project on poetry and the visual arts.

Ellen Carol Jones has taught as Associate Professor of English and International Studies at Saint Louis University; her Ph.D. is from Cornell University. She has edited or co-edited *Twenty-First Joyce* (2004), *Joyce: Feminism/Post/Colonialism* (1998), and four special volumes of *MFS*: *The Politics of Modernism* (1992), *Virginia Woolf* (1992), *Feminist Readings of Joyce* (1989), and *Feminism and Modern Fiction* (1988). She is the author of numerous essays on Joyce and Woolf; "Empty Shoes," on iconic representations of the Shoah, was published in *Footnotes: On Shoes* (2001).

John Kenny is a native of Glenamaddy, Co Galway and is a graduate of the National University of Ireland. His doctoral thesis was on the work of John Banville. His areas of special interest are contemporary Irish fiction, twentieth-century Irish literature and culture, modern British and world fiction, and twentieth-century literary theories. He has published essays on Irish fiction and society and on the theory and practice of literary reviewing. He regularly writes on new Irish fiction for the *Irish Times* and the *Times Literary Supplement*. He is currently a lecturer at the Department of English, NUI Galway where he teaches in the areas of contemporary literature, modernist and postmodernist cultures, literary theory, and the history of the critical essay. He has recently begun an introductory book on the work of Patrick McCabe.

Vivian Valvano Lynch is Associate Professor of English at St. John's University. She is the author of *Portraits of Artists: Warriors in the Novels of William Kennedy* (Rowman and Littlefield, 1999) and numerous essays on James Joyce, as well as on contemporary Irish and Irish-American fiction and drama. A co-editor of *The Irish Literary Supplement*, she regularly reviews books and performances for that publication.

Marisol Morales Ladrón is a Senior Lecturer at the University of Alcalá (Madrid, Spain) where she teaches English, Irish and Comparative literature. Her publications include the books: *Breve introducción a la literature comparada [A Brief Introduction to Comparative Literature]* (1999), and *Las poéticas de James Joyce y Luis Martín-Santos [The Poetics of James Joyce and Luis Martín-Santos]* (forthcoming). She has co-edited two volumes on feminist criticism: *Mosaicos y taraceas: Desconstrucción feminista de los discursos del género [Mosaics and Inlayings: Feminist Deconstruction of Gender Discourses]* (2000), and *(Trans)formaciones de las sexualidades y el género [(Trans)Formations of Sexualities and Genders]* (2001). She has also published articles on a number of Irish authors such as: Oscar Wilde, James Joyce, W. B. Yeats, Bernard Mac Laverty, Brian Friel and Emma Donoghue, among others.

Donald E. Morse, Visiting Professor of American, Irish, and English literature, University of Debrecen, Hungary and Emeritus Professor of English and Rhetoric, Oakland University, Michigan, USA, has been twice Fulbright Professor and twice Soros Professor, UD and the recipient of a Rockefeller Study Fellowship. Author or editor of nine books and over a hundred scholarly articles, his Irish scholarship includes *Worlds Visible and Invisible* (1994) and with Csilla Bertha *More Real than Reality: The Fantastic in Irish Literature and the Arts* (1991), and the IASIL volume *A Small Nation's Contribution to the World* (1993). In 1989 and 2003 he and Bertha hosted IASIL conferences in Debrecen. In 1999 the University of Debrecen awarded him an Honorary Doctorate in recognition of his service to Hungarian higher education and his international scholarship.

Paul Murphy is a Lecturer in Drama at Queen's University, Belfast. His recent publications include: 'J.M. Synge and the Pitfalls of National Consciousness', *Theatre Research*

International, Summer 2003; 'The Myth of Benightedness After the Irish Renaissance: the drama of George Shiels', *Moving Worlds*, Autumn 2003; 'Nostalgic vs. Nomadic Subjectivities in Late 20th Century Irish Drama', *Australasian Drama Studies Journal*, Autumn 2003. He is currently working on a monograph entitled *Land of Heart's Desire: Hegemony and Fantasy in Irish Drama, 1899-1949*, and is co-author of the forthcoming revision of *A Commentary on the Collected Plays of W.B. Yeats*, for Macmillan. His future research will focus on the production of four volumes of a documentary history of Irish drama from 1926-1951, which will continue the renowned six volume Modern Irish Drama series pioneered by the late Robert Hogan.

Erin V. Obermueller has recently completed her Ph.D. at Saint Louis University. Her dissertation examined Victorian women's writing and the visual arts, with particular regard to the way models, artists, and museum visitors complicate the domestic ideal.

Maryna Romanets, Ph.D. teaches in the Department of English, University of Northern British Columbia, Canada. She has published articles on contemporary Irish, British and Ukrainian literatures focusing on the issues of representation and gender, politics and language, and intertextual relations, as well as on the mechanisms of textual production and translation theory and praxis. She is currently completing the book *Displaced Subjects, Anamorphosic Texts, Reconfigured Visions: Improvised Traditions in Contemporary Irish and Ukrainian Literature*.

Robert Tracy is Professor Emeritus of English and of Celtic Studies at the University of California, Berkeley. He has served as Co-Director of the UC Dickens Project. His publications include *Trollope's Later Novels* (1978); editions of works by Synge, Trollope, Le Fanu, and Flann O'Brien.

Simon Trezise, who died in 2003, was a lecturer in literature at the Department of Lifelong Learning at the University of Exeter. His PhD was on Shaw, but most of his work was based in a deep knowledge of the mid- to late nineteenth century; in particular he was a Hardy specialist. He wrote *The West Country as a Literary Invention: Putting Fiction in its Place* (University of Exeter Press, 2000), and at the time of his death was working on a book entitled *Thomas Hardy's Cornwall*. He was passionately interested in regional literature, and was an inspiring teacher of adult students. Simon had also worked for the WEA and the Open University.

Clare Wallace is a lecturer in the Department of English and American Studies at Charles University in Prague. She is the co-editor (with Louis Armand) of *Giacomo Joyce: Envoys of the Other* (Bethesda: Academica, 2002) and is an advisory editor for the online journals *Rhizomes: Cultural Studies in Emerging Knowledge* and *Hypermedia Joyce Studies*. She has published on Marina Carr, Patrick McCabe and James Joyce and is currently engaged in research on the relation between new writing for theatre in Britain and Ireland in the 1990s and postmodernity.

Kim Wallace teaches English at Carmel College, Merseyside. She completed a PhD in 2000 entitled *Constructing Identities: History and Metafiction in Irish Novels 1980-1999*. She has published an article on Colm Toibin's *The Story of the Night* in *BELLS*.